Internet and E-mail for Seniors
with Windows 7

Studio Visual Steps

Internet and E-mail
for Seniors with
Windows 7

For everyone who wants to learn to use the Internet at a later age

This book has been written using the Visual Steps™ method.
Cover design by Studio Willemien Haagsma bNO
© 2010 Visual Steps
Edited by Jolanda Ligthart, Mara Kok and Rilana Groot
Translated by Chris Hollingsworth, *1ˢᵗ Resources* and Irene Venditti, *i-write* translation services.
Editor in chief: Ria Beentjes
Second printing: October 2010

ISBN 978 90 5905 116 4

Resources used: Some of the computer terms and definitions seen here in this book have been taken from descriptions found online at the Windows Help and Support website. (http://windowshelp.microsoft.com/Windows/en-US/default.mspx) Additional technical resources include:

Would you like more information?
www.visualsteps.com

Do you have questions or suggestions?
E-mail: info@visualsteps.com

Website for this book:
www.visualsteps.com/internet7
Here you can register your book.

Register your book
We will keep you aware of any important changes that are necessary to you as a user of the book. You can also take advantage of our periodic newsletter informing you of our product releases, company news, tips & tricks, special offers, etc.
www.visualsteps.com/internet7

Table of Contents

Appendices

Bonus Online Chapter

At the website accompanied to this book, you will find a bonus online chapter and an extra appendix. In *Chapter 9 Bonus Online Chapter and Extra Information* you can read how to open this chapter and appendix.

Extra Appendix

Setting Up a Webmail Account in Windows Live Mail

Foreword

The Internet has ushered in a whole new era. Until a few years ago, most computers were isolated from one another. Since the emergence of the Internet, people are able to communicate with other connected computer users on a worldwide basis. The Internet has gradually become so vast that you can browse in even the most obscure libraries and communicate with people and organizations no matter where in the world they are.

More and more applications are being created that have advantages for computer non-experts as well. For example, e-mail is increasingly replacing the telephone, regular mail and the fax.

The purpose of this book is to acquaint you with the Internet. Then we will teach you the essential skills needed to take full advantage of what the Internet can offer. We have also given a lot of attention to Internet safety and privacy. We will alert you to potential dangers when using the internet. Finally, we will show you what kind of measures you can take to protect your computer.

We have created a special website to accompany this book, where you can safely practice what you have learned before you set out on your own on the Internet.

This book makes use of the Visual Steps™ method specifically developed for adult learners by Addo Stuur.
We hope you enjoy this book and wish you a pleasant journey on the Internet.

The Studio Visual Steps Authors

P.S. Your comments and suggestions are most welcome.
Our e-mail address is: mail@visualsteps.com

Visual Steps Newsletter

All Visual Steps books follow the same methodology: clear and concise step-by-step instructions with screenshots to demonstrate each task.
A complete list of all our books can be found on our website **www.visualsteps.com**
You can also sign up to receive our **free Visual Steps Newsletter**.

In this Newsletter you will receive periodic information by e-mail regarding:
- the latest titles and previously released books;
- special offers, supplemental chapters, tips and free informative booklets.

Also our Newsletter subscribers may download any of the documents listed on the web pages **www.visualsteps.com/info_downloads** and **www.visualsteps.com/tips**

If you subscribe to our newsletter, be assured that we will never use your e-mail address for any purpose other than sending you the information as previously described. We will not share this address with any third-party. Each newsletter also contains a one-click link to unsubscribe.

Introduction to Visual Steps™

The Visual Steps manuals and handbooks offer the best instruction available for anyone new to computers. Nowhere else in the world will you find better support while getting to know the computer, the Internet, *Windows* and other computer programs.

Visual Steps manuals are special because of their:
- **Content**
  The adult learners needs, desires, know-how and skills have been taken into account.
- **Structure**
  Get started right away. No lengthy explanations. The chapters are organized in such a way that you can skip a chapter or redo a chapter without worry. Easy step- by-step instructions and practice exercises to reinforce what you have learned.
- **Illustrations**
  Every single step is accompanied by a screenshot. These illustrations will guide you in finding the right buttons or menus, and will quickly show you if you are still on the right track.
- **Format**
  A sizable format and pleasantly large letters enhance readability.

In short, I believe these manuals will be excellent guides.

Dr. H. van der Meij

Faculty of Applied Education, Department of Instruction Technology, University of Twente, the Netherlands

What You Will Need

In order to work through this book, you will need a number of things on your computer.

The primary requirement for working with this book is having one of the US versions of *Windows 7* installed on your computer:
- *Windows 7 Starter*
- *Windows 7 Home Premium*
- *Windows 7 Professional*
- *Windows 7 Ultimate/Enterprise*

You can check this yourself by turning on your computer and looking at the start-up screen.

Network and Internet
View network status and tasks
Choose homegroup and sharing options

You need a functioning **Internet connection**. Contact your Internet Service Provider or your local computer store if you need help.

If you need help setting up your dial-up connection, you can read *Appendix A Setting up a Dial-up Connection* at the end of this book.

If you need help setting up your broadband Internet connection (cable, DSL or ISDN), please contact your Internet Service Provider or consult the manual you have received. Each provider has a different protocol for setting up a connection. Detailed documentation containing this type of technical information goes beyond the scope of this book.

 Internet Explorer

 Windows Live Mail

In order to work with the Internet, you must have the following two programs installed on your computer:
- *Windows Internet Explorer version 8 or 9*
- *Windows Live Mail*

Windows Live Mail might not be installed to your computer yet. If so, follow the instructions in *Appendix C Downloading and Installing Windows Live Mail* to install this program.

You also need:

A computer mouse. If you are working on a laptop with touchpad, you may want to purchase an external mouse in order to more easily follow the steps in this book.

How This Book Is Organized

This book is set up in such a way that you do not necessarily have to work through it from the beginning to the end. It is a good idea, however, to work through the chapters containing basic techniques first.

The Basics
- connecting to the Internet — Chapter 1
- surfing the Internet — Chapters 1 and 2
- sending e-mail — Chapter 5

After you have mastered these basic techniques, you can choose among the following chapters. Each one can be worked through separately. These cover the following subjects:

Optional Subjects
- searching the Internet — Chapter 3
- saving text and pictures — Chapter 4
- your *Windows Live Contacts* folder and e-mail attachments — Chapter 6
- formatting e-mail — Chapter 7
- using *Windows Calendar* — Chapter 7
- downloading files — Chapter 8
- security and privacy — Bonus Online Chapter 10

Please note: You can find the Bonus Online Chapter at the website that goes with this book: **www.visualsteps.com/internet7**
In *Chapter 9 Bonus Online Chapter and Extra Information* you can read how to open these chapter.

Website

At the website that accompanies this book, **www.visualsteps.com/internet7**, you will find a Bonus Online Chapter and more information about the book. This website will also keep you informed of changes you need to know of as a user of the book. Please, also take a look at our website **www.visualsteps.com** from time to time to read about new books and gather other useful information.

How to Use This Book

This book has been written using the Visual Steps™ method. It is important that you work through each chapter **step-by-step**. If you follow all the steps, you will not encounter any surprises. In this way, you will quickly learn how to use the Internet without any problems.

In this Visual Steps™ book, you will see various icons. This is what they mean:

Techniques
These icons indicate an action to be carried out:

 The mouse icon means you should do something with the mouse.

 The keyboard icon means you should type something on the keyboard.

 The hand icon means you should do something else, for example turn on the computer.

In addition to these actions, in some spots in the book **extra assistance** is provided so that you can successfully work through each chapter.

Help
These icons indicate that extra help is available:

The arrow icon warns you about something.

The bandage icon can help you if something has gone wrong.

 Have you forgotten how to do something? The number next to the footsteps icon tells you where you can find it in the appendix *How Do I Do That Again?*

In separate boxes you find tips or additional, background information.

Extra Information
Information boxes are denoted by these icons:

The book icon gives you extra background information that you can read at your convenience. This extra information is not necessary for working through the book.

 The light bulb icon indicates an extra tip for using *Windows* and the Internet.

Prior Computer Experience

This book assumes a minimum of prior computer experience. Nonetheless, there are a few basic techniques you should know in order to use this book. You do not need to have any prior experience with the Internet. But you do need to be able to:

- click with the mouse
- start and stop programs
- type and edit text
- start up and shut down *Windows*

If you do not know how to do these things yet, you can read the book ***Windows 7 for Seniors*** first:

ISBN 978 90 5905 116 4

Paperback

US $19.95
Canada $21.95

Windows 7 for Seniors has been specifically written for people who are taking their first computer steps at a later age. It is a real "how to" book. By working through this book, you will learn all the techniques needed to operate your computer. You will gradually become more confident and comfortable using the computer. The step-by-step method makes instruction easy to process so you quickly gain basic computer skills.

What You Will Learn
When you finish this book, you will have the skills to:
• work independently with your computer
• write a letter using your computer
• adjust your computer settings so you can work with it most comfortably

For more information, visit
www.visualsteps.com/windows7

The Screen Shots

The screen shots in this book were made on a computer running *Windows 7 Ultimate*. The screen shots used in this book indicate which button, folder, file or hyperlink you need to click on your computer screen. In the instruction text (in **bold** letters) you will see a small image of the item you need to click. The black line will point you to the right place on your screen.
The small screen shots that are printed in this book are not meant to be completely legible all the time. This is not necessary, as you will see these images on your own computer screen in real size and fully legible.

Here you see an example of an instruction text and a screen shot. The black line indicates where to find this item on your own computer screen:

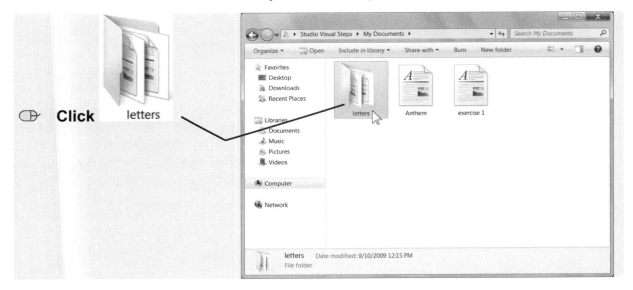

Sometimes the screen shot shows only a portion of a window. Here is an example:

It really will **not be necessary** for you to read all the information in the screen shots in this book. Always use the screen shots in combination with the image you see on your own computer screen.

Test Your Knowledge

Have you finished reading this book? Test your knowledge then with the online tests *Internet Explorer 8* and *Windows Live Mail*. Visit the website:
www.ccforseniors.com

These multiple-choice tests will show you how good your knowledge of Internet and e-mail is. If you pass the test, you will receive your free computer certificate by e-mail.

For Teachers

This book is designed as a self-study guide. It is also well suited for use in a group or a classroom setting. For this purpose, we offer a free teacher's manual containing information about how to prepare for the course (including didactic teaching methods) and testing materials. You can download this teacher's manual (PDF file) from the website which accompanies this book: **www.visualsteps.com/internet7**

Register Your Book

You can register your book. We will keep you aware of any important changes that are necessary to you as a user of the book. You can also take advantage of:
Our periodic newsletter informing you of our product releases, company news, tips & tricks, special offers, etcetera.

1. Starting Out on the World Wide Web

The Internet consists of thousands of computers that are connected to one another by cables, the telephone network and satellite links. The *World Wide Web* is one of the most enjoyable and widely-used parts of the Internet. The World Wide Web is just that: a 'spider web' of computers containing information on many diverse subjects.

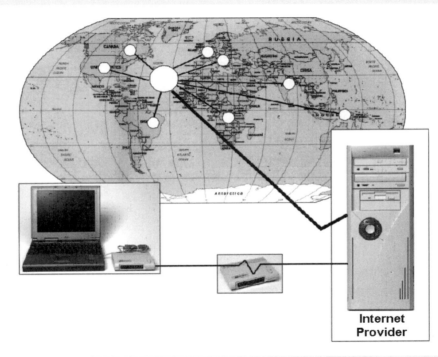

A computer connected to an Internet Service Provider

You can use your computer to open and read these specially formatted documents on the Internet no matter where you are in the world. These documents are called web pages. A website consists of one or more web pages. You can move from one web page to another with a click of the mouse. You can move from one website to another just as easily. This is called *surfing the web*.

In order to access the Internet, you will need to connect to a computer that is already connected to the Internet. An *Internet Service Provider*, also called an ISP, offers this type of service.

If you want to use the Internet, you will need a subscription with an Internet Service Provider. You will be given a user name and a password, and the ISP will provide software to set up your computer. This gives you access to the Internet.
If you have a regular dial-up (telephone) connection to your ISP, you will have to manually connect in order to surf the Internet. If you have a DSL or cable connection, you do not have to do anything. Your computer automatically connects to the Internet. Once you are connected to the Internet, you are online. In this chapter, you will go online and learn how to *surf* the Internet.

In this chapter, you will learn how to:

- start *Internet Explorer*
- connect to your Internet Service Provider
- use a web address
- browse forward and back
- use tabbed browsing
- use the scroll bar
- move from one window to another
- zoom in and out
- disconnect from the Internet

Please note:

You must have a working Internet connection in order to use this book.
Contact your Internet Service Provider or your computer supplier if you need help.
If you need help setting up your dial-up connection, you can read *Appendix A Setting up a Dial-up Connection* at the end of this book. If you need help setting up your broadband Internet connection (cable, DSL or ISDN), please contact your Internet Service Provider or consult the manual you have received. Each provider has a different protocol for setting up a connection. Therefore we have chosen not to describe setting up these connections in great detail.

Please note:

This book assumes that you are working with a computer mouse. If you are working on a laptop with touchpad, you may want to purchase an external mouse to be able to follow the steps in this book more easily. If you want to learn about using the touchpad to operate your laptop, surf to the website **www.visualsteps.com/internet7/news** and read the *Tip Working with a Touchpad*.

1.1 Starting Windows

Windows starts automatically when you turn on your computer.

☞ **Turn on your computer**

If you have set up user accounts on your computer, you will see the screen below first, where you can choose your own account.
If you did not set up any user accounts on your computer, you will immediately see the *desktop* of *Windows 7*. In that case, continue reading on the next page.

If you see this screen:

☞ **Click the icon of your user account**

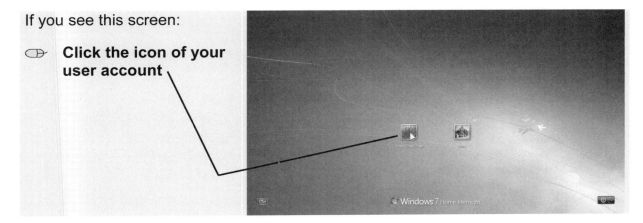

If you have set up a password for the user account, you will have to type it right now:

⌨ **Type the password**

☞ **Click**

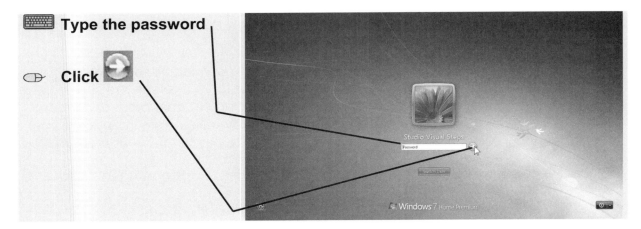

You now see the desktop of *Windows 7* containing several icons:

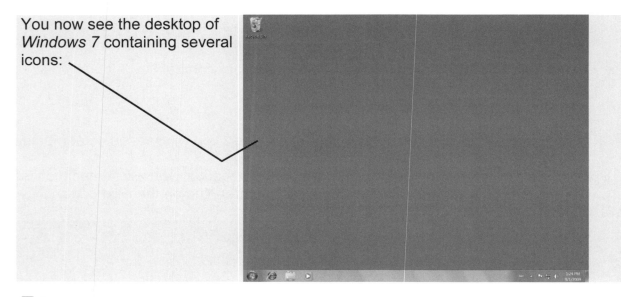

Please note:

The desktop you see on your screen may look different than the desktop you see in the image above. The settings for the appearance of *Windows 7* can be adjusted in many ways. In order to increase the clarity of the images used in this book, a solid color has been chosen as a background for the desktop instead of a photograph.

The Internet changes on a daily basis. For this reason, the images in this book taken from the Internet at the time of this writing may differ from those you see on your own computer.

1.2 Is Your Modem Ready?

Many people use a *modem* and a telephone line to connect to the Internet. A modem is a device that connects your computer to your telephone line or cable network. Sometimes it is in a separate box, called an *external modem*. In many modern computers, however, the modem is already built in - an internal modem. Before you connect to the Internet, it is important to check that your modem is *ready*.

☞ **Make sure your modem is connected to the telephone line or cable network**
You can read the tips on *Connecting over a telephone line* at the end of this chapter if you need more information about dial-up connections.

Do you have an external modem?
☞ **Turn the modem on**

Do you have an internal modem?
☞ **You do not have to do anything**

1.3 Starting Internet Explorer

The program you will use to contact the World Wide Web is called *Internet Explorer*. Here is how you start this program:

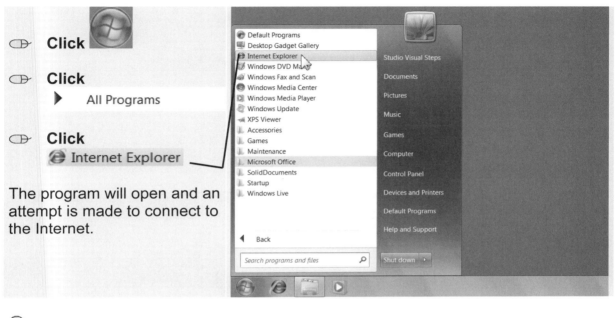

☞ **Click**

☞ **Click**

▶   All Programs

☞ **Click**

🙾 Internet Explorer

The program will open and an attempt is made to connect to the Internet.

🔘 **Tip**

Starting from the taskbar

You can also start *Internet Explorer* by clicking 🙾 on the taskbar.

If you are using *Internet Explorer* for the first time and you have a *broadband* connection to the Internet (DSL or cable), you will probably see a window like this floating on top of the *Internet Explorer* window:

☞ **Click** Connect

Webpage unavailable while offline

The webpage you requested is not available offline. To view this page, click Connect.

Connect   Stay Offline

If you are using *dial-up networking* to connect to the Internet, you will see a *Dial-up Connection* window.

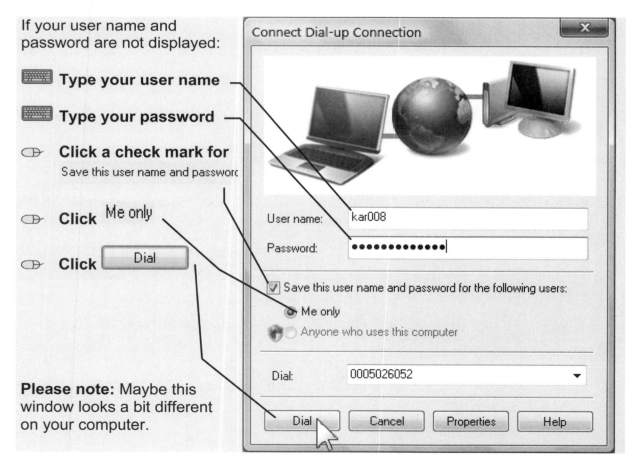

Click Connect

Please note: Maybe this window looks a bit different on your computer.

Dial-up Connection

Select the service you want to connect to.

Connect to: Dial-up Connection ▼

☐ Connect automatically

Connect   Settings...   Work Offline

If you have an Internet access subscription, your ISP has given you a *user name* and a *password*. If everything is set up properly, both of these will already be displayed in the next window.

If your user name and password are not displayed:

Type your user name

Type your password

Click a check mark for
Save this user name and password

Click Me only

Click Dial

Please note: Maybe this window looks a bit different on your computer.

Connect Dial-up Connection

User name: kar008

Password: ●●●●●●●●●●●●●

☑ Save this user name and password for the following users:

○ Me only

○ Anyone who uses this computer

Dial: 0005026052   ▼

Dial   Cancel   Properties   Help

A connection is made to your Internet Service Provider.

HELP! I do not see windows like these.

Are these windows not shown on your screen? If you are connected to the Internet by cable or DSL, then this *Dial-up Connection* window will not appear. You will have a different set up on your computer. *Internet Explorer* automatically connects with the Internet when you open it.

☞ **Just continue reading**

1.4 Connecting to Your Internet Service Provider

If you are using dial-up networking to connect to the Internet, your computer will now try to contact your ISP by using the modem. The modem goes through the following steps:

- the modem dials your ISP's telephone number
- then it connects to your ISP's computer
- your computer sends your user name and password to the ISP's computer
- the ISP's computer checks your user name and password
- if they are correct, your connection to the Internet is established

If your modem is connected to the telephone line, you will usually hear quite a bit of static noise. Your modem is busy converting the signal to a form that allows it to travel over the phone line.

You can follow the progress of your connection in the window:

Connecting to Dial-up Connection...

Dialing 1-456-456-4556

Cancel

If you have a cable, ISDN or DSL connection, *Internet Explorer* automatically connects to the Internet and you will not hear any noise.

Once you are connected to the Internet, the home page will be displayed in the *Internet Explorer* window. This is the window of *Internet Explorer version 8*:

If you have not made any changes to your settings, this is probably a page from *Microsoft*, the company that makes *Internet Explorer*.

At the bottom right-hand corner of the taskbar, you will see an Internet acces icon

indicating that you are *online*:

If you are using *Internet Explorer version 9*, your window probably looks like this:

If so, please take a look at *section 1.26 Internet Explorer 9* and follow the steps in this section to make sure your window looks more the same as the windows used in this book.

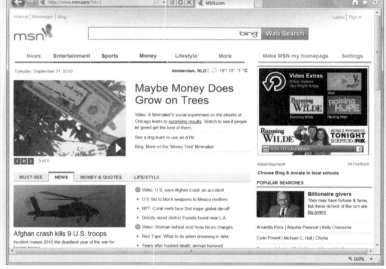

Please note:

The home page on your computer may not be the same as the one in the illustration. You might, for example, see the website of your Internet Service Provider.

HELP! Invalid user name or password.

If you connect but receive the following message 'Invalid User name or Password', re-enter your user name and password in the *Dial-up Connection* window and try to connect to the Internet again.

HELP! There is no connection.

Were you unable to connect to the Internet?
This could be because your ISP's number is 'busy'.
When that happens, try again a little later.

HELP! Still no connection?

If you have tried to connect to the Internet a number of times and you still are unable to establish a connection, most likely the settings on your computer are not correct. You will need to contact your ISP for assistance.

1.5 Typing an Address

Every website has its own web address on the World Wide Web. These are the addresses that start with www that you see everywhere.
You can use these addresses to find a website on any computer that is connected to the Internet. The web address of the Visual Steps publishing company is:

www.visualsteps.com

At the top left of the window:

☞ **Click the Address bar**

The web address
 http://www.msn.com/defaultc.aspx
will turn blue as a sign that it is selected.

You can type the address into this box:

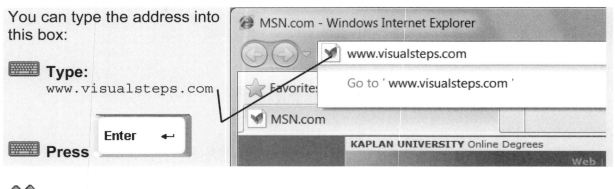

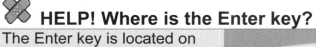 **Type:**
www.visualsteps.com

 **Press**

HELP! Where is the Enter key?

The Enter key is located on the right-hand side of your keyboard:

After a few moments, you see the opening page for this website:

Please note: this web page is updated frequently. The picture you see on your computer may be different than the one in this illustration.

1.6 Maximizing the Window

You can maximize the *Internet Explorer* window at any time, so that it fills the entire screen. This makes it easier to view a web page. Here is how you do this:

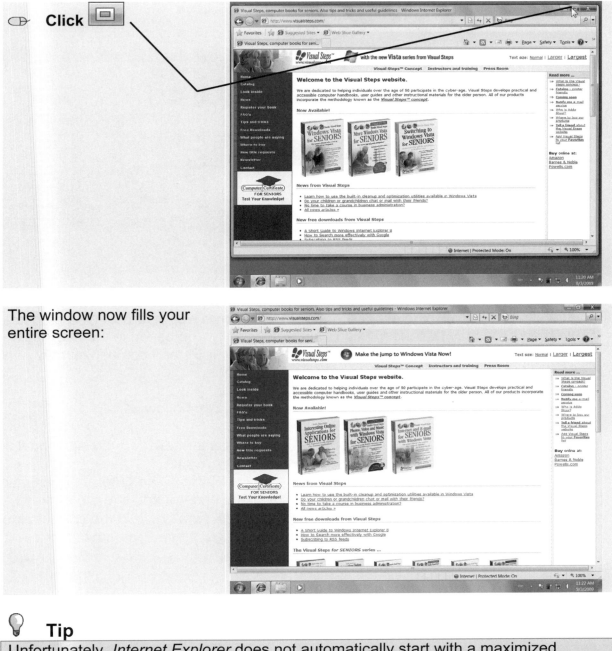

The window now fills your entire screen:

💡 **Tip**

Unfortunately, *Internet Explorer* does not automatically start with a maximized window. Go ahead and click 🔲 right after it opens.

You can restore the window to its original size with just one click:

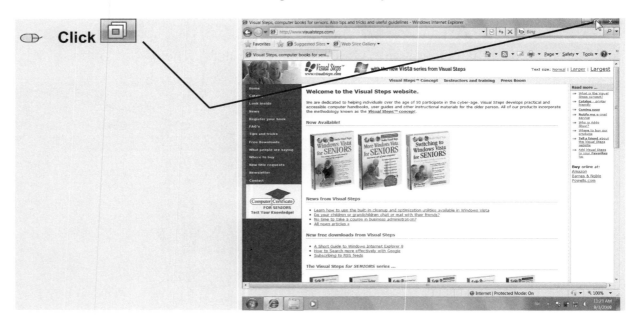

1.7 A Wrong Address

Once in a while a typing error is made when typing a web address. Or a particular web address may no longer exist. This is especially true because the Internet is highly dynamic, changing every day. Private individuals and companies may need to change their web addresses for a variety of reasons.

When typing a web address, pay close attention to the following:

- Sometimes you will see an address that starts with http://. That is additional information indicating that the address is for a website.
- With *Internet Explorer,* you do not need to type http://. The program automatically understands that you are looking for a website and will add it to the address.
- Make sure that any dots (.) or forward slashes (/) are typed in the correct places. If they are not, you will receive an error message. Never type spaces in a web address.

Please note:

Internet Explorer version 9 is smarter than version 8. If you see the screenshot shown on page 34 directly, then continue to read this section further.

If even one dot is missing, an error message may appear. Try it:

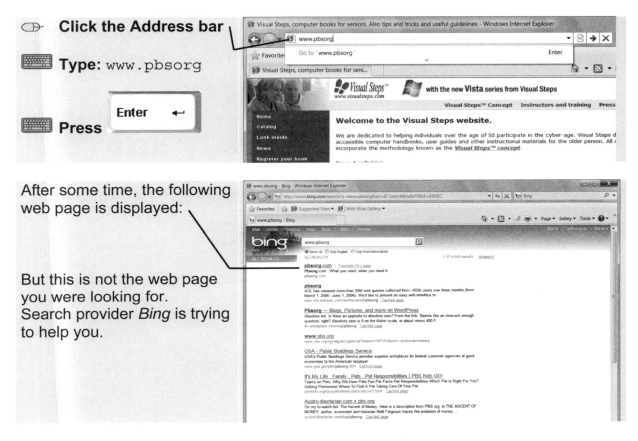

Click the Address bar

Type: `www.pbsorg`

Press Enter ↵

After some time, the following web page is displayed:

But this is not the web page you were looking for.
Search provider *Bing* is trying to help you.

Bing has made these suggestions because the address you typed - www.pbsorg - was incorrect, but very similar to an address they already had stored in their database. The dot before org is missing. The correct address for the Public Broadcasting Service website is:

www.pbs.org

Try the correct address:

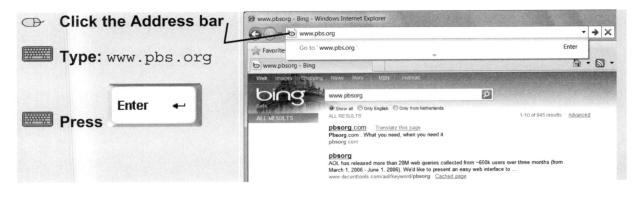

Click the Address bar

Type: `www.pbs.org`

Press Enter ↵

After a short while, you see the home page for the Public Broadcasting Service.

At the time of this writing, this is how the page looked:

Remember, if you forget just one dot the program may not be able to find the website you want.

Please note:
The website shown above may look different now. The Internet changes all the time.

1.8 Refreshing a Page

Sometimes a page is not displayed on your screen as it should be. When that happens, you can tell *Internet Explorer* to reload the page again: to *refresh* it. Just watch what happens:

In *Internet Explorer 8*:

☞ **Click**

In *Internet Explorer 9*:

☞ **Click** ↻

You will see that the window will be refreshed and the information is collected once again.

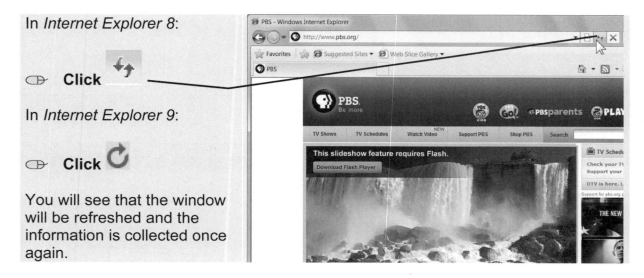

Everything that is shown on your screen must be sent in through the telephone line or the cable. This may take a while. Sometimes it will seem like nothing is happening. But there is a way to check if *Internet Explorer* is still busy loading a page that you have requested:

At the bottom of the screen, the green bar indicates that information is being received:

In *Internet Explorer 9*, you will not see this bar.

Not all information appears immediately on your screen. It may take time to load the entire page, especially if you are using dial-up networking to connect to the Internet.

1.9 Forward and Back

You do not need to retype the web address of a website if you want to revisit it. *Internet Explorer* has a number of buttons that help you *navigate* the Internet.

At the top left of the window:

⊂⊃ **Click**

The previous web page you viewed will be opened.

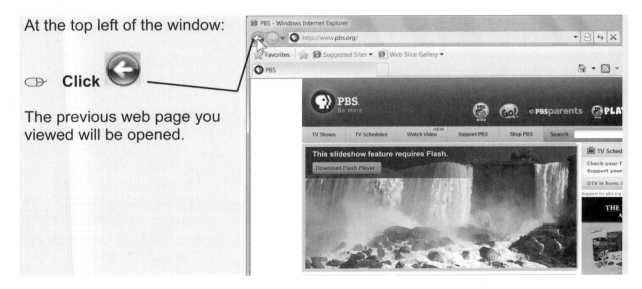

What you see now is the website where search provider *Bing* was helping you:

In *Internet Explorer 9*, you will probably see the window of the Visual Steps website on the next page.

Perhaps you noticed how quickly this is done. *Internet Explorer* retains the websites you recently visited in its memory so that you can quickly look at them again without the need of requesting the information through your telephone line or cable.

In *Internet Explorer 8*:

☞ **Click** two more times

In *Internet Explorer 9*:

☞ **Click** once again

Now you will go back to the website you first visited.

Once again, the start page is displayed:

Now you can no longer browse back. That is because this was the first website you opened.

The button is gray and can no longer be used:

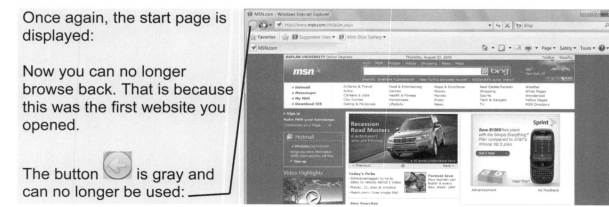

You can, however, browse the other way. There is a special button for this as well.

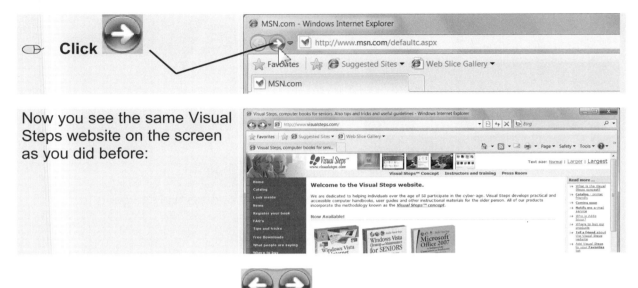

Click

Now you see the same Visual Steps website on the screen as you did before:

As you have seen, the buttons ⬅️➡️ can easily be used to switch back and forth between the websites you have viewed. This is called "surfing" the Internet. However, these websites will not remain in memory forever. When you close *Internet Explorer,* the websites will be removed from the browser's memory.

1.10 Tabbed Browsing

Internet Explorer has an interesting feature that allows you to open multiple websites in a single browser window. This is called *tabbed browsing*. You can start by opening a new, blank tab:

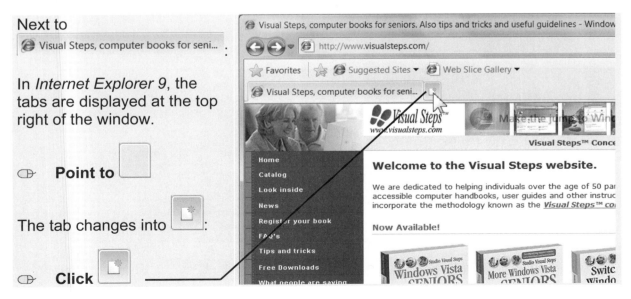

Next to

 Visual Steps, computer books for seni... .

In *Internet Explorer 9*, the tabs are displayed at the top right of the window.

Point to

The tab changes into :

Click

In the new tab you will see a web page with information about tabs, your most visited web pages or other things.

The web address 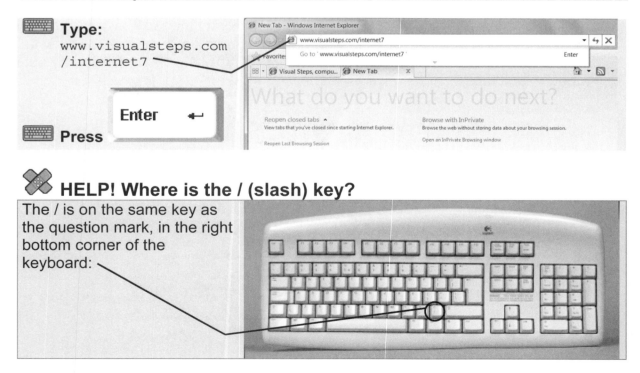 aboutTabs is blue, so you could start typing a new web address right away:

In the next paragraph, you will use the new tab to open a web page in the *subdirectory* of the Visual Steps publishing company website.

1.11 Subdirectories

Some websites have an additional website added onto the main web address. This extra website is in a subdirectory. The subdirectory is separated from the main address by a / (*slash*). Take, for example, the website for this book:

www.visualsteps.com/internet7

Type:
www.visualsteps.com
/internet7

Enter ←

Press

❌ HELP! Where is the / (slash) key?

The / is on the same key as the question mark, in the right bottom corner of the keyboard:

After a short while, you see a website with information about this book:

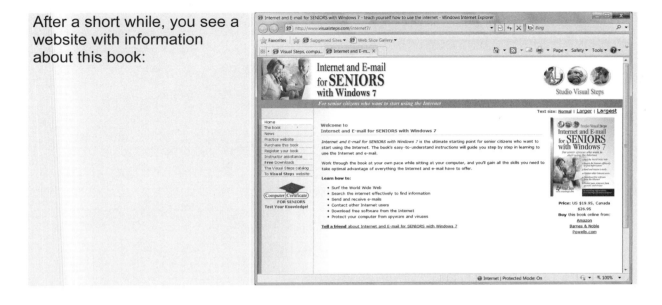

1.12 Browsing by Clicking

Nearly every website will have a navigation list, a sort of *table of contents* summarizing the subjects you can find on the site. This website has one too. You can see the subjects in a column on the left-hand side. By clicking on one of the subjects, you can go to another page:

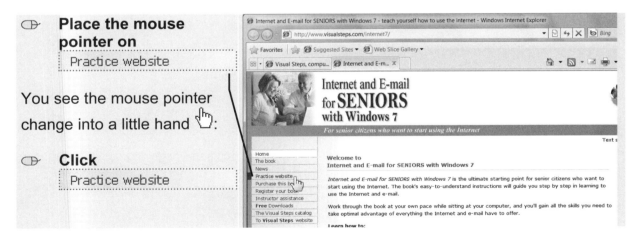

Place the mouse pointer on

Practice website

You see the mouse pointer change into a little hand 🖑:

Click

Practice website

You can click anywhere on a web page where you see the little hand appear. Not only buttons, but also bits of text or images may be 'clickable'. A word, a button or an image that you can click is called a *link*. Sometimes the word *hyperlink* is used.

The practice website for this book is opened in the second tab, replacing the website for this book:

On the page you see various buttons that link to other pages:

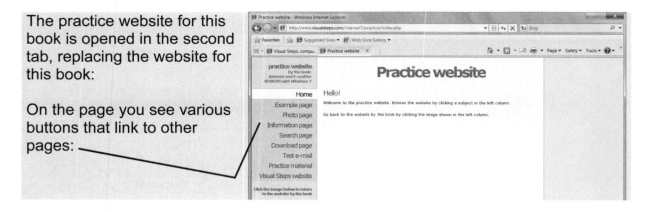

1.13 Opening a Link in a New Tab

When you click a link, the new web page will replace the old web page in the tab you are working in. *Internet Explorer* has a trick to open a link directly in a new tab. Try that with one of the links on the exercise page:

Press and hold

Ctrl

Click

Example page

Release

Ctrl

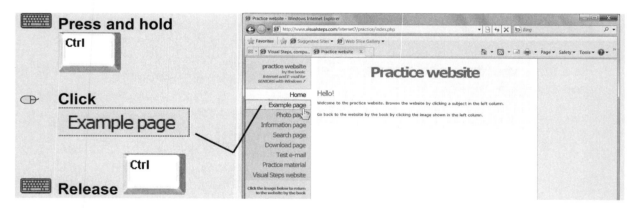

The example page opens in a new tab.

Click the third tab

Now you can read what is on
the example page:

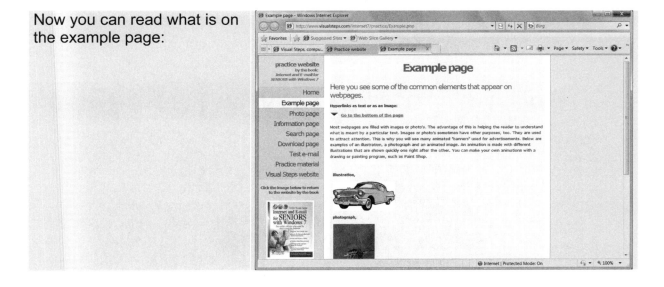

1.14 Using the Scroll Bars

When you view pages on the Internet, you may need to use the *scroll bar*. Even if
you maximize the browser window, it might not be large enough to hold all of the
information. In order to see the rest of the page, you must use the vertical scroll bar.

At the bottom of the scroll
box:

☞ **Click**

You see the page slide
upwards:

You can move the page back down so you can see the top again.

At the top of the scroll box:

☞ **Click** ▲

You see the page slide back down:

You can move the page very precisely by dragging with the mouse. Here is how you drag:

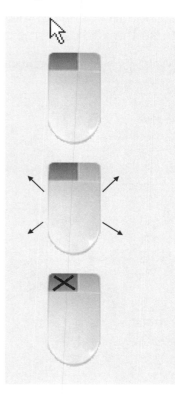

- Point to something with the mouse pointer.

- Press the left mouse button and keep it pressed.

- Move the mouse.

- Release the mouse button when you are finished.

By dragging with the mouse, you can move the slidable part of the scroll box, called the *scroll bar*. Give it a try:

 Drag the scroll bar down

The page slides in the opposite direction. Now you can read the bottom part of the text:

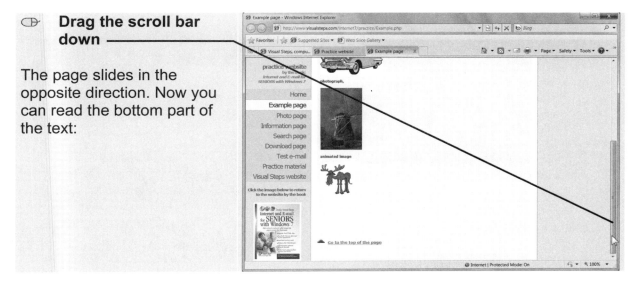

This window sliding is called *scrolling* in computer language.

⍛ Tip

The scroll wheel
The rapidly growing popularity of the Internet has resulted in various new additions to the mouse, including one called the scroll wheel.
By turning the wheel with your finger, the contents of the window will scroll. This is the same thing that happens when you use the scroll bar, but it is much easier and quicker.

Once you have gotten used to a mouse wheel, you will never want to do without.
To scroll down, roll the wheel backward (toward you).
To scroll up, roll the wheel forward (away from you).

⍛ Tip

Clicking with the scroll wheel
The mouse wheel can also be used to click a link:

 Place your mouse pointer on a link

 Press the scroll wheel down

Now the link automatically opens in a new tab.

♀ Tip

Other types of mice

In addition to the classic mouse shape, there are also *ergonomically*-shaped mice with extra buttons for your thumb, for example. You can give these different buttons specific functions.

A *trackball* is a kind of "reverse" mouse. The device does not move on your desk, instead you roll the ball with your fingers to move the mouse pointer. The trackball also has a scroll wheel for the Internet and multiple buttons.

1.15 Back to the Home Page

A good website is made in such a way that you can easily move from one page to the next without getting lost. Most websites, for example, have a button marked *Home* or *Start* that when clicked will return you to the website's *home page*.

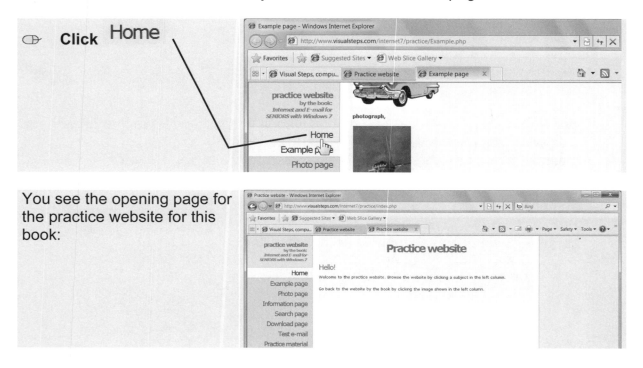

☞ **Click Home**

You see the opening page for the practice website for this book:

1.16 A Second Window

Up to this point, you have viewed all the web pages in tabs in a single *Internet Explorer* window. However, a website can be designed so that a new browser window is opened when you click a hyperlink. You do not have any control over this, because it has been programmed into the website and happens automatically. There is a hyperlink like this on the exercise page. Give it a try:

Please note:

In *Internet Explorer 9,* the photo does not open automatically in a new window, but instead in a new tab. You have no influence over this. You can proceed further with

⇧ **Shift**

the next actions by using the ⇧ Shift -key.

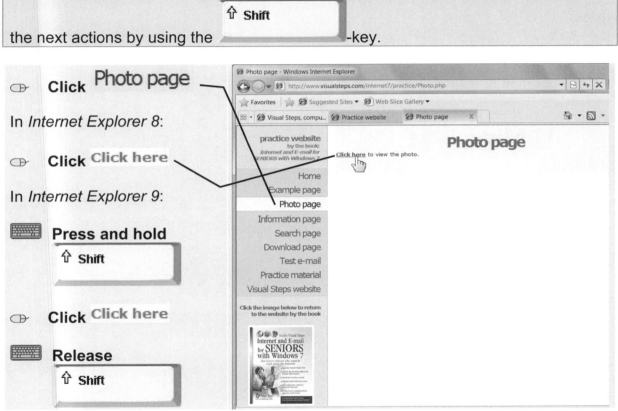

Click **Photo page**

In *Internet Explorer 8:*

Click **Click here**

In *Internet Explorer 9:*

Press and hold ⇧ **Shift**

Click **Click here**

Release ⇧ **Shift**

You see a new window
containing a photo:

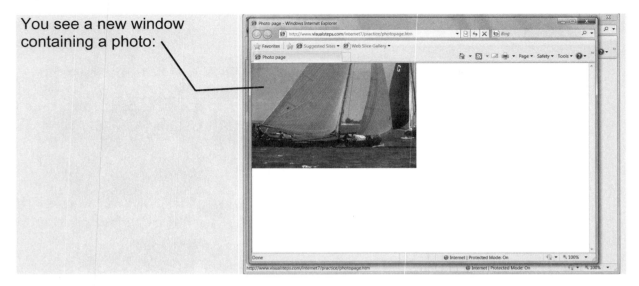

If you do not want to close this page, and would like to keep this window available,
you can minimize it.

1.17 Minimizing a Window

Making a window small is called *minimizing*.

⬚ **Click** [—]

The window containing the
photo will be minimized.

Now you see the window with
the practice website and the
other tabs again:

You can also minimize this window:

⬚ **Click** [—]

The window will be
minimized.

Now you have minimized two windows, the window with the photo and the window with the practice website and the other tabs.

Both windows have been minimized:

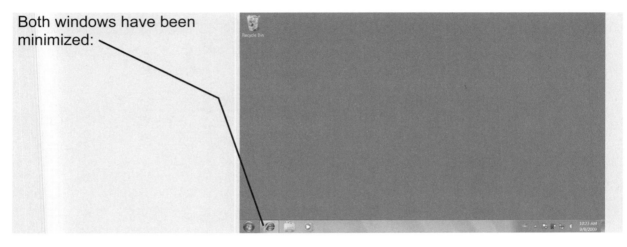

 The gray bar next to is called the *taskbar*. The taskbar always contains the buttons for the programs you are currently using.

1.18 Opening a Window

You can quickly re-open a window by using the buttons on the taskbar:

On the taskbar:

☞ **Point to**

Now, a miniature version of the windows is displayed above the taskbar:

☞ **Click**

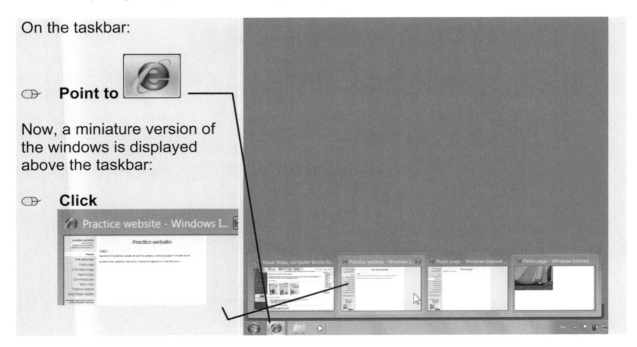

You see the window for the practice website again. Now you can open the window with the photo the same way:

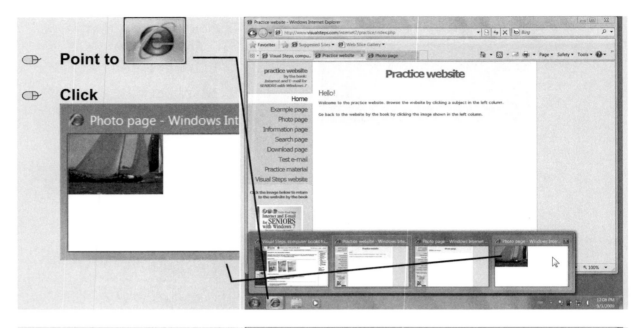

Point to

Click

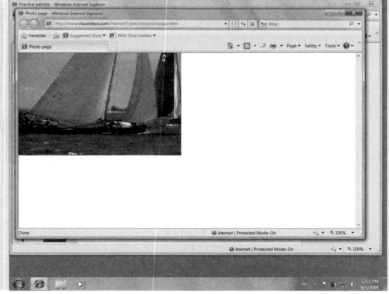

The window with the photo now appears on top of the other window:

1.19 Closing Windows

When you have several windows opened, you can always close the ones you no longer need.

➥ Please note:

Always keep at least one *Internet Explorer* window open, or the connection to the Internet may be broken.

In this case, you can close the window with the photo.

In the window with the photo:

☞ Click ❌

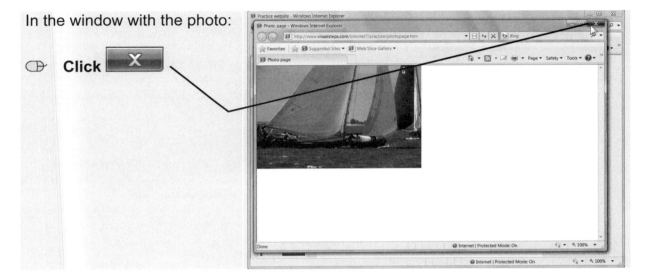

The window closes.

💡 Tip

Opening a link in a new window
Even when it has not been programmed into the website, you can always open a link in a new browser window, instead of in the same window or a new tab. Here is how to do this:

⌨ Press and hold ⇧ Shift

☞ Click the link

⌨ Release ⇧ Shift

A new browser window opens and you see the website to the link you just clicked.

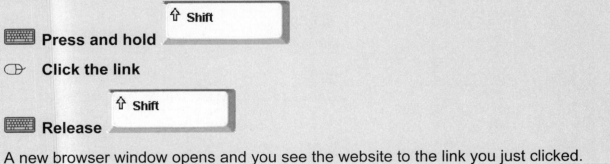

1.20 Closing Tabs

A tab you no longer need can also be closed. Try that with the first tab:

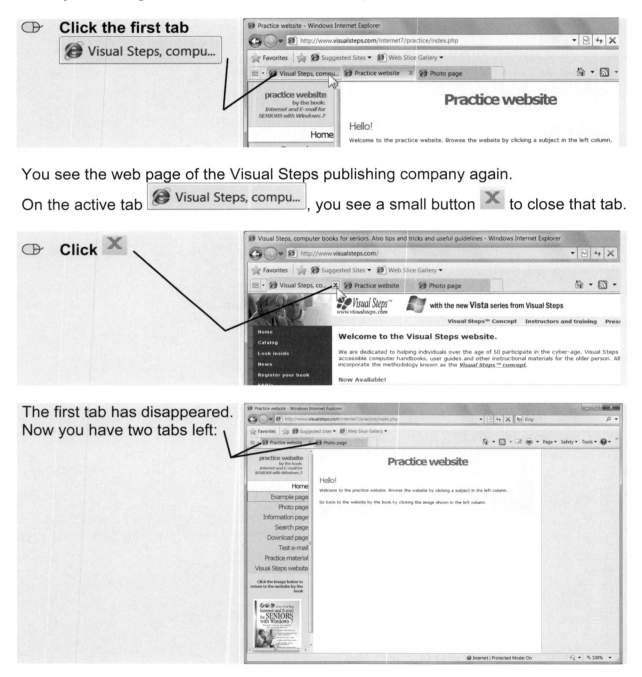

You see the web page of the Visual Steps publishing company again.

On the active tab, you see a small button to close that tab.

The first tab has disappeared. Now you have two tabs left:

💡 **Tip**

Quick Tabs

When you have multiple web pages open on separate tabs, *Quick Tabs* provides a miniature view of all your open tabs. This makes it easier to find the web page that you want to view.

Please note: *Internet Explorer 9* does not contain this function.

Click 🔲

Quick Tabs shows you a miniature version of each opened tab:

You can switch to a tab by clicking its miniature.

Click

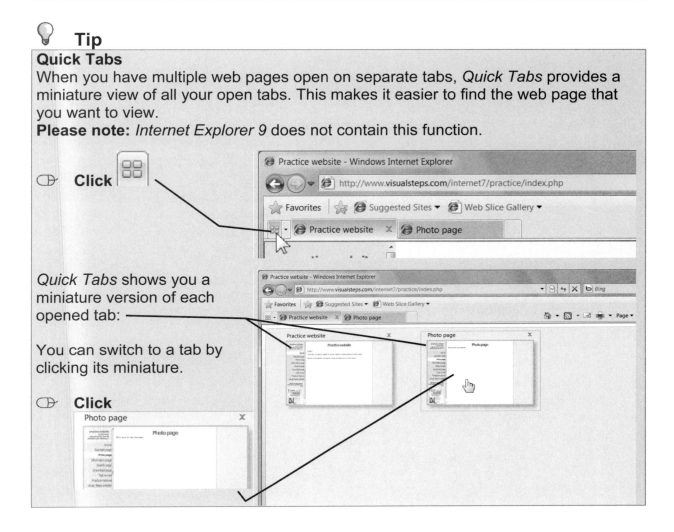

1.21 Zooming In and Out

Images and text on web pages can be very small. By zooming in on part of the website, you can see more detail or read the text more easily. You can give that a try on the example page:

You see the practice website:

Click Example page

You see this page:

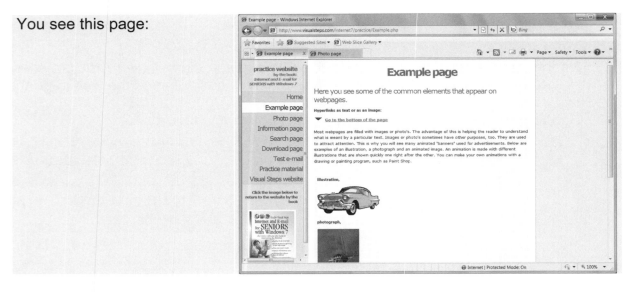

Zooming in will enlarge the text and the objects on your screen.

In the bottom right hand corner:

☞ **Click** 🔍 100%

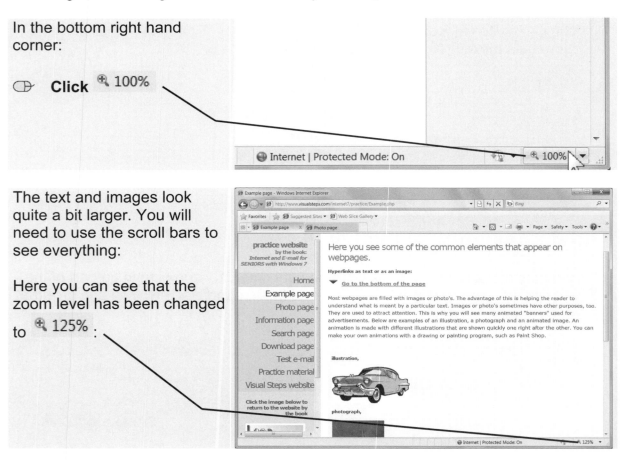

The text and images look quite a bit larger. You will need to use the scroll bars to see everything:

Here you can see that the zoom level has been changed to 🔍 125% :

You can zoom in even more:

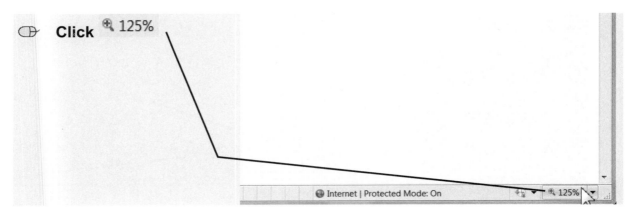

Now the zoom level has increased to 🔍 150%. Clicking this button again will not increase the zoom level anymore. Instead, you will go back to the original level of 🔍 100%. Try that:

Everything has returned to its normal size:

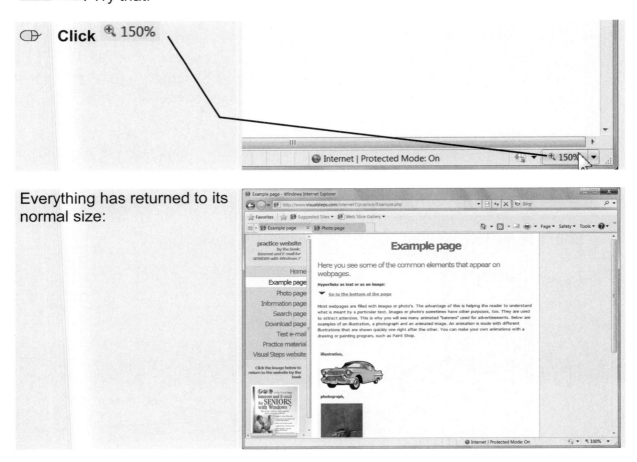

It is possible to zoom in beyond 150%, even up to 400%. This is how you do that:

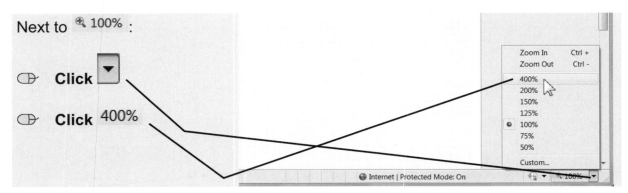

You have zoomed in so far that you can only see a small part of the web page.

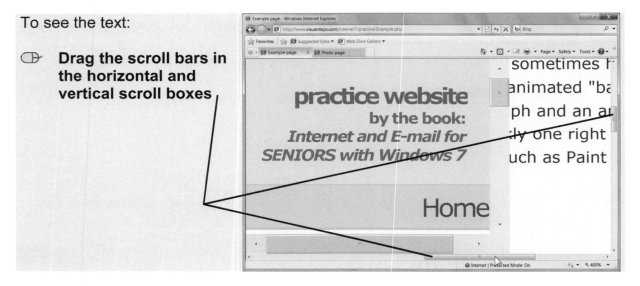

With a zoom level of 50% you can see most of the web page.

However, most of the text is now very small and difficult to read. Just one click will bring you back to a zoom level of 100%:

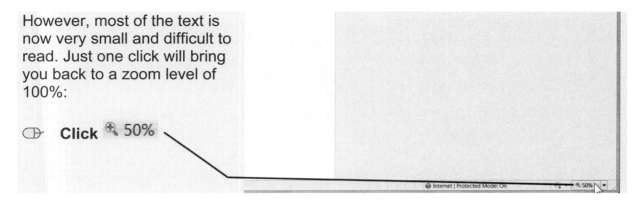

☞ **Click** 🔍 50%

The website is now shown in its normal size.

1.22 Disconnecting from the Internet

If you have a common analog dial-up connection to the Internet, you have to disconnect each time you stop using the Internet. No other calls can come through to you as long as you are connected to the Internet.

If you have a broadband connection like DSL or cable, you are always connected to the Internet, whether you are using the web or not. You do not have to disconnect.

Follow these steps to close the *Internet Explorer* window and disconnect.

☞ **Click** X

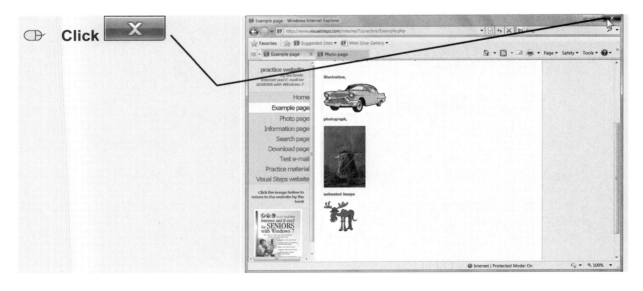

When multiple tabs are in use, *Internet Explorer* checks if you want to close all of them:

☞ **Click** Close all tabs

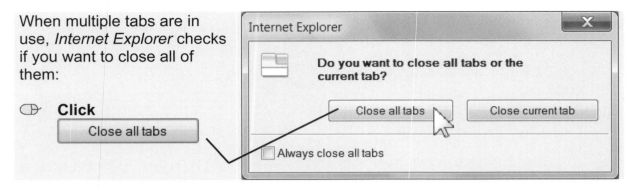

If you have a dial-up connection, you see the *Auto Disconnect* window:

☞ **Click** Disconnect Now

The connection has been broken.

Please note: Maybe this window looks a bit different on your computer.

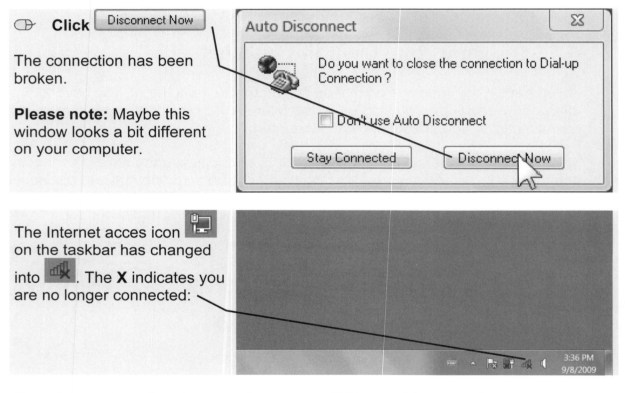

The Internet acces icon on the taskbar has changed into . The **X** indicates you are no longer connected:

If you have a broadband connection such as DSL or cable, you will not see the *Auto Disconnect* window. You will still see in the notification area on the far right side of the taskbar because you are continuously online.

HELP! The connection is not broken.

Do you have a dial-up connection to the Internet and you do not see the *Auto Disconnect* window?

Do you still see the Internet acces icon 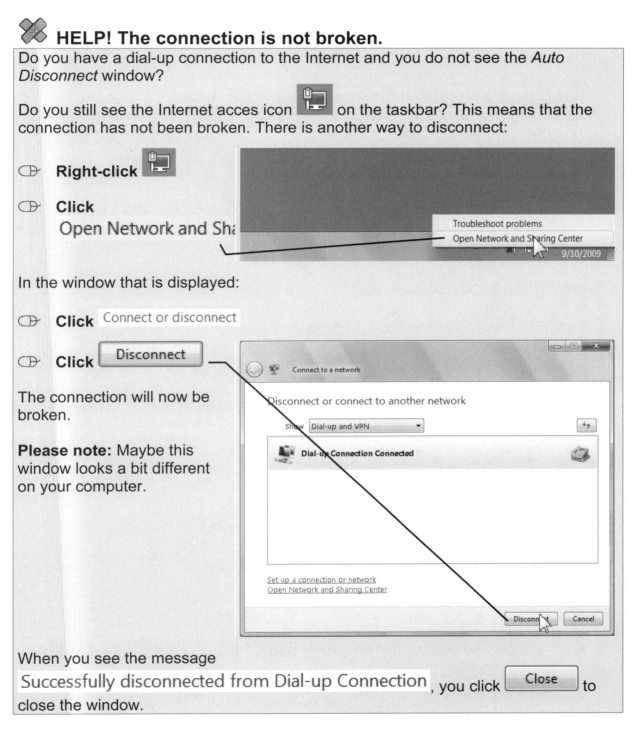 on the taskbar? This means that the connection has not been broken. There is another way to disconnect:

☞ **Right-click**

☞ **Click**
   Open Network and Sha

Troubleshoot problems
Open Network and Sharing Center

9/10/2009

In the window that is displayed:

☞ **Click** Connect or disconnect

☞ **Click** Disconnect

The connection will now be broken.

Please note: Maybe this window looks a bit different on your computer.

Connect to a network

Disconnect or connect to another network

Show   Dial-up and VPN

Dial-up Connection Connected

Set up a connection or network
Open Network and Sharing Center

Disconnect   Cancel

When you see the message
Successfully disconnected from Dial-up Connection , you click Close to close the window.

In this chapter you learned how to surf the Internet. With the following exercises you can practice what you have learned.

1.23 Exercises

The following exercises will help you master what you have just learned. Have you forgotten how to do something? Use the number beside the footsteps to look it up in the appendix *How Do I Do That Again?*

Exercise: Surfing

Going from one website to another is called surfing. In this exercise, you will surf to websites you visited previously.

☞ Start *Internet Explorer*. $\mathscr{C}\mathscr{C}^1$

☞ If necessary, connect to the Internet. $\mathscr{C}\mathscr{C}^3$

☞ Type in the address of the Public Broadcasting Service: www.pbs.org $\mathscr{C}\mathscr{C}^4$

☞ Type in the address: www.visualsteps.com/internet7 $\mathscr{C}\mathscr{C}^4$

☞ Go back to www.pbs.org $\mathscr{C}\mathscr{C}^6$

☞ Refresh the page. $\mathscr{C}\mathscr{C}^8$

☞ Go forward to www.visualsteps.com/internet7 $\mathscr{C}\mathscr{C}^7$

☞ Click Practice website .

☞ Click Example page .

☞ Scroll to the bottom of the example page. $\mathscr{C}\mathscr{C}^9$

☞ Go back to the Public Broadcasting Service website. $\mathscr{C}\mathscr{C}^6$

☞ Close *Internet Explorer*. $\mathscr{C}\mathscr{C}^2$

☞ If necessary, close the connection to the Internet. $\mathscr{C}\mathscr{C}^5$

Exercise: Tabs and Windows

In this exercise, you will practice working with tabs and windows.

☞ Start *Internet Explorer* 👣1 and if necessary, connect to the Internet. 👣3

☞ Type in the address: www.visualsteps.com 👣4

☞ Open a new tab. 👣61

☞ Type in the address: www.visualsteps.com/internet7 👣4

☞ Click Practice website.

☞ Open the link Example page in a new tab. 👣62

☞ Click Photo page.

If you are using *Internet Explorer 9*:

☞ Press and hold ⇧ Shift

☞ Click Click here.

☞ Minimize the photo page window. 👣11

☞ Switch to the first tab. 👣63

☞ Minimize the *Internet Explorer* window. 👣11

☞ Open the window with the photo by using the taskbar. 👣12

☞ Close the window with the photo. 👣13

☞ Open the *Photo page* window by using the taskbar. 👣12

☞ Close the second tab. 👣64

☞ Close *Internet Explorer* 👣2 and if necessary, close the Internet connection. 👣5

1.24 Background Information

Glossary

Address bar	The Address bar is located near the top of the *Internet Explorer* window. It displays the web address of the web page you are currently viewing. By typing a new web address and pressing the Enter key you can open another web page.
Back button	Use the Back button ⬅ to return to the previous web page.
Broadband connection	A high speed Internet connection. Broadband connections are typically 256 kilobytes per second (KBps) or faster. Broadband includes DSL and cable modem service.
Browser, Web browser	A program used to display web pages and to navigate the Internet. *Internet Explorer* is a web browser.
Cable Internet	Cable Internet access is a broadband connection that uses the same wiring as cable TV. To use cable, you need an account with a cable Internet Service Provider in your area. The ISP usually provides any necessary equipment, and often sends a technician to set it up for you.
Desktop	The desktop is the main screen area that you see after you turn on your computer and log on to *Windows 7*. When you open programs or folders, they appear on the desktop.
Dial-up connection	Connecting to the Internet by using a modem and a telephone line. Usually a low speed analog connection.
Dragging	Moving an item on the screen by selecting the item and then pressing and holding down the left mouse button while sliding or moving the mouse.
DSL	Digital Subscriber Line - a type of high speed Internet connection using standard telephone wires. This is a broadband connection. The ISP is usually a phone company.
Forward button	Use the Forward button ➡ to go to the website you visited after the one you are now viewing.

- Continue reading on the next page -

Home page	The first page or opening page of a website. Also the page that is displayed when you first start *Internet Explorer.*
Hyperlink, Link	A hyperlink or link, is a navigation element in a web page that automatically displays the referred information when the user clicks on the hyperlink. A hyperlink can be text or images like buttons, icons or pictures. You can recognize a hyperlink when the mouse pointer turns into a hand 🖑.
Icon	A small picture that represents a folder, program, or object.
Internet	A network of computer networks which operates worldwide using a common set of communications protocols. The part of the Internet that most people are familiar with is the World Wide Web (WWW).
Internet Explorer	A program used to display web pages and to navigate the Internet.
ISP	An Internet Service Provider (ISP) is a company that provides you with access to the Internet, usually for a fee. The most common ways to connect to an ISP are by using a phone line (dial-up) or broadband connection (cable or DSL). Many ISPs provide additional services such as e-mail accounts, virtual hosting, and space for you to create a website.
Maximize	Increase the size of a window to full-screen size.
Minimize	Reduce a window to a button on the taskbar.
Modem	A modem is a device that connects your computer to your telephone line or cable network.
Password	A string of characters that a user must enter to gain access to a resource that is password protected. Passwords help ensure that unauthorized users do not access your Internet connection or your computer.
Program	A set of instructions that a computer uses to perform a specific task, such as word processing or calculating.
Quick Tabs	*Quick Tabs* gives a miniature view of all your open tabs. Not available in *Internet Explorer 9.*
Refreshing	Reloading a web page.
Restore	Return a window to its former size.

- Continue reading on the next page -

Scroll bars	When a web page picture exceeds the size of its window, scroll bars appear to allow you to see the information that is currently out of view. You can drag the horizontal or vertical scroll bar to display the desired part of the web page.
Surfing	Going from one website to another.
Tab	Part of the *Internet Explorer* window on which a separate website can be opened.
Tabbed browsing	Tabbed browsing allows you to open multiple websites in a single browser window. You can open web pages on new tabs, and switch between them by clicking the tab.
Taskbar	The taskbar is the long horizontal bar at the bottom of your screen. The taskbar is usually visible.
User name	Login name.
Web address	The web address of a website uniquely identifies a location on the Internet. An example of a web address is: **www.visualsteps.com**. A web address is also called an URL (Uniform Resource Locator). People use URLs to find websites, but computers use IP addresses to find websites. An IP address usually consists of four groups of numbers separated by periods, such as 192.200.44.69. Special computers on the Internet translate URLs into IP addresses (and vice versa).
Web page	A web page is a resource of information that is suitable for the World Wide Web and can be accessed through a browser.
Website	A website is a collection of interconnected web pages, typically common to a particular domain name on the World Wide Web on the Internet.
Window	A rectangular box or frame on a computer screen in which programs and content appear.
Windows 7	Operating system: the computer program that manages all other computer programs on your computer. The operating system stores files, allows you to use programs, and coordinates the use of computer hardware (mouse, keyboard).
WWW	World Wide Web - web of computers, connected to each other - containing an infinite amount of web pages.
Zooming in or out	Enlarge or reduce the view of a web page. Zoom enlarges or reduces everything on the page, including text and images.

Source: Windows Help and Support

The history of the Internet
Soon after the introduction of the first computers, people in offices began connecting them using cables so that every employee could exchange information with others. Computers that are connected to one another are called a *network*.

The first of these networks began in the USA at the end of the 1960s. The Department of Defense had a network called ARPANET. ARPANET was an experiment. The DoD wanted to develop a technology that would allow all the defense computers to communicate with one another, even if part of the connection fell away because of a nuclear attack, for example. The problem was solved by a method that works just like the highway network. If a road is blocked, you can usually still get to your destination by taking a different route. This technique worked. Similar networks appeared in other countries.

At the end of the 1980s, all these networks were connected to one another. The Internet was born. At first, mainly universities and research institutions were connected to the Internet, but in 1990 individuals and commercial companies also gained access to it. From that moment on, the number of users has grown phenomenally, a growth that continues up to this day.

Domain names
A web address associated with a particular name is called a domain name. Every web address has a suffix such as *.com*.

For example: www.visualsteps.**com**

There are several variations on this suffix. In Europe, a country code is often used:

For example: www.visualsteps.**nl**

Other country codes include **.be** for Belgium and **.de** for Germany.
Outside Europe and in the United States, a different system is used. The suffix indicates the type of organization:
.com .... commercial company
.edu .... educational institution
.org .... non-profit organization

Internet Service Providers

Connecting to the Internet is done over a telephone line or cable. Computers can communicate with one another over the home network. Connecting your computer to others usually happens with the help of an Internet Service Provider (ISP). This ISP gives access to the Internet by means of a large number of computers, all of which are connected to the Internet. When you make contact with one of the ISP's computers, you gain access to the Internet.

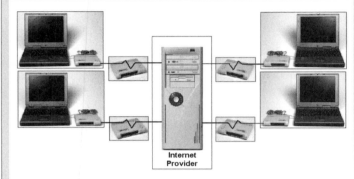

The Internet Service Provider offers access to many users

There are two kinds of subscriptions: free and premium. In practice they offer the same options, though some providers distinguish between them. With a premium subscription, the paying customer will get faster access and more disk space for his own website. You do not have to feel sorry for the free providers, though - they make their money on advertisements placed directly on your screen.
If you have a DSL or cable connection, you pay a fixed amount every month.

Dial-up networking

Most large ISPs have so many *access numbers* (the telephone number for the ISP that your own computer will call) that you can always call locally. If there is no local number in your area, the ISP usually offers a toll-free number you can call. That means accessing the Internet will not cost you a lot of money on your telephone bill.

What services do ISPs provide?
- access to the World Wide Web (viewing information on the Internet)
- e-mail (electronic mail)
- FTP (download files from other computers)
- newsgroups (discuss topics with a group of other users)

During the time you are connected to the Internet, you, the *client*, are in contact with your ISP's computers. These computers are called *servers*. The computers work together according to the *client-server* model.

The modem

It is easy to understand why the telephone network is used to connect computers that may be thousands of miles apart. After all, nearly everyone has a telephone line. Cable TV providers have also entered the Internet market, using the cable network for Internet connections.

You need a special device to connect to the Internet via a telephone line or a cable connection: the *modem*. A modem makes it possible for your computer to communicate with your ISP's computer. There are two kinds of modems:

The first is a separate box that is connected to your computer with a cable. This is called an *external modem*.

Another cable connects the modem to the outlet for the telephone line or the cable TV connection.

External modem

Almost all new computers have a built-in modem. This is called an *internal modem*.

The only part of this you see is a plug for a telephone cable or for a cable connection. These may be found in the back of your desktop computer or on the side of your laptop.

Internal modem

The modem to make a dial-up connection is connected to the telephone jack in your home by a regular telephone cable. You can also use a splitter if you want to keep your telephone connected to this same jack.

Telephone splitter

How to connect the modem

If you have an internal modem, a cable runs from the modem in your computer to the telephone jack. If you use a splitter, you can plug both your telephone and the modem into the same jack.

Computer with internal modem and splitter

If you have an external modem, the modem box is located somewhere between your computer and the telephone jack:

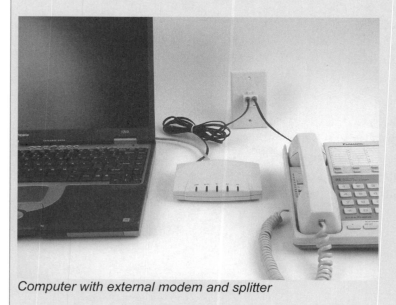

Computer with external modem and splitter

The modem is connected to the computer with a separate cable.

Connecting over a telephone line

The internal or external modem always has an outlet for a *UTP* cable. This is an ordinary telephone cable. There are telephone plugs (also known as *RJ-11* plugs) on both ends. You plug one end of the telephone cable into the modem:

A UTP cable with telephone plugs

The UTP outlet on the modem

Plug the other end of the cable into the telephone jack on your wall:

The telephone plug

The telephone jack

If you want to connect your telephone to this same telephone jack, you can use a splitter. Some splitters fit directly into the phone jack. Others allow you to place it wherever you like, and connect it to the wall jack with another regular telephone cable:

A telephone splitter you can place anywhere

A splitter that connects directly to the phone jack

If you need a longer cable because your computer is too far from the phone jack, you can buy one in a variety of lengths at most appliance stores. Remember, all you need is a regular telephone cable.

1.25 Tips

💡 Tip

Displaying the menu bar permanently
Like other *Windows* programs, *Internet Explorer* has a *menu bar* that can be used to access various functions: File Edit View Favorites Tools Help . The menu bar is not visible when you use the standard settings of *Internet Explorer*.
Please note: this is not possible in *Internet Explorer 9*. If you are using *Internet Explorer 9*, see the *Tip* on the next page to display the menu bar temporarily.

This is how you display the menu bar in *Internet Explorer 8*:

In the top right corner:

☞ **Click** Tools ▾

☞ **Click** Toolbars

☞ **Click** Menu Bar

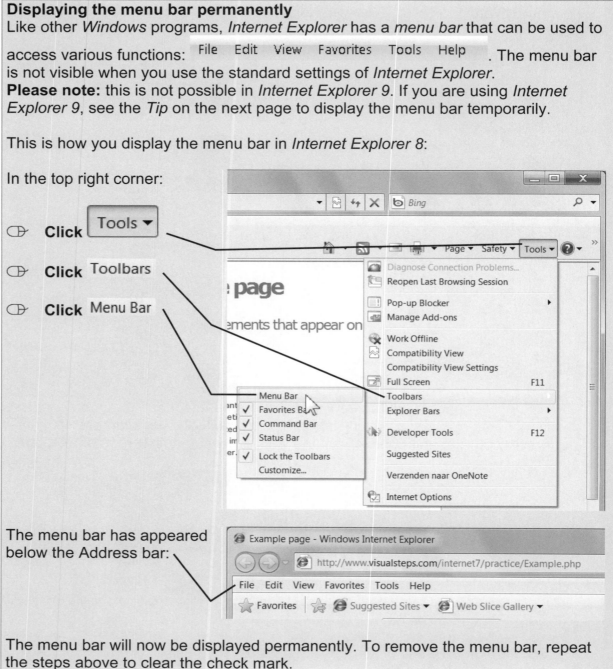

The menu bar has appeared below the Address bar:

The menu bar will now be displayed permanently. To remove the menu bar, repeat the steps above to clear the check mark.

💡 Tip
Displaying the menu bar temporarily
If you want to use the menu bar once without permanently displaying it:

⌨ **Press** `Alt`

💡 Tip
Increase text size
In this chapter you have learned how to adjust the zoom level on a web page. There is also another method for making the letters of the text on web pages larger or smaller. This does not enlarge images, or text on buttons. Here is how to choose the largest text size:

☞ **If necessary, display the menu bar** 🦶**68**

🖰 **Click** View

🖰 **Click** Text Size

🖰 **Click** Largest

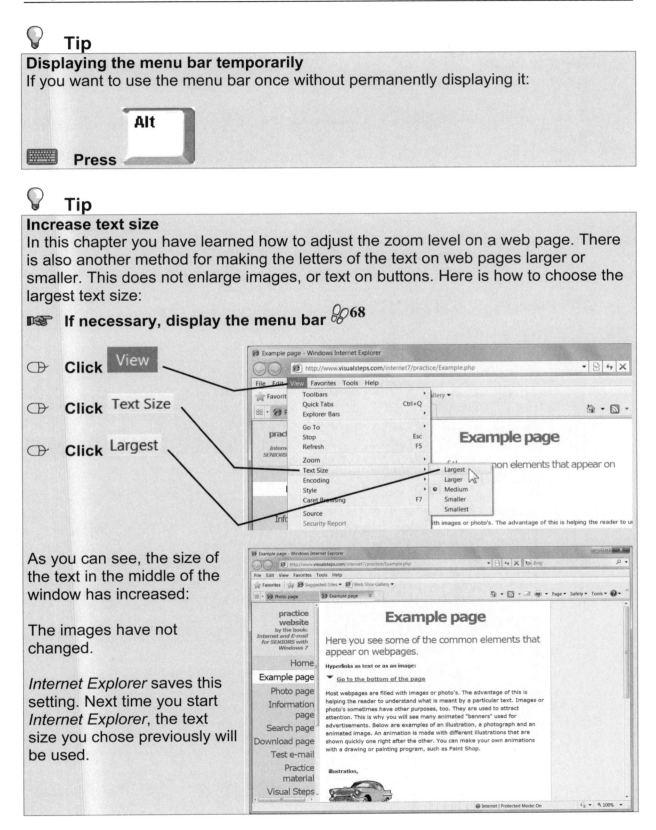

As you can see, the size of the text in the middle of the window has increased:

The images have not changed.

Internet Explorer saves this setting. Next time you start *Internet Explorer*, the text size you chose previously will be used.

💡 Tip

Selected button
Sometimes you can do things very quickly without having to use the mouse.

Do you see that one button has a darker color?

This means this button is already *selected*. Now you can press the Enter key instead of clicking the button with the mouse pointer.

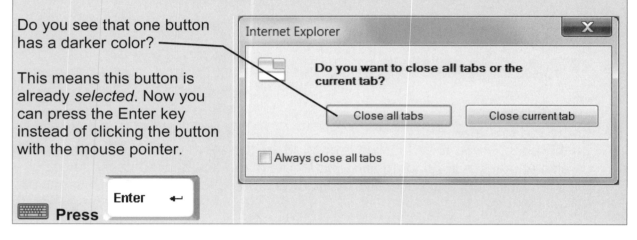

 Press

💡 Tip

An extension reel
Make sure the telephone cable is neatly stored against the wall so you can not trip over it. Buy an extension cord if you need one. There are also telephone extension reels, with one or more telephone jacks on the reel and a telephone plug on the end of the cable. These allow you to keep your telephone cable at just the right length.

💡 Tip

A busy signal
Is your Internet connection made through your telephone line (dial-up)?
If you are connected to the Internet and someone tries to call you, they will get a busy signal. If you are expecting a call, you should wait to connect to the Internet.

Is your Internet connection made through an ISDN line?
Then you can connect to the Internet and call or be called at the same time.

Is your Internet connection made through a DSL line?
Then you can connect to the Internet and call or be called at the same time.

Is your Internet connection made through the cable TV line?
Then, of course, you can always call or be called.

Tip

Zooming in up to 1000%
Zooming in is not limited to 400%. You can zoom in as much as 1000%.

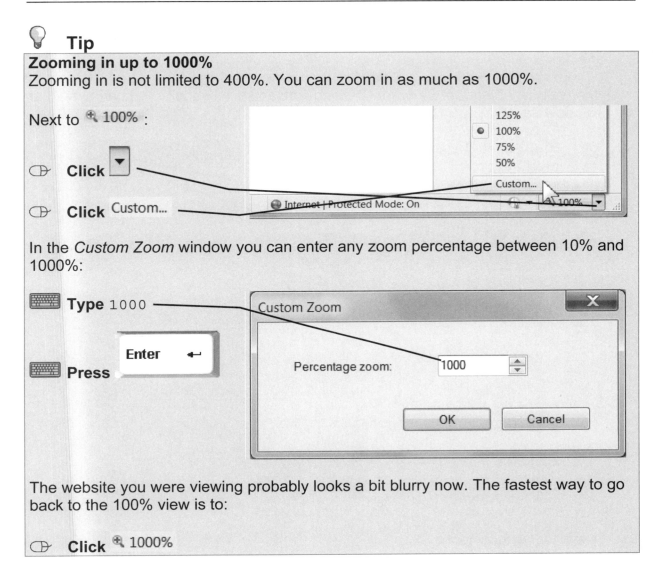

Next to 🔍 100% :

⊕ **Click** ▼

⊕ **Click** Custom...

In the *Custom Zoom* window you can enter any zoom percentage between 10% and 1000%:

⌨ **Type** 1000

⌨ **Press** Enter ←

The website you were viewing probably looks a bit blurry now. The fastest way to go back to the 100% view is to:

⊕ **Click** 🔍 1000%

1.26 Internet Explorer 9

If you are using *Internet Explorer 9*, your window might look a little bit different than the window of *Internet Explorer 8*, which is used for this book. You can change the window as follows:

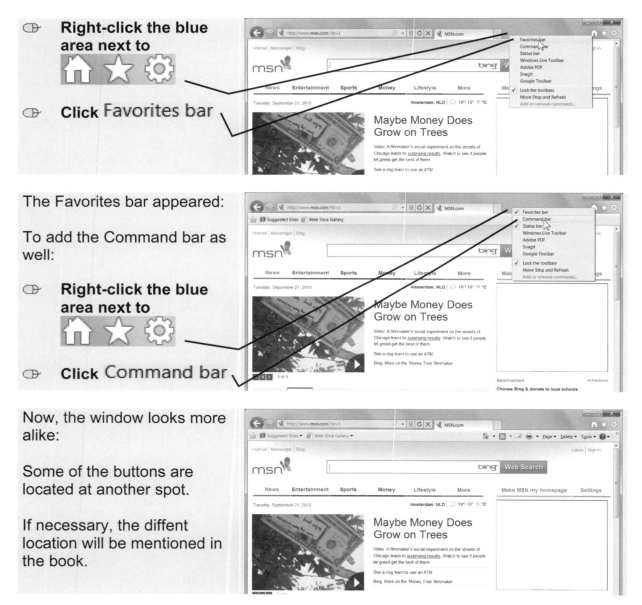

☞ **Right-click the blue area next to**
    🏠 ⭐ ⚙️

☞ **Click** Favorites bar

The Favorites bar appeared:

To add the Command bar as well:

☞ **Right-click the blue area next to**
    🏠 ⭐ ⚙️

☞ **Click** Command bar

Now, the window looks more alike:

Some of the buttons are located at another spot.

If necessary, the diffent location will be mentioned in the book.

2. Navigating the Internet

Surfing the Internet is a fun and enjoyable activity. By clicking on various hyperlinks, you can visit many interesting websites and personal home pages. By *website* we mean an extensive system of web pages for a company or organization. A personal *home page* may consist of only a few web pages. It usually belongs to an individual, or contains only a little commercial information about a company.

The World Wide Web is infinitely large and increases by thousands of websites daily. After surfing for a while, you will no doubt want to revisit an interesting website from time to time. All those hyperlinks make it easy to lose your way, however.

Fortunately, *Internet Explorer* has several built-in options to help you get to where you want to go. In this chapter, you will learn how to use these convenient features, allowing you to 'navigate' straight to your target: back to the web pages you visited earlier.

In this chapter, you will learn how to:

- open a website from the list of addresses previously typed
- save a web address
- open a favorite
- organize your favorites
- use RSS feeds
- temporarily disconnect
- change the *Internet Explorer* home page
- use the *History*
- give a website its own shortcut

2.1 Starting Internet Explorer

☞ **Turn on the computer**

Do you have an external modem?
☞ **Turn on the modem**

Now you can start *Internet Explorer*:

☞ **Start *Internet Explorer*** 👣¹

Internet Explorer starts, and you can connect to the Internet:

☞ **Click** [Connect]

Please note: Maybe this
window looks a bit different
on your computer.

Dial-up Connection   ✕

Select the service you want to connect
to.

Connect to: [Dial-up Connection   ▼]

☐ Connect automatically

[Connect]   [Settings...]   [Work Offline]

➥ **Please note:**

If you are connected to the Internet by cable or DSL, then this *Dial-up Connection*
window will not appear. Your computer is already connected to the Internet.

If your user name and
password are not displayed:

⌨ **Type your user name**

⌨ **Type your password**

☞ **Click a check mark for**
Save this user name and password

☞ **Click** Me only

☞ **Click** [Dial]

Please note: Maybe this
window looks a bit different
on your computer.

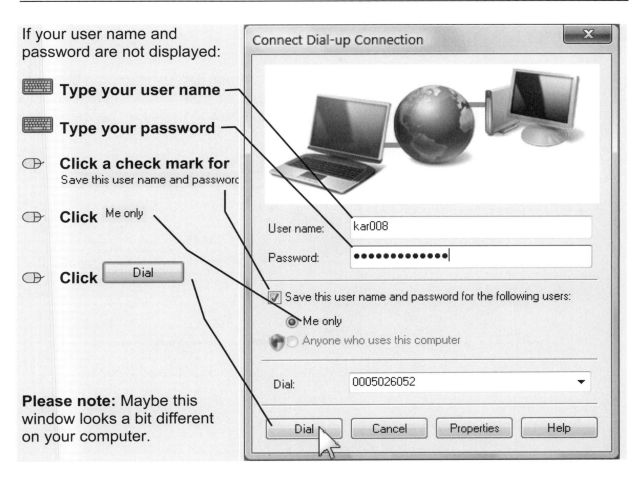

A connection is made to your ISP (Internet Service Provider).

You see the home page as it
is set up on your computer:

This page might be different
on your computer.

You will learn later how to
change the page that appears
when you start *Internet
Explorer*.

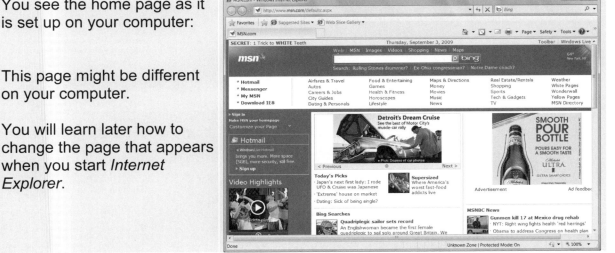

2.2 The Address Bar

Internet Explorer has a useful feature on the Address bar. By clicking a button on the Address bar, you will see a list of website addresses that you have previously typed. You can use this list to reopen a website without having to retype the web address.

At the end of the Address bar:

⊕ **Click**

You see a list of web addresses you have visited before:

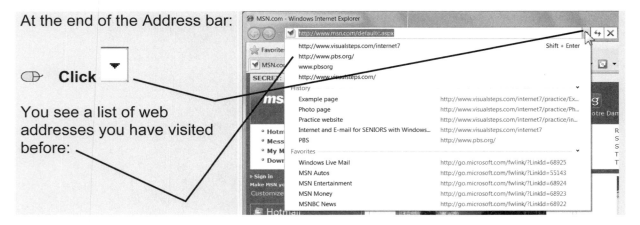

You can click one of these addresses to reopen the associated website:

⊕ **Click**
    http://www.visualsteps.com/

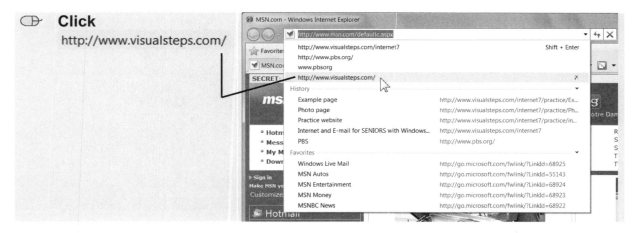

The website for the Visual Steps publishing company will be opened. This method only works for a website that you recently visited. If you would like to keep a web address for a longer time, it is a better idea to save it.

2.3 Saving a Web Address

Once you have found an interesting website, you can save its address. From then on, you can quickly reopen this website anytime without having to remember the web address or retyping it. Saved websites are called favorites in *Internet Explorer*.

Please note:

You can only save a web address when the associated website is displayed in the *Internet Explorer* window.

In this case, you see the Visual Steps website:

In *Internet Explorer 8*:

Click **Favorites**

In *Internet Explorer 9*, at the top right of the window:

Click

Click **Add to Favorites...**

Now you see a small window on top of the web page in which the name of the website has already been inserted:

Click **Add**

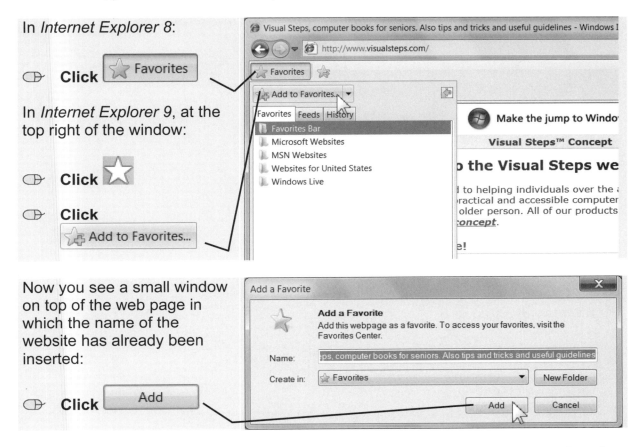

Later, you will see how to quickly reopen this favorite website. To see how a favorite works, you will first need to go to a different website. You can go, for example, to the special website for seniors, *SeniorNet*:

Click the Address bar

Type:
www.seniornet.org

Press Enter

You see the *SeniorNet* home
page:

Now you can open the favorite you just saved.

2.4 Opening a Favorite

You can quickly open your favorite websites using the Favorites Center:

In *Internet Explorer 8*:

⊂⊃ **Click** [☆ Favorites]

In *Internet Explorer 9*, at the
top right of the window:

⊂⊃ **Click** ☆

The Favorites Center is
opened. In Internet Explorer 8
it is displayed at the left side
of the window. In version 9 at
the right side.

⊂⊃ **If necessary, click**
    [Favorites]

⊂⊃ **Click**
    🌐 Visual Steps, computer b

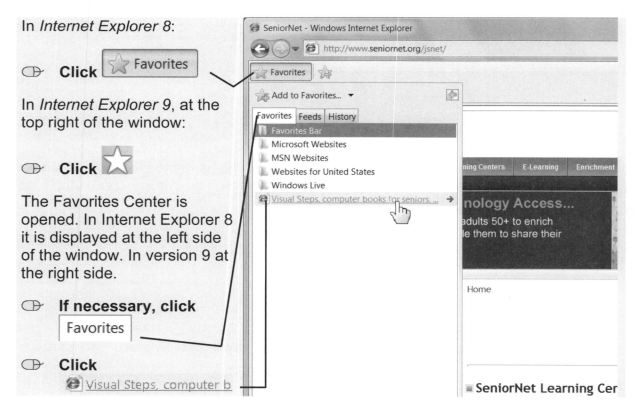

Internet Explorer immediately jumps to the Visual Steps website:

Internet Explorer remembers your favorites even after you have closed the program. This allows you to create an entire collection of websites that you can visit again later.

2.5 Organizing Your Favorites

You can save all your favorite websites in one long list in the Favorites Center, but in the long term this is not very practical. It is better to organize your favorites in separate folders. You can save websites according to subject, for example.
You can also use folders to separate your own favorites from those of other users on the same computer.

For practice, you are going to create a folder for websites related to this book.

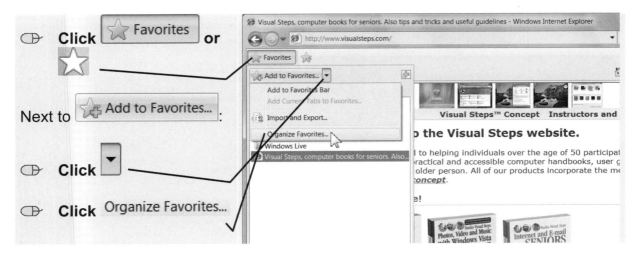

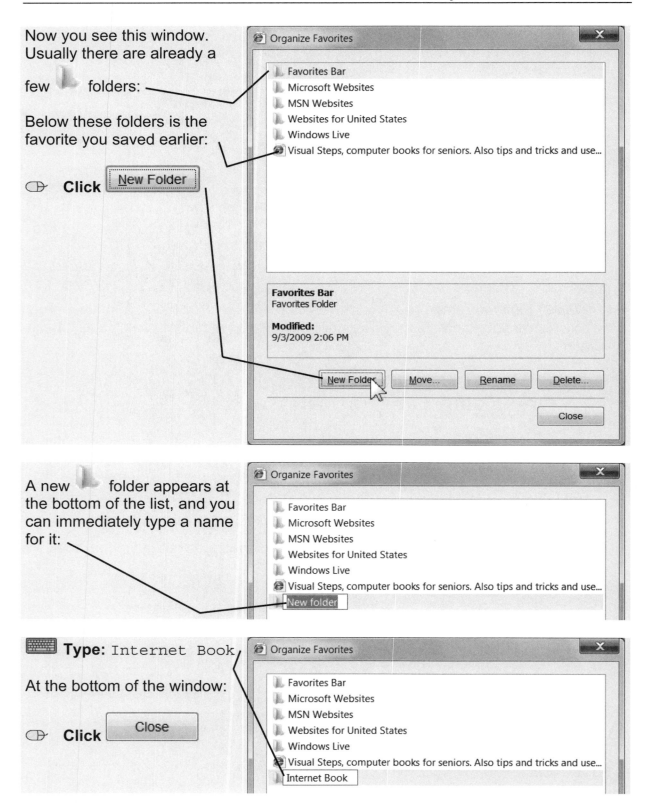

Now you see this window.
Usually there are already a
few [folder icon] folders:

Below these folders is the
favorite you saved earlier:

☞ **Click** New Folder

A new [folder icon] folder appears at
the bottom of the list, and you
can immediately type a name
for it:

⌨ **Type:** Internet Book

At the bottom of the window:

☞ **Click** Close

The folder has now been created. You can check this right away in the Favorites Center:

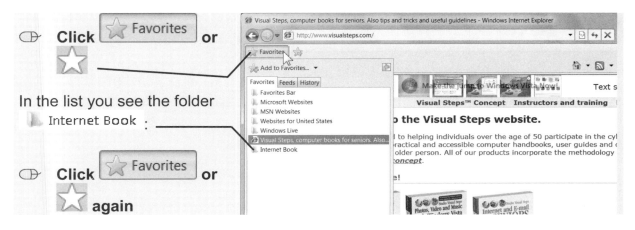

☞ **Click** [⭐ Favorites] **or** ⭐

In the list you see the folder 📁 Internet Book :

☞ **Click** [⭐ Favorites] **or** ⭐ **again**

You have seen that the folder has been created. A little later on, you will read how you can save all the websites related to this book in this new folder.

2.6 Typing Part of a Web Address

At the beginning of this chapter you read about the list of web addresses previously visited. This list can get very long, making it hard to find the address you need. Take a look now at what happens when you start typing just part of a web address:

☞ **Click the Address bar**

⌨ **Type:** `www.visu`

Under the Address bar, a list of web addresses appears that begins with `www.visu`:

Now you just need to click the desired web address in the list:

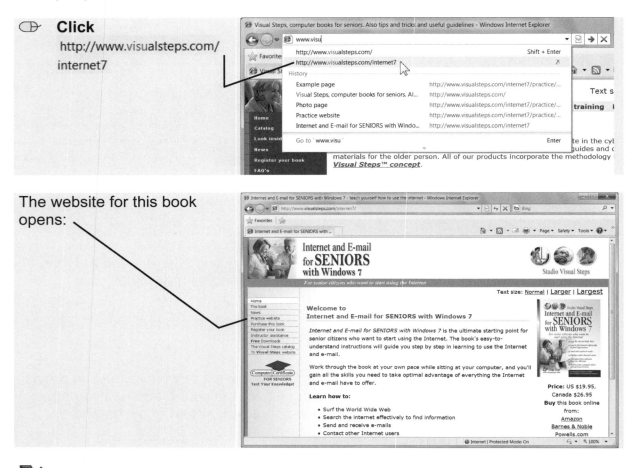

⊂⊅ Click

http://www.visualsteps.com/
internet7

The website for this book
opens:

➥ Please note:

Pay attention to which address you click - *Internet Explorer* also remembers
incorrectly typed web addresses.

2.7 Saving a Web Address in a Folder

It is pretty easy to save a website in the new folder in the Favorites Center.

➥ Please note:

You can only save a web address when the associated website is displayed in the *Internet Explorer* window.

In this case, you now see the website for this book in the window. You can save this website in the new *Internet Book* folder.

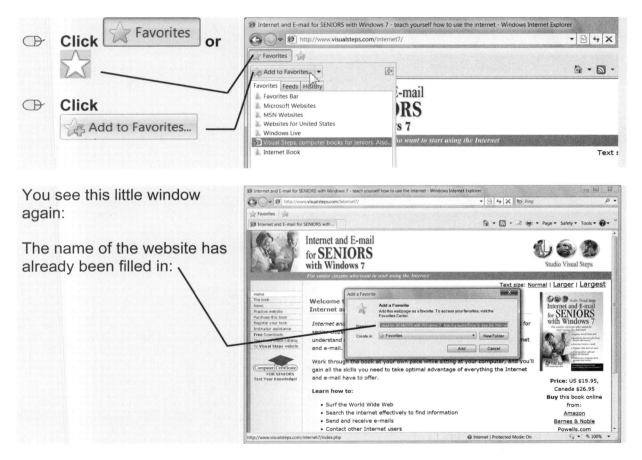

☞ **Click** ⭐ Favorites or ☆

☞ **Click** ⭐ Add to Favorites...

You see this little window again:

The name of the website has already been filled in:

Now you open the folder where you want to save this favorite:

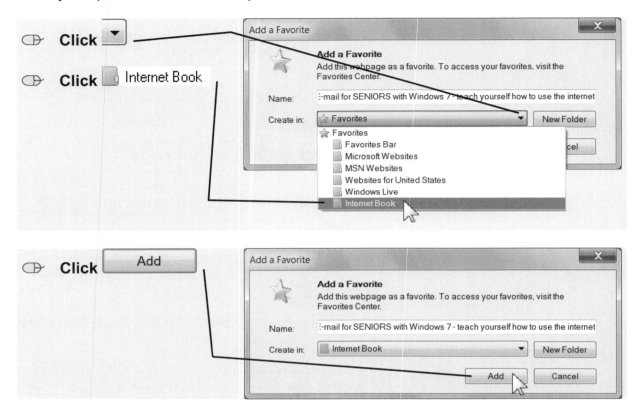

Later on you will check if the website has been saved in the folder. First you open another website, for example the CNN website:

Now you can open the Favorites Center to see if the favorite has been stored in the right folder:

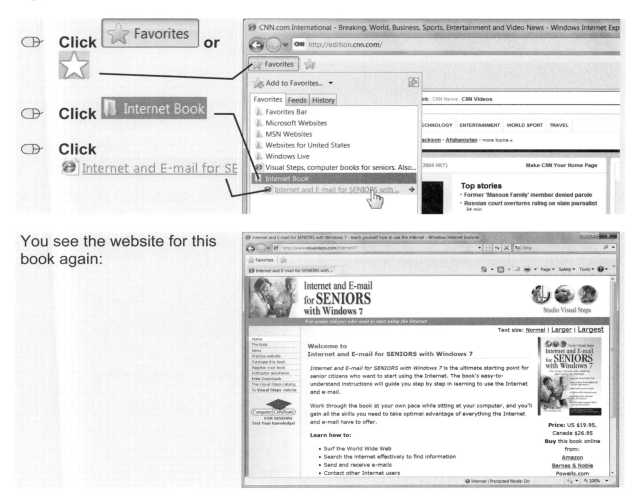

In the next paragraph you will go to the Visual Steps website to learn more about RSS feeds.

2.8 RSS Feeds

Internet is quickly becoming a treasure trove of interesting applications. News agencies like CNN and other dynamic websites offer a service called *RSS feeds*, also called web feeds. The acronym RSS stands for *Really Simple Syndication*, a format used to publish frequently updated digital content. *Internet Explorer* has a built-in feed reader that can display these feeds. Feeds are often used to publish news updates or sports scores. But feeds can also be used to publish other types of digital content, like images and audio or video files. Most RSS feed applications are offered for free. When you subscribe to the Visual Steps Computer tips feeds for exemple, the latest computer tips are automatically sent to your computer when you connect to the Internet.

Internet Explorer looks for RSS feeds on every web page you visit. When available feeds are found, the *RSS Feed* button will change from gray to orange (or green). You can use the Visual Steps website to practice with RSS feeds:

☞ **Go to www.visualsteps.com** 🦶4

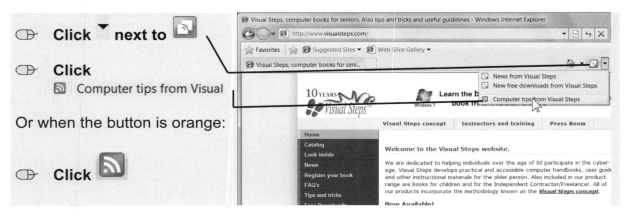

Click next to

Click
Computer tips from Visual

Or when the button is orange:

Click

This will open the web page where you can view the feeds and subscribe to them. Subscribing to a feed is usually free.

The RSS feeds from **visualsteps.com** consist of computer tips:

Click
🔖 Subscribe to this feed

The name of the feed has
already been entered: ——

⊙ **Click** Subscribe

> **Subscribe to this Feed**   ✕
>
> **Subscribe to this Feed**
> When you subscribe to a feed, it is automatically added to
> the Favorites Center and kept up to date.
>
> Name: Computer tips from Visual Steps
>
> Create in: 🔲 Feeds   ▼   New folder
>
>   ☐ Add to Favorites Bar
>
> What is a Feed?   Subscribe   Cancel

You see a confirmation
message:

> 🌐 Computer tips from Visual Steps - Windows Internet Explorer
>
> ← ○ ▾ 🌐 http://www.visualsteps.com/feeds/tips.xml
>
> ⭐ Favorites ☆
>
> 🌐 Computer tips from Visual Steps
>
> **You've successfully subscribed to this feed!**
> Updated content can be viewed in Internet Explorer and other programs that use the Common Feed List.
>
> ⭐ View my feeds

Now that you have subscribed to this feed, it has been added to the *Common Feed List* in the Favorites Center. You can verify this:

⊙ **Click** ⭐ Favorites **or**
☆

The RSS feeds have a
separate section with a button
in the Favorites Center:

⊙ **Click** Feeds ——

> 🌐 Computer tips from Visual Steps - Windows Internet Explorer
>
> ← ○ ▾ 🌐 http://www.visualsteps.com/feeds/tips.xml   ▾ ✦ ✕
>
> ⭐ Favorites ☆
>
> 🌟 Add to Favorites Bar ▾   ⊞
>
> Favorites | Feeds | History
>   📁 Favorites Bar
>   📁 Microsoft Websites   other programs that use the Common Feed List.
>   📁 MSN Websites
>   📁 Websites for United States
>   📁 Windows Live   👣 Visua
>   🌐 Visual Steps, computer books for seniors. Also...   www.visuals
>   📕 Internet Book
>   🌐 Internet and E-mail for SENIORS with Wind...

When you have subscribed to
a feed, they will be listed
here. In this case, there is
only the Visual Steps feed:

⊙ **Click**
🔲 **Computer tips from Visual !**

> 🌐 Computer tips from Visual Steps - Windows Internet Explorer
>
> ← ○ ▾ 🌐 http://www.visualsteps.com/feeds/tips.xml
>
> ⭐ Favorites ☆
>
> 🌟 Add to Favorites Bar ▾   ⊞
>
> Favorites | Feeds | History
>   📁 **Feeds for United States**
>   📁 **Microsoft Feeds**   other programs that use the Common Feed List.
>   🔲 Computer tips from Visual Steps   ✦

The Visual Steps Computer
tips are displayed:

Updated information from the
feed is automatically
downloaded to your
computer, even when you are
not using *Internet Explorer*.

💡 Tip

Feed facts

- Clicking a tip will open all the tips on the Visual Steps website.

- By default, the feed will be updated once a day. To change this default setting, click View feed properties... on the feeds page.

- After you visit the feeds page, all feeds on the page will be marked as read. Next time you visit the feeds page, these old headlines will be gray instead of blue. This makes it easier to recognize the feeds you have not read yet.

- Many websites offer RSS feeds. Make sure to check the website for your local newspaper, or you favorite sports or news channel.

💡 Tip

Feed Headlines on your desktop

Now that you have subscribed to the Visual Steps feed, these headlines are also shown in the *gadget* named *Feed Headlines* on your desktop.

If you want this gadget to display only the Visual Steps tips, then do as follows:

👉 **Right-click the desktop**

A menu appears:

👉 **Click** Gadgets

👉 **Double-click**

Feed Headlines

👉 **Click** ✕

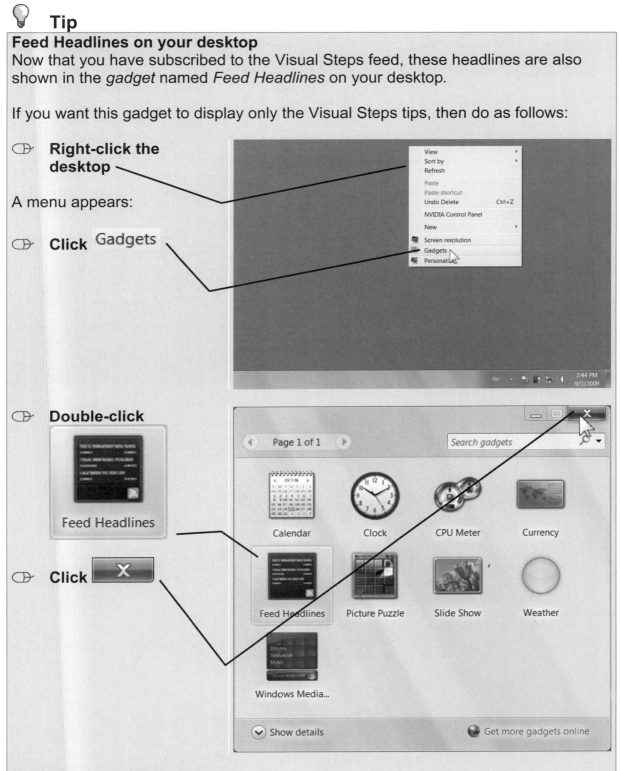

- Continue reading on the next page -

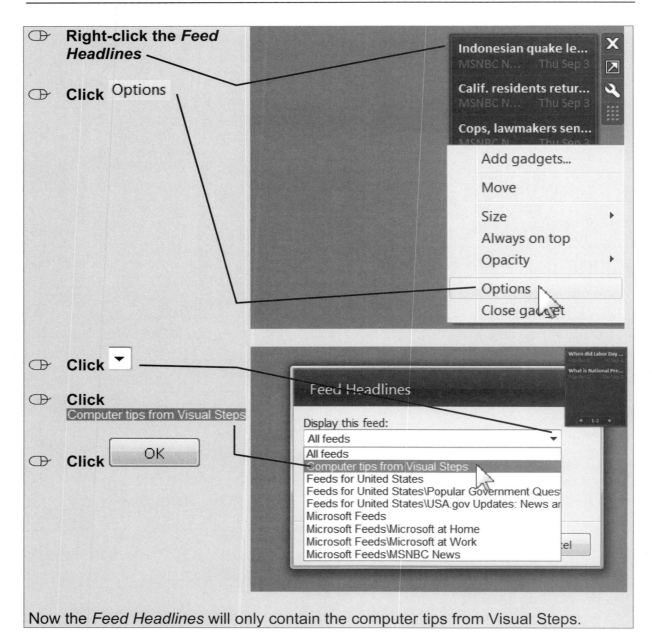

Now the *Feed Headlines* will only contain the computer tips from Visual Steps.

2.9 Temporarily Disconnecting

➥ Please note:

This section only applies when you use a dial-up connection.
If you have a DSL or cable connection, you do not have to worry about your telephone line being busy. You can just read through this section.

If you have a dial-up connection where you have to manually connect to the Internet, you may sometimes want to temporarily break the connection to the Internet to save on telephone charges. For example if you want to do something else, or when a web page takes a long time to read. This way you also free up your telephone line in case someone wants to call you. You do not have to close *Internet Explorer* to do so:

☞ **Right-click**

☞ **Click**
Open Network and Sha

> Troubleshoot problems
> Open Network and Sharing Center
> 9/10/2009

In the window that is displayed:

☞ **Click** Connect or disconnect

This window appears:

☞ **Click** Disconnect

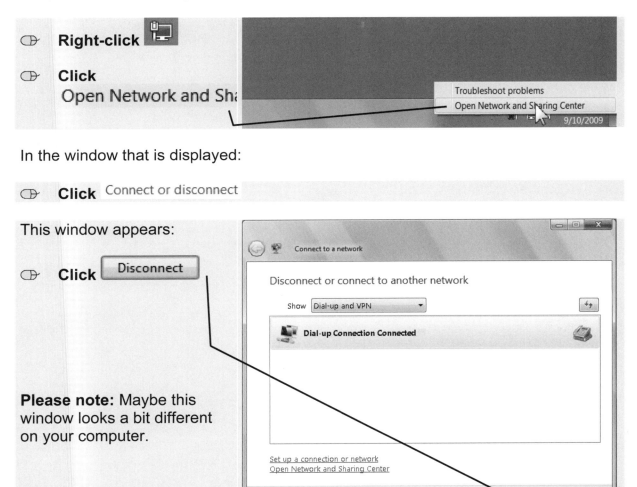

Connect to a network

Disconnect or connect to another network

Show Dial-up and VPN

Dial-up Connection Connected

Set up a connection or network
Open Network and Sharing Center

Disconnect   Cancel

Please note: Maybe this window looks a bit different on your computer.

When you see the message

Successfully disconnected from Dial-up Connection , the connection is broken.

With the button Close you can close this window.

The Internet acces icon on the taskbar has changed into . The **X** indicates you are no longer connected:

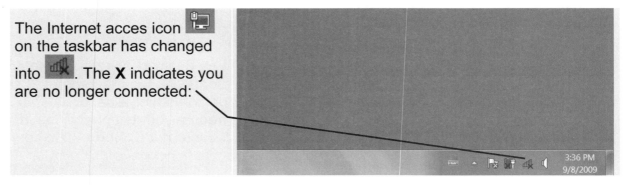

To reconnect, do the following. In the *Connect to a network* window:

☞ **Click**

Now you see this window for the dial-up connection:

☞ **Click** Connect

Please note: Maybe this window looks a bit different on your computer.

Dial-up Connection

Select the service you want to connect to.

Connect to: Dial-up Connection ▼

☐ Connect automatically

Connect   Settings...   Work Offline

If necessary:

Type your user name

Type your password

Click a check mark for
Save this user name and password for

Click Me only

Click Dial

Please note: Maybe this window looks a bit different on your computer.

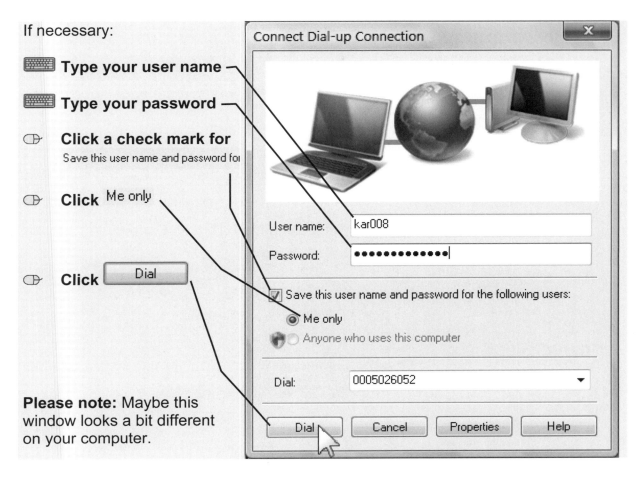

The connection to the Internet is re-established.

2.10 Changing the Home Page

When opened *Internet Explorer* displays a particular web page, called the *home page*. You can change this setting and make this your favorite page, for example the practice website for this book.

➥ Please note:

You can make a page your home page when it is displayed in the *Internet Explorer* window.

First you open the website for this book using the Favorites Center:

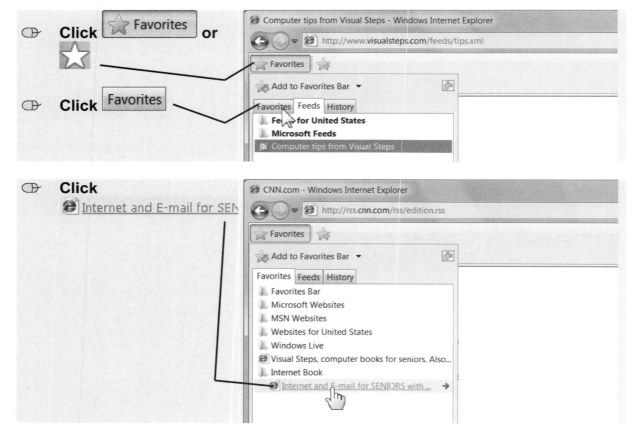

The web page for this book opens.

⭐ Tip

Take a moment to register your book
You can register your book. Visual Steps will keep you aware of any important changes that are necessary to you as a user of the book. You will also receive our periodic newsletter (e-mail) informing you of our product releases, company news, tips & tricks, free guides, special offers, etcetera.

On the left side of the web page you see a list:

☞ **Click**
Register your book

You will see a window like this:

⌨ **Type your e-mail address** ——

☞ **Click** Submit

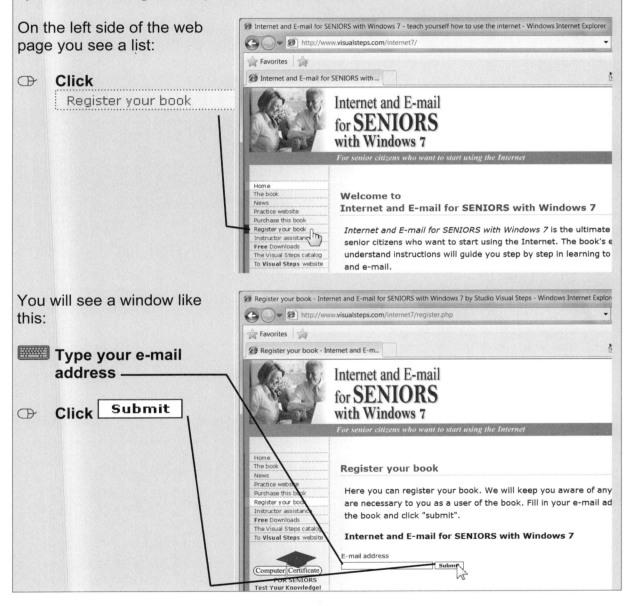

There is also a link to the practice website:

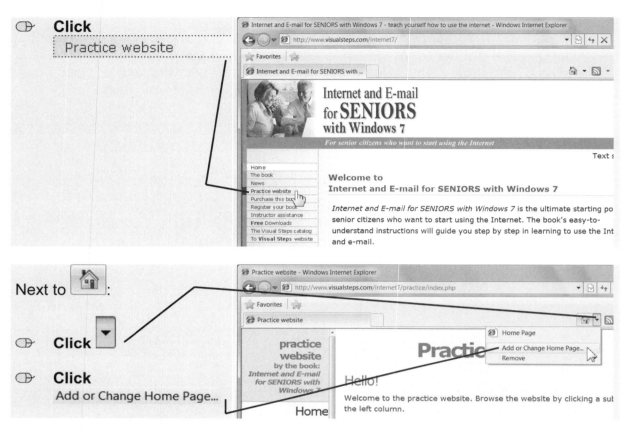

Click

Practice website

Next to [🏠]:

Click [▼]

Click

Add or Change Home Page...

Now you see this window:

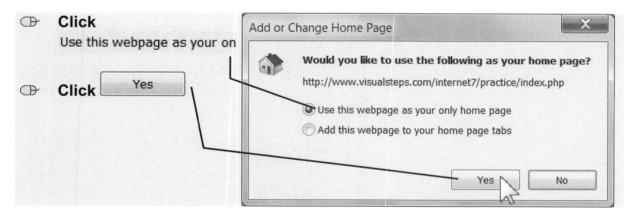

Click

Use this webpage as your on

Click | Yes |

The practice website has now been stored as the home page.

💡 Tip

Keeping your favorites on display
If you want to keep the Favorites Center in your viewing window:

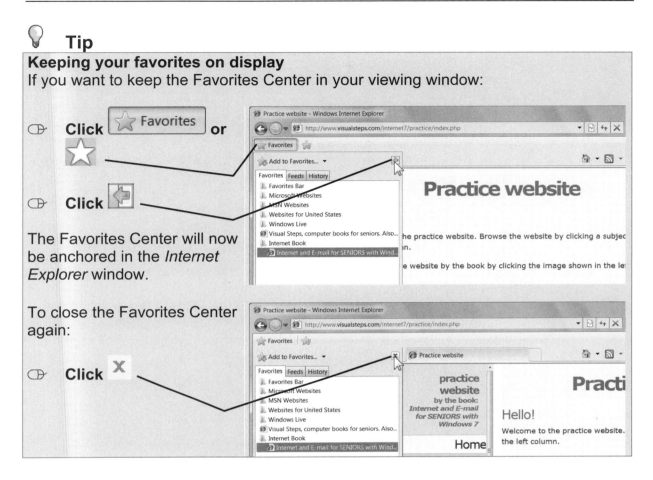

👆 **Click** Favorites or ⭐

👆 **Click** ⬅️

The Favorites Center will now be anchored in the *Internet Explorer* window.

To close the Favorites Center again:

👆 **Click** X

2.11 History

Besides the favorites and RSS feeds, the Favorites Center also has a section with a button called *History*. This is where *Internet Explorer* stores links to the websites you have recently visited.

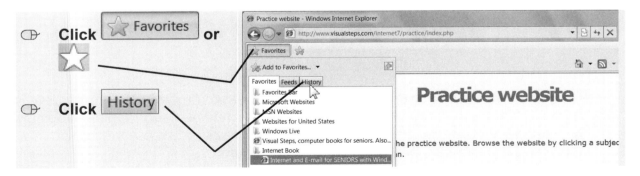

👆 **Click** Favorites or ⭐

👆 **Click** History

The *History* is presented as a chronological list, where the websites are neatly organized under today, previous days, or previous weeks.

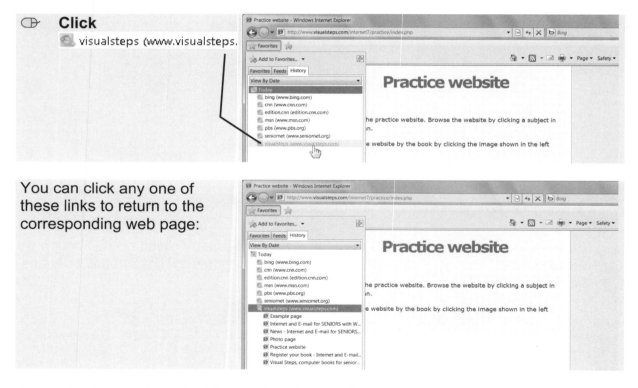

☞ **Click** [Today]

In [Today], you see the folders for the websites you have visited, arranged in alphabetical order:

When you open one of these folders, you can see the specific web pages you have visited on that website. Take a look:

☞ **Click**

  visualsteps (www.visualsteps.

You can click any one of these links to return to the corresponding web page:

Returning to a website in this way is only useful if you remember when you last visited it. If you are on the Internet daily, however, and you surf to many websites, this method is not as useful. In that case, it is a lot easier to store these web addresses as favorites, like you have practiced before.

A website that you look at frequently can also be saved as a shortcut on your desktop. Continue to the next paragraph to read more about that.

2.12 Shortcuts

You can also put an icon called a *shortcut* for your favorite website on your desktop. Once you have started *Windows*, you just have to double-click this icon to view the website. For practice, you can make a shortcut for the *Internet for Seniors* website. You can make a shortcut when the web page is displayed in the *Internet Explorer* window. Here is how to make a shortcut:

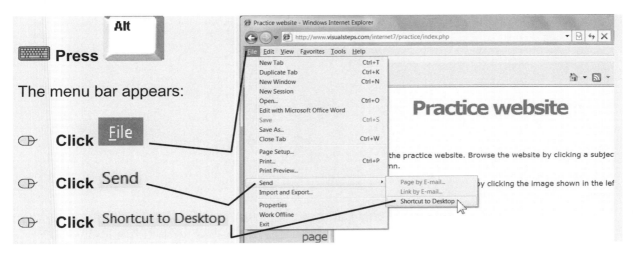

⌨ **Press** Alt

The menu bar appears:

☞ **Click** File

☞ **Click** Send

☞ **Click** Shortcut to Desktop

Internet Explorer asks you to confirm this action:

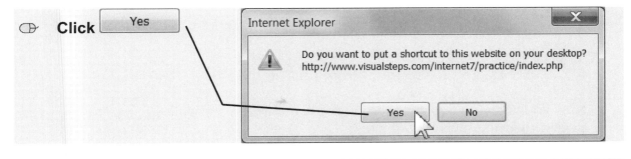

☞ **Click** Yes

☞ **Minimize the *Internet Explorer* window** ♘♘¹¹

When the *Internet Explorer* window is minimized, you see the desktop:

The shortcut has been placed on the desktop:

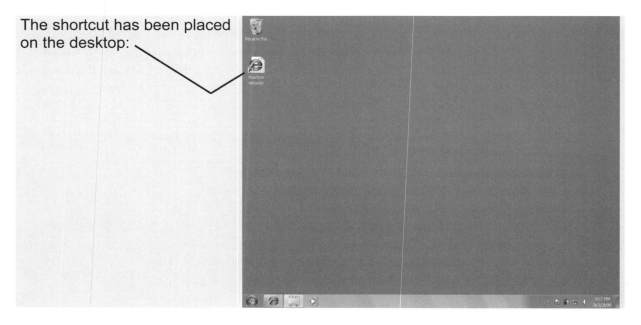

By double-clicking this icon, you can open the *Internet for Seniors* website without even having to open *Internet Explorer* itself. That happens automatically.

☞ **Start *Internet Explorer* from the taskbar** 🐾¹²

☞ **Close *Internet Explorer*** 🐾²

☞ **If necessary, disconnect from the Internet** 🐾⁵

Now you know several ways to navigate the Internet effectively, and to find your way back and forth between websites.

You can practice these techniques in the following exercises.

2.13 Exercises

The following exercises will help you master what you have just learned. Have you forgotten how to perform a particular action? Use the number beside the footsteps to look it up in the appendix *How Do I Do That Again?*

Exercise: The SeniorNet Favorite

In this exercise, you will open the websites for SeniorNet and CNN and add them to your favorites.

☞ Start *Internet Explorer*. ᵒᵒ¹

☞ If necessary, connect to the Internet. ᵒᵒ³

☞ Use the hidden list under the Address bar to open: www.seniornet.org ᵒᵒ⁶⁵

☞ Make the address for SeniorNet a favorite. ᵒᵒ¹⁵

☞ Use the hidden list under the Address bar to open: www.cnn.com ᵒᵒ⁶⁵

☞ Make the address for CNN a favorite. ᵒᵒ¹⁵

☞ If needed, temporarily disconnect from the Internet. ᵒᵒ¹⁶

☞ Reconnect to the Internet. ᵒᵒ⁶⁷

☞ Open the favorite SeniorNet. ᵒᵒ¹⁷

☞ Open the favorite CNN. ᵒᵒ¹⁷

☞ Close *Internet Explorer*. ᵒᵒ²

☞ If necessary, disconnect from the Internet. ᵒᵒ⁵

Exercise: A New Favorite

In this exercise, you will open the National Geographic website and add it to your favorites in the folder related to this book.

☞   Start *Internet Explorer.* 👣[1]

☞   If necessary, connect to the Internet. 👣[3]

☞   Type the address: www.nationalgeographic.com 👣[4]

☞   Now you see this website:

☞   Save the address for the National Geographic website as a favorite in the
      📁 Internet Book folder. 👣[18]

☞   Open the favorite CNN. 👣[17]

☞   Open the favorite SeniorNet. 👣[17]

☞   Open the favorite National Geographic. 👣[19]

☞   Close *Internet Explorer.* 👣[2]

☞   If necessary, disconnect from the Internet. 👣[5]

2.14 Background Information

Glossary

Favorites	*Internet Explorer* favorites are links (bookmarks) to websites that you visit frequently. By adding a website to your favorites list, you can go to that site by simply clicking its name, instead of having to type its address in the Address bar.
Favorites Center	The *Internet Explorer* area where you can view and organize your favorites.
Feed Headlines	*Feed Headlines* is one of the gadgets in *Windows 7* that is displayed on the desktop. You can see continuously updated headlines from a website that supplies RSS feeds.
History	The section of the Favorites Center that displays the websites you recently visited. By default, the *History* listing is sorted by date.
Home page	The web page that is displayed each time you open *Internet Explorer* or click the button or .
Information bar	In *Internet Explorer*, the information bar appears below the Address bar and displays information about downloads, blocked pop-up windows, and other activities.
Pop-up	A pop-up is a small web browser window that appears on top of the website you are viewing. A pop-up window, often used for advertising purposes, may open as soon as you visit a website.
RSS feeds	RSS feeds contain frequently updated content published by a website, such as news headlines or sports scores. The acronym RSS stands for *Really Simple Syndication*, the format used to publish these feeds.
Shortcut	A shortcut is a link to a website, file or program, represented by an icon. Double-clicking a shortcut will open the file or program.

Source: Windows Help and Support

Why do I have to wait so long sometimes?
Sometimes it takes quite a long time before a page you want loads into your browser. This depends on a number of things:

- Modems can have various speeds. The faster the speed of the modem, the faster text and pictures are transmitted. The speed of the connection type also plays an important part.
  To date, a modem connected with the normal analog telephone line is the slowest type. Other types of connections, such as ISDN, cable and DSL, are significantly faster.
  New developments will present a range of fast transmission possibilities through the regular analog telephone line.

- Some websites have more pictures and illustrations than others. Some pages have numerous pictures or various graphic effects. All those dancing figures, revolving text, pop-up assistants and other graphic effects require information to be sent to your computer, and it all has to be sent via the telephone line if that is how you are connected.
  Receiving pictures takes a particularly long time. The more efficient the web page is designed, the faster it will appear on your screen.

- Sometimes it is very busy on the Internet. So many people are surfing at the same time that traffic jams occur. When that happens, you will have to wait longer than usual.

What can be done about this?

- You do not always have to wait until all the pictures have been received. Sometimes you immediately see the topic you are looking for.

  ☞ **If this is the case, click ☒ next to the Address bar**
  No more information is sent and you can click to go to a different page.

- Sometimes a website's opening page will have a button that says: *Text only*. If you click that button, only the text will be sent, not the illustrations. That takes much less time.

How does the WWW work?

The World Wide Web (WWW) is one of the more recent and most popular Internet applications. The idea for the web was developed in 1989 by Tim Berners Lee and Robert Cailliau at CERN (the European Organization for Nuclear Research) in Geneva, Switzerland.

The information on the WWW comes to us in the form of *hypermedia*. The word hypermedia is derived from *hypertext*.

A hypertext is a text containing *jump text* (or *hyperlinks*). The words in a hyperlink refer to the address of a different web page. By clicking on the jump text, you tell *Internet Explorer* to open that other web page. This page might be located on any Internet-connected computer in the world, even one on the other side of the world.

Words are not the only things that can be used as a hyperlink. Drawings and photos can also be used. Web pages usually contain not only text, but also images, sound and moving images (*multimedia*). That is why you sometimes hear the term *hypermedia* these days. It is a contraction of the words *hyper*text and multi*media*.

How does the Internet system always find the right page? The WWW contains millions of pages. Each page has its own unique address, called an *URL* (Uniform Resource Allocator).

An example of an URL is: **http://www.visualsteps.com**.
You can read this as follows:

http	HyperText Transfer Protocol
www	World Wide Web
internetforseniors	The domain name or "brand name" of the organization
com	A commercial website (as opposed to e.g. educational)

Based upon the URL, your ISP's computer knows on which computer the website is stored. In order to make communication between computers possible, every computer receives a unique address, the *Internet Protocol Number* (IP number or IP address). You will not use this number in daily practice. Instead, people use the URL, for example www.internetforseniors.com. When computers communicate with one another, this name is automatically converted to the numeric IP address. Sometimes you will see these numbers displayed at the bottom of the *Internet Explorer* window.

HTML
Web pages are written in a special language. This makes it possible for the pages to look the same on completely different computers. *Internet Explorer* translates this language into a readable page for you. This language is called *HTML* or *HyperText Markup Language*.
Every HTML page looks the same in its simplest form.

```
<HTML>
     <HEAD>
           <TITLE>Internet for Seniors</TITLE>
     </head>

     <BODY>
          <p>This will be the text.</p>
     </body>
</HTML>
```

This language is fairly complicated, and therefore not very practical to use. Fortunately, we do not have to wrestle with all these unintelligible codes any more. Software companies like *Microsoft* have created special programs that make it possible to write web pages without the need to know a single word of HTML. We call this kind of program a *web editor*. One example of a web editor is *Dreamweaver*. A web editor works just like a text editing program such as *Microsoft Word*. You type in text, add images, and make sure that everything looks nice. The web editor translates all your work into HTML. It could not be easier.

Bandwidth

In the early days of telecommunications, telephone lines were only used for speech. Now that the arrival of the Internet has appropriated these lines for other purposes in recent years - such as sending text, images, audio and video - it has become apparent that the bandwidth of these lines is too limited.

What do we mean by bandwidth?

The term can best be compared to a hallway between two rooms. Imagine that a hundred people are standing in one room. The time it will take for all these people to move to the other room depends primarily on how wide the hallway is. The wider the hallway, the better the flow. People have been searching for years for techniques to increase bandwidth for the Internet.

ISDN

One of these techniques is ISDN (Integrated Services Digital Network). ISDN allows much more information to be sent on the same copper wire in a given amount of time (up to 64 Kilobits per second). It is also possible to send different signals at the same time. That is how ISDN makes it possible to call someone on the phone and use the Internet at the same time. ISDN does have special requirements, however, such as a special modem and a different telephone subscription.

DSL

DSL (Digital Subscriber Line) is another technique for making broadband Internet possible. Here, the connection is split in two: an *upstream* channel (for sending information) and a *downstream* channel (for receiving information). Just as with ISDN, it is possible to call on the phone and use the Internet at the same time. Like ISDN, DSL has special equipment requirements. It also has a unique feature. With DSL, the user has a private line between two modems: one at home and the other at the exchange. This makes the channel secure. Your data goes over your own private line, in contrast to other techniques in which the line is shared with other users. Because you have your own line to the exchange, its speed is not affected by other users.

Cable

High-speed connections are also available through the television cable infrastructure. This connection, however, becomes faster or slower depending on how many other people are using the same cable.

2.15 Tips

Tip

Clearing the History
You might not like the fact that all the websites you visit are stored in a list. Another user on your computer could easily view your surfing behavior.
Fortunately, you can also clear your surfing history. *Bonus Online Chapter 10 Security and Privacy* on the website that goes with this book will show you how.

Tip

The Home button
If you click the Home button 🏠 or 🏠, your default home page will be displayed.

Tip

Organizing favorites
You might want to remove, rename or move some of your favorites from time to time. Here is how to do this:

Click [⭐ Favorites] or [⭐][▼] next to [⭐ Add to Favorites...], Organize Favorites...

You see this window:

With the [Delete...] button, you can remove a selected favorites:

With the [Rename] button, you can give a favorites a different name:

With the [Move...] button you can move a favorites to a different folder:

With the [New Folder] button you can create a new folder for a group of favorites:

Organize Favorites

- Favorites Bar
- Microsoft Websites
- MSN Websites
- Websites for United States
- Windows Live
- Visual Steps, computer books for seniors. Also tips and tricks and use...
- Internet Book

Favorites Bar
Favorites Folder

Modified:
9/3/2009 2:06 PM

[New Folder] [Move...] [Rename] [Delete...]

3. Searching and Finding on the Internet

The Internet is sometimes compared to a large library full of information on all kinds of subjects. Unfortunately, this library has no librarian. The books in this library are all jumbled up together. This comparison is a pretty good one. There is indeed no supervisory organization that organizes the information on the Internet. Everyone can place his own information on the Internet, which is immediately available to everyone else. This does not make searching on the Internet any easier.

There are a large number of companies and organizations that try to assist Internet users by organizing this enormous mountain of information. This occurs in several ways. The first way is via a *search engine*. This is a computer that is constantly busy indexing web pages. You can use the search engine's web page to search for all the web pages that contain certain words, your *search terms* which you have typed into the search term box.

A second method for organizing information on the Internet is a *directory*. In this case, a company has already selected a large number of web pages and categorized them according to subject.

Despite these various resources, searching on the Internet can still be frustrating at times. You know, for example, that information on a particular subject must be out there somewhere, yet you can not find the web page in question. This chapter will help you perform better searches. It covers various techniques for searching for information. The more you practice these techniques the better you will become at finding the information you want.

In this chapter, you will learn how to:

- use the instant Search box
- search for information, images and news with *Bing*
- change your default search engine to *Google*
- do an advanced search in *Google*
- use directories
- search within a web page

3.1 Starting Internet Explorer

☞ **Turn on the computer**

Do you have an external modem?
☞ **Turn on the modem**

Now you can start *Internet Explorer*.

☞ **Start *Internet Explorer*** ✂¹

After *Internet Explorer* starts, you can connect to the Internet:

◯ **Click** [Connect]

Please note: Maybe this window looks a bit different on your computer.

Dial-up Connection [X]

Select the service you want to connect to.

Connect to: [Dial-up Connection   ▾]

☐ Connect automatically

[Connect]   [Settings...]   [Work Offline]

➥ **Please note:**

If you are connected to the Internet by cable or DSL, then this *Dial-up Connection* window will not appear. Your computer is already connected to the Internet.

If your user name and password are not displayed:

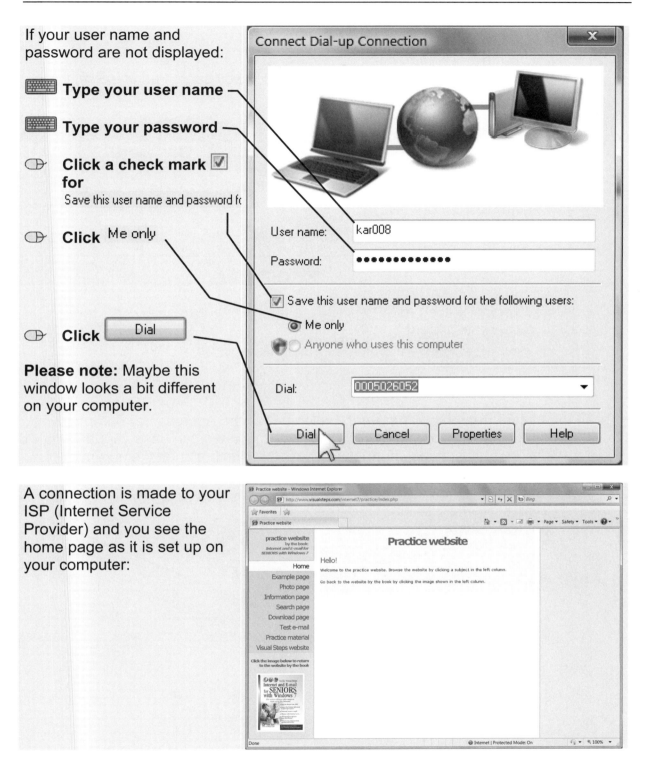

⌨ **Type your user name**

⌨ **Type your password**

🖰 **Click a check mark ☑ for**
Save this user name and password for

🖰 **Click** Me only

🖰 **Click** ⎣ Dial ⎦

Please note: Maybe this window looks a bit different on your computer.

A connection is made to your ISP (Internet Service Provider) and you see the home page as it is set up on your computer:

3.2 The Instant Search Box

Internet Explorer offers direct access to the *Microsoft* search engine *Bing* through the instant Search box.

In *Internet Explorer 8*, you can find the instant Search box in the top right corner of the window:

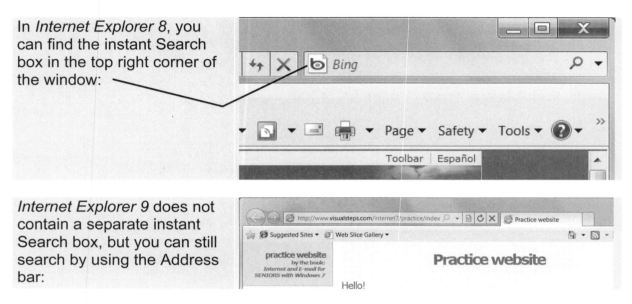

Internet Explorer 9 does not contain a separate instant Search box, but you can still search by using the Address bar:

In the instant Search box (*Internet Explorer 8*) or the Address bar (*Internet Explorer 9*), you can type one or more words with which you want to base your search. For example, try to find some information about the Dutch painter Rembrandt:

In *Internet Explorer 8*:

☞ **Click the instant Search box**

⌨ **Type:** Rembrandt

☞ **Click** 🔍

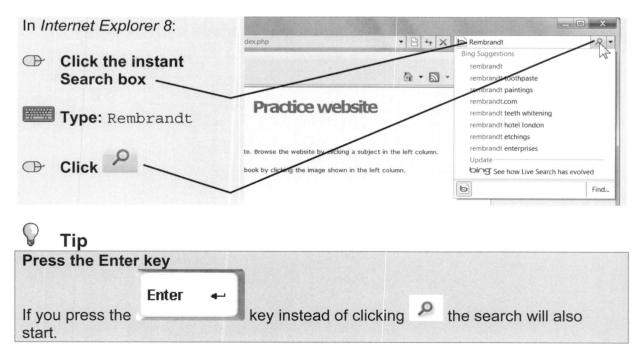

💡 **Tip**

Press the Enter key

If you press the [**Enter** ↵] key instead of clicking 🔍 the search will also start.

In *Internet Explorer 9*:

Click the Address bar

Type: Rembrandt

Click

Within a few seconds, *Bing* presents the search results:

On top of the page you see some links of SPONSORED SITES, that probably have very little to do with Rembrandt:

Try this search result:

If necessary, drag the scroll bar down to see more results

Click Rembrandt - Wikipedia, the

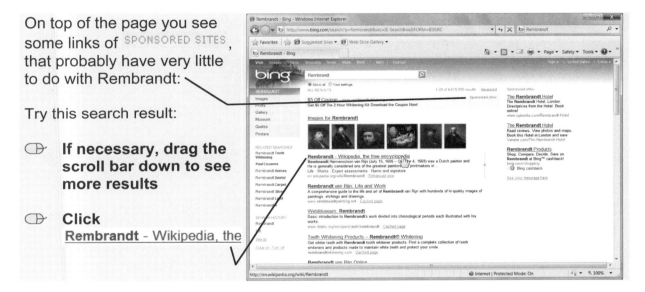

If you can not find this page, you can try to find the page by using the words 'Rembrandt Wikipedia' to search instead of only the word 'Rembrandt'.

You see the *Wikipedia* page for Rembrandt van Rijn:

 **Please note:**

Wikipedia is a free encyclopedia collaboratively written by many of its readers from around the world. Each blue word in the text is a link to a new article about that word. *Wikipedia* has rapidly grown into one of the largest reference websites on the Internet. New information is added to the *Wikipedia* website regularly. Qualified users may edit existing pages at any time. Therefore, the image you see above may look different from what you see now on your screen.

3.3 Searching for News

Instead of doing a general search, you can also search for news about Rembrandt.

☞ **Go back to the website with the search results** 𝒬𝒬6

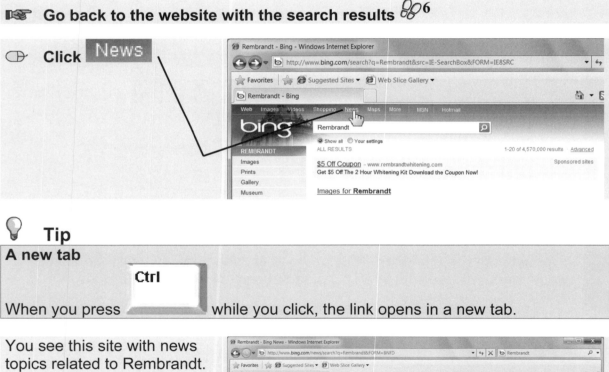

☞ **Click** `News`

💡 **Tip**

A new tab

`Ctrl`

When you press ___ while you click, the link opens in a new tab.

You see this site with news topics related to Rembrandt.

Unfortunately, the news is not limited to Rembrandt the painter. There could also be news about a toothpaste or a racehorse named Rembrandt, for example.

3.4 Changing the Default Search Engine

Bing is the default search engine in *Internet Explorer*. That is understandable, since *Bing* is made by *Microsoft*, the maker of *Internet Explorer*. With a few clicks, you can change the default search engine to the very popular *Google Search*:

In *Internet Explorer 8*, next to

☞ **Click** ▼

☞ **Click**
Find More Providers...

In *Internet Explorer 9*, in the Address bar:

☞ **Click** ▼

☞ **Click Add**

On this page you can choose which search provider you would like to add to *Internet Explorer*:

☞ **If necessary, drag the scroll bar down**

Next to Google :

☞ **Click**
Add to Internet Explorer

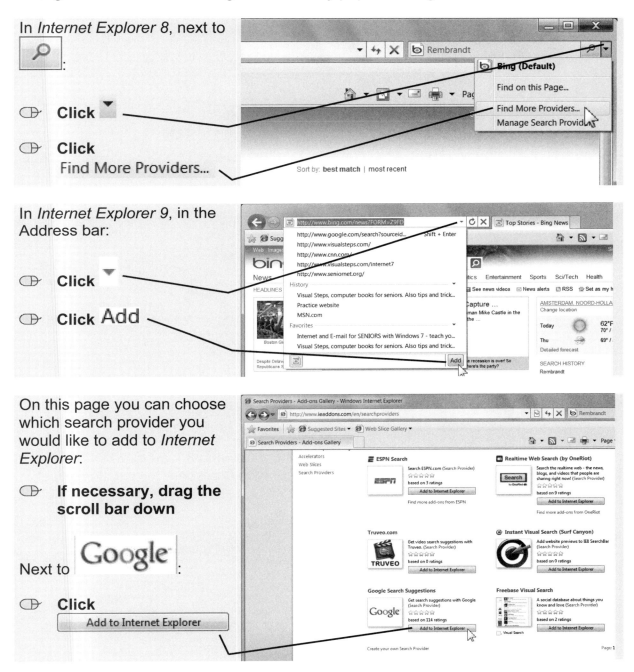

The *Add Search Provider* window appears:

Here you can choose to make *Google* your default search provider:

☞ **Click a check mark ☑ for**
Make this my default sear

☞ **Click** [Add]

Google has become your default search engine. Here is a quick way to check that:

☞ **Click ▼ in the instant Search box or Address bar**

Google 🔳 **has been selected as default search engine:**

3.5 Searching with Google

Google works pretty much the same as *Bing,* but without the advertisements. You can start your *Google* search. For example, try to find some information about another famous Dutch painter, Vincent Van Gogh:

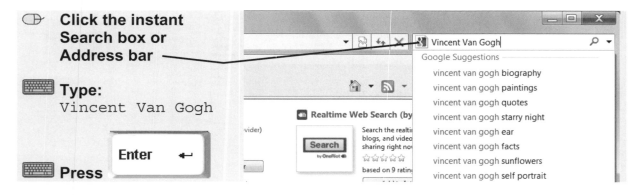

☞ **Click the instant Search box or Address bar**

⌨ **Type:**
Vincent Van Gogh

☞ **Press** [Enter ↵]

💡 **Tip**

Display search results in a new tab

To display the results of your search in a new tab you do the following:

⌨ **Type your search terms in the instant Search box or Address bar**

⌨ **Press and hold** `Alt`

⌨ **Press** `Enter ←` **, then release** `Alt`

On this *Google* page you see that this search nets over 3 million *hits* (search results).

The first ten of these results are displayed:

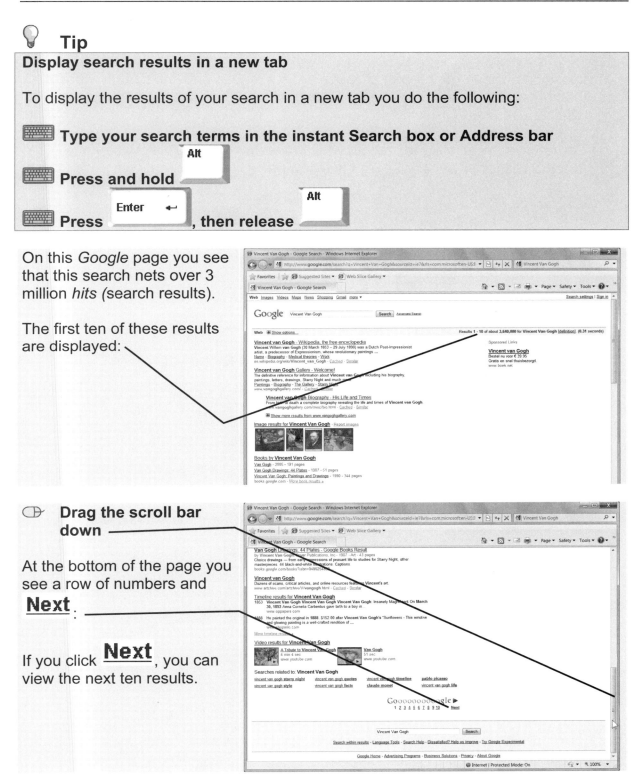

👆 **Drag the scroll bar down**

At the bottom of the page you see a row of numbers and **Next**:

If you click **Next**, you can view the next ten results.

3.6 Narrowing Down the Search Results

It is impossible to go through all these search results and find exactly what you want to know about Vincent Van Gogh. To narrow down your search, you can search within these search results.

Perhaps you would like to find out which museum you can visit to see one of his famous sunflower paintings. Try the following:

Click
Search within results

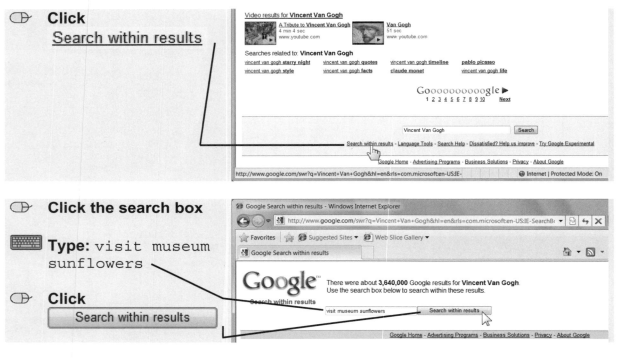

Click the search box

Type: visit museum
sunflowers

Click
Search within results

Now the number of hits has been narrowed down to about 11,000:

Most likely, a *Wikipedia* entry appears in the top of the search results. Try another one this time:

For example, click
The Paintings: Sunflowers

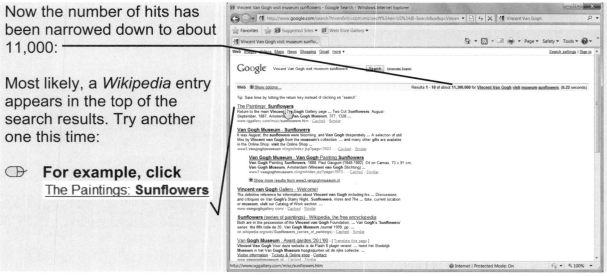

 **Please note:**

The Internet grows and changes all the time. It is possible that the results for this search have changed since this book was published. If you can not find this search result, try another one.

On this web page of the *Vincent Van Gogh Gallery* you can find the location of all eleven sunflower paintings:

☞ **Use the scroll bar to scroll down**

When you are finished reading:

☞ **Click**

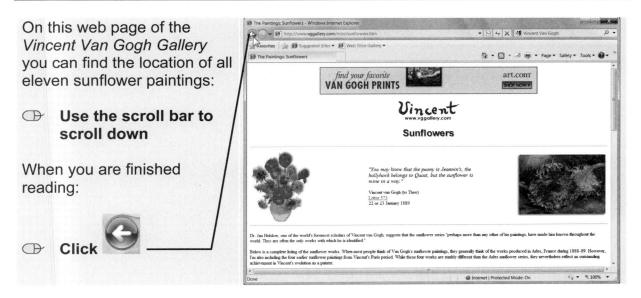

You then return to the web page with the *Google* search results.

3.7 Advanced Search

Searching and narrowing down the search results is a good way to eventually find what you are looking for. But if you know exactly what you want and more importantly what you do not want to find, you are ready to try an *Advanced Search* in *Google*.

☞ **Click**

Advanced Search

The *Advanced Search* page opens:

The words you used on your last search are entered into one of the boxes:

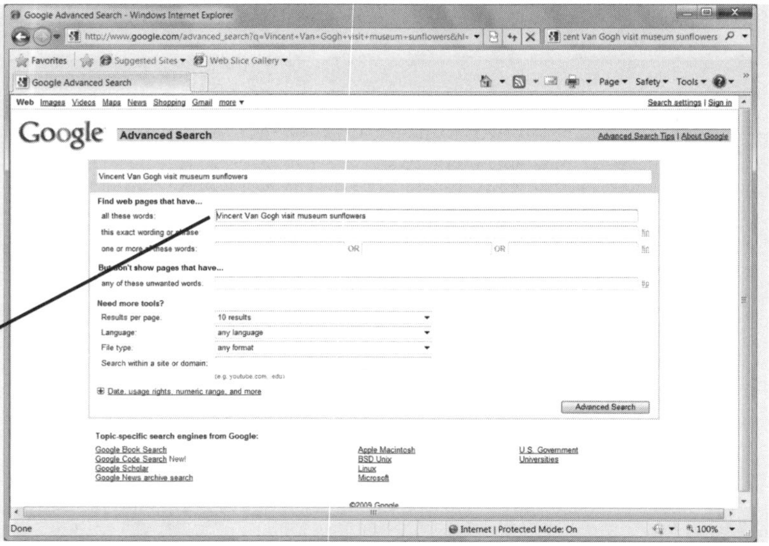

Since you are going to do a different search, you can clear that entry:

☞ **Click the box**

Vincent Van Gogh visit museum su

three times

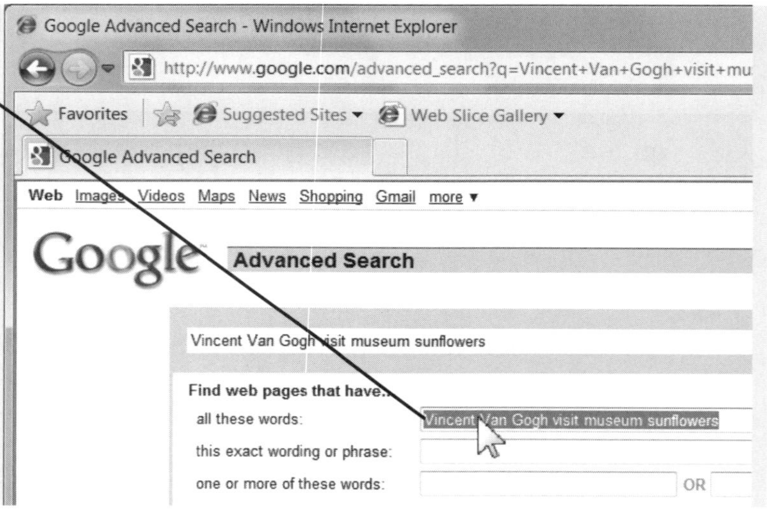

The entry is selected and turns blue. Now you can delete it:

⌨ **Press** `Delete`

Say for example, you are going to visit Amsterdam for a weekend and you would like to know when the Rijksmuseum is open for visitors. This museum has many paintings by the Dutch master Rembrandt. The *Advanced Search* might be able to help you out.

First you enter the name and the location of the museum. The search field **all these words:** will make sure that both of those words are found, but not necessarily in that order.

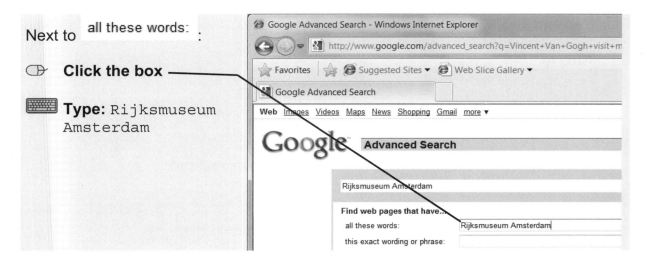

Next to all these words: :

Click the box ———

Type: Rijksmuseum Amsterdam

In the next box you can enter multiple search terms that should be treated as a unit. Since you are looking for the opening hours of the museum, you want to get search results that contain both words in that exact order. Most search engines call this an 'exact phrase'.

Next to
this exact wording or phrase: .

Click the box ———

Type: opening hours

You can also enter a few words, one of which should show up in the search results:

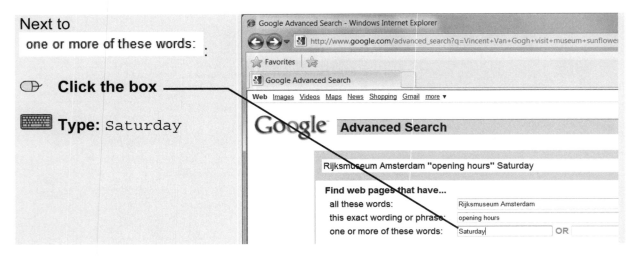

The museum might give the opening hours separately for each day, or combined for weekdays and the weekend. Either way, by using this method you will find out what time the museum opens on Saturday.

You can start the search:

The search results are shown.

Click the first result

In this example, the first search result leads you directly to the website of the Rijksmuseum. But since the Internet changes all the time, it is possible that the results for this search have changed since this book was published.

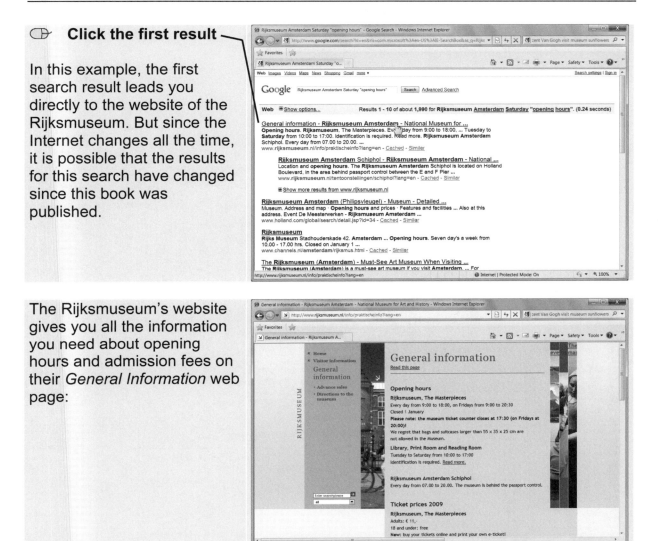

The Rijksmuseum's website gives you all the information you need about opening hours and admission fees on their *General Information* web page:

In the next section you will do a specific search for images.

3.8 Searching for Images

It is possible to limit your search to images that have something to do with Vincent Van Gogh:

☞ **Go back to the website with the search results**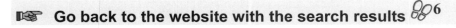

In the instant Search box (*Internet Explorer 8*) or Address bar (*Internet Explorer 9*):

⌨ **Type:** Vincent Van Gogh

🖱 **Click** 🔍 **or** 📇

You see the search results for Vincent Van Gogh:

🖱 **Click** Images

You see the search results with images of Van Gogh's paintings:

🖱 **Click one of the images**

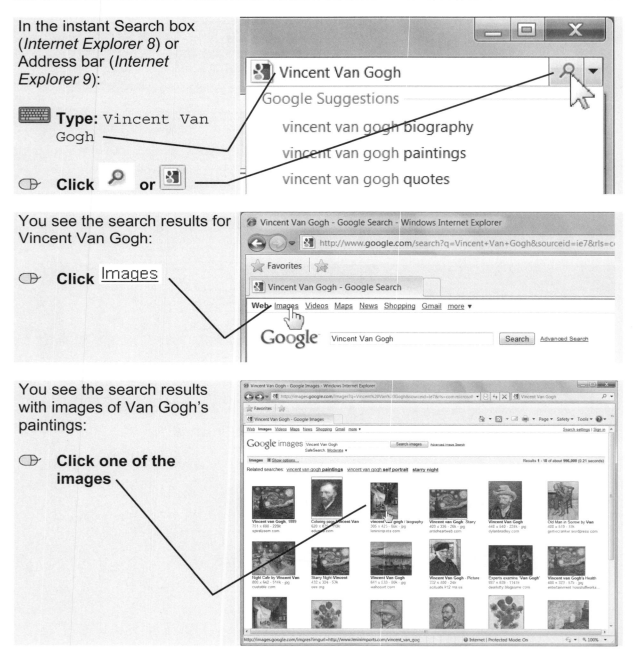

On this page you see a preview of the website where the image has been found:

⊕ **Click** <u>**See full size image**</u>

The image loads into the window. This may take a moment if it is a very large image and you are using a dial-up connection:

☞ **Go back to the previous page** ✌️6

If you want to visit the website where the image has been found you can use the link that is displayed here:

☞ **Go back to the previous page** ✌️6

3.9 Searching for Video Clips

In addition to images, you can also use *Google* to look for video clips.

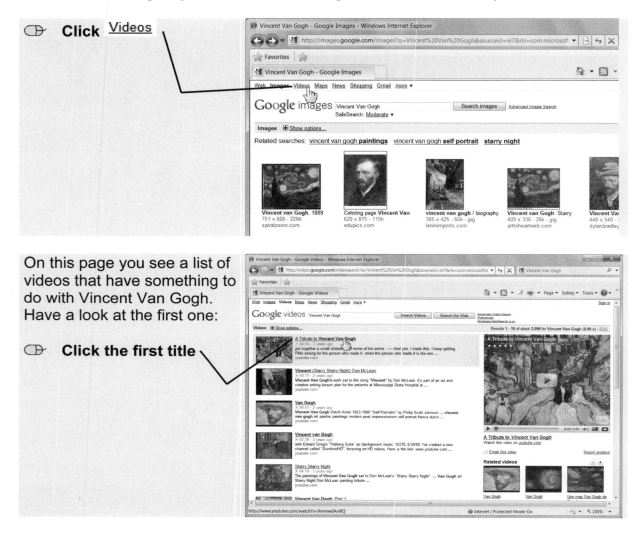

Click Videos

On this page you see a list of
videos that have something to
do with Vincent Van Gogh.
Have a look at the first one:

Click the first title

The video will be played in the window:

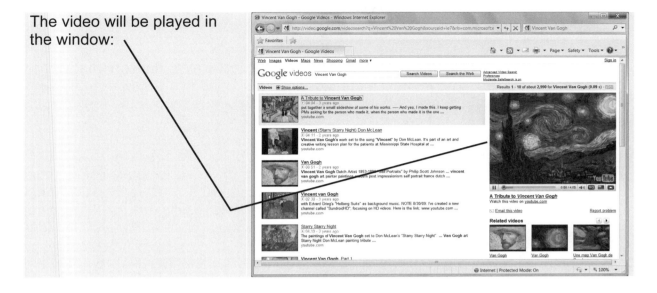

💡 **Tip**

YouTube

YouTube (www.youtube.com) is a free and very popular source for video material. Users can upload, view and share video clips. For each video you can see the average rating and the number of times a video has been watched.

You can search for a video using a search term.

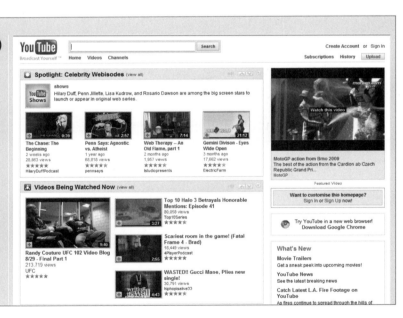

3.10 Directories

In practice, search engines are not always the fastest way to find information about a particular subject. The immense number of pages found in a single search makes it very difficult to find exactly what you need. The reason is simple: the searching is done by computers, not people.

A different way of searching is becoming more popular: the *directory*.
A directory is a website containing a large number of web addresses categorized by subject. This categorizing is done by a large editorial staff who work on the directory by organizing, evaluating and checking websites. This results in a useful summary. That is why many people use this kind of page as their *Internet Explorer* home page.

Another name for a directory is a *portal*. A portal is a useful gateway to the Internet, because you can see in one glance which websites offer what kind of information. America's most extensive portal website is the *Open Directory Project*. There is a link to this directory on the exercise page of this book.

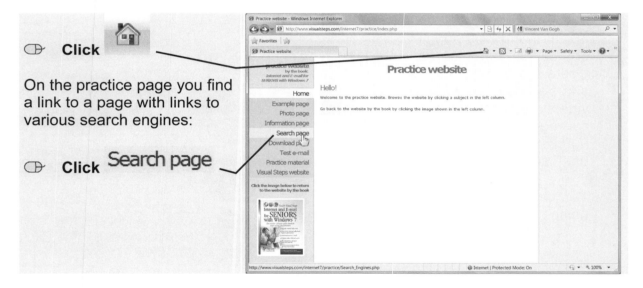

☞ **Click** 🏠

On the practice page you find a link to a page with links to various search engines:

☞ **Click** Search page

💡 **Tip**

New search features
Visit this page regularly. If important new search features are developed for the Internet, they will most certainly be included on this page.

The link to the *Open Directory Project* can be found near the bottom of the page:

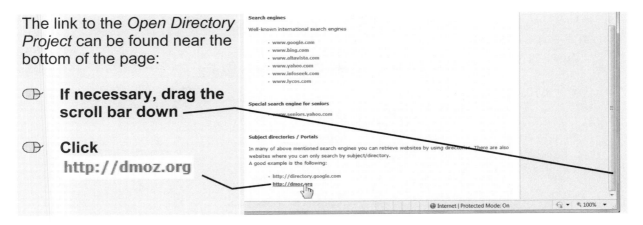

☞ **If necessary, drag the scroll bar down**

☞ **Click**
   http://dmoz.org

The *Open Directory Project* page opens in a new browser window. Here is how you use the search function on this website to find a restaurant on the tropical island of Bonaire:

☞ **Click the text box**

⌨ **Type:** Bonaire

☞ **Click** Search

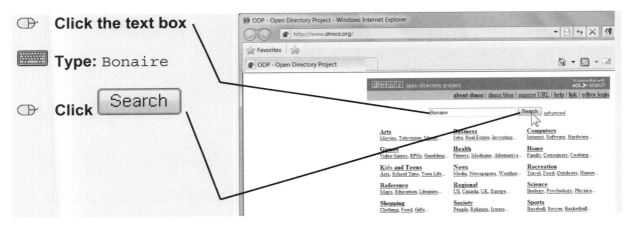

Now it will search for pages containing information about Bonaire.

You see a window with a list of website categories:

☞ **Click**
   1. **Regional: Caribbean**

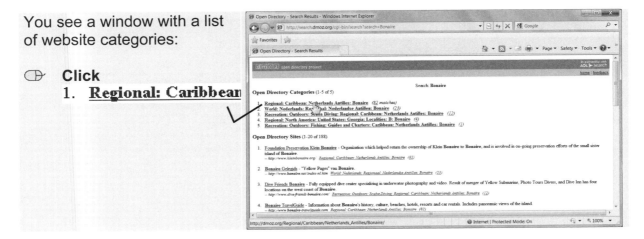

Now you see a page with more categories about Bonaire:

☞ **Click**
  • **Travel and Tourism**

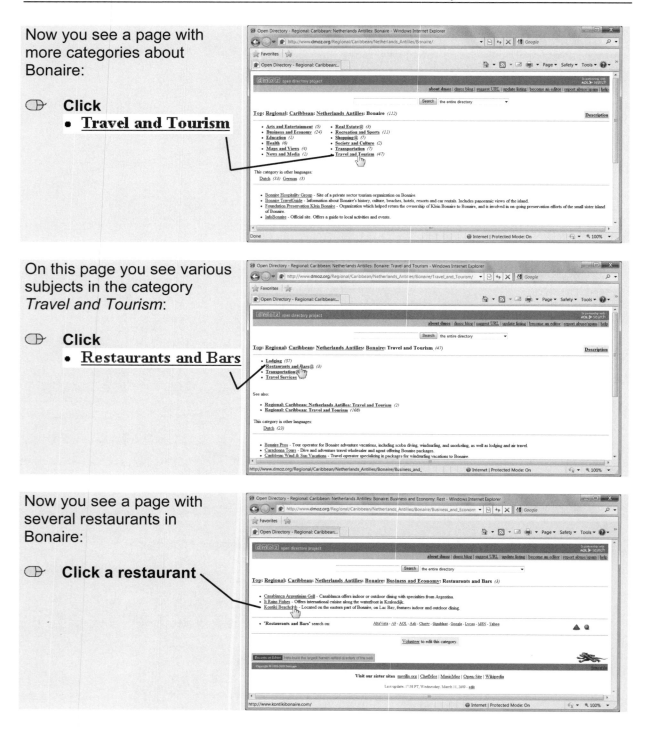

On this page you see various subjects in the category *Travel and Tourism*:

☞ **Click**
  • **Restaurants and Bars**

Now you see a page with several restaurants in Bonaire:

☞ **Click a restaurant**

The page for the restaurant opens:

In *Internet Explorer 8* it will be displayed in a new window.

In *Internet Explorer 9* it will be displayed in a new tab.

You can close this window now.

☞ **Close the window** 🐾^{32} **or tab** 🐾^{64}

You see the search page for this book again:

☞ **Click** **Home**

You are back on the exercise page:

You have seen how to search using a directory. In addition to www.dmoz.org, there are many other directory websites. There is another handy trick in *Internet Explorer* that you can use when you want to search for something on the Internet.

3.11 Searching Within a Page in Internet Explorer

Sometimes a web page has so much text that it is hard to find your search term. *Internet Explorer* has a solution for that. You can search the text in a window for a particular word or phrase. Here is how you do it:

Click Information page

You see a text in the window which tells you the story of Anne Frank.

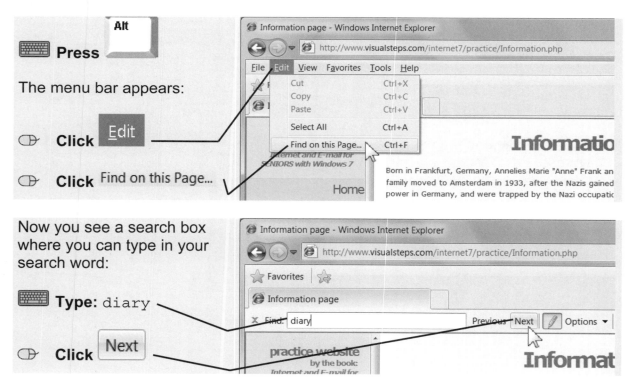

Press Alt

The menu bar appears:

Click Edit

Click Find on this Page...

Now you see a search box where you can type in your search word:

Type: diary

Click Next

If the word is found, it will be highlighted in the text:

Continue searching to see if the word occurs again:

☞ **Click** Next **a couple of times**

When the search has reached the bottom of the page, it will start again at the top. You can stop the search by closing the search box:

☞ **Click** X

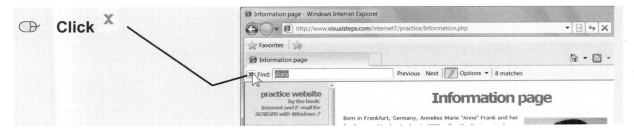

This search can be very useful.

☞ **Close *Internet Explorer*** ⿻²

☞ **If necessary, disconnect from the Internet** ⿻⁵

You can practice searching on the Internet in the following exercises.

💡 **Tip**

Using the search box
If you click the option Match Whole Word Only, it will search for an entire word. Then only the word box will be found, and not e.g. boxing.

If you click the option Match Case, attention will be paid to the use of capital letters. Then box will be found, but not Box.

3.12 Exercises

Have you forgotten how to perform a particular action? Use the number beside the footsteps to look it up in the appendix *How Do I Do That Again?*

Exercise: Searching with the Instant Search Box

In this exercise, you will practice searching for information.

☞ Start *Internet Explorer*. [1]

☞ If necessary, connect to the Internet. [3]

☞ Click the instant Search box [20] or Address bar.

☞ Search for the word *bridge*. [21]

☞ Take a look at a couple of the websites that were found. [23]

☞ Begin a new search. [22]

☞ Search for *Karel Appel*. [21]

☞ Take a look at a couple of the websites that were found. [23]

Exercise: Searching with a Directory

In this exercise, you will practice searching using the *Open Directory Project*.

☞ Open from *History*: *dmoz.org* 🐾**14**

☞ Search for *Ford*. 🐾**21**

☞ Choose the category *Recreation: Autos: Makes and Models: Ford*. 🐾**24**

☞ Choose the category *Explorer*. 🐾**24**

☞ Take a look at a couple of the websites that were found. 🐾**23**

Exercise: A Different Search Engine

In this exercise, you will use a different search engine, namely *Lycos*.

☞ Click 🏠.

☞ Click Search page .

☞ Click www.lycos.com .

☞ Click the box next to | Search |.

☞ Search for the word *butterflies*. 🐾**21**

☞ Take a look at a couple of the websites that were found. 🐾**23**

☞ Search for *Empire State Building*. 🐾**21**

☞ Take a look at a couple of the websites that were found. 🐾**23**

☞ Close *Internet Explorer*. 🐾**2**

☞ If necessary, disconnect from the Internet. 🐾**5**

3.13 Background Information

Glossary

Advanced Search	More detailed search, that you can customize for example by adding an exact phrase that should be found, or omitting a word that should not be found in the search results.
Bing	Search engine made by *Microsoft*.
Case sensitive	Words can differ in meaning based on the differing use of uppercase and lowercase letters. Searches performed by *Google* and *Bing* are not case sensitive.
Default search engine	Search provider that is used by default when using the instant Search box. You can set your favorite search engine as default search engine.
Directory	An collection of links to other websites, listed by category and sub-category. This categorizing is done by a large editorial staff who work on the directory by organizing, evaluating and checking websites. This results in a useful summary. The *Open Directory Project* is a good example.
Exact Phrase	Search terms that are treated as a unit. To search for an exact phrase, enclose it in quotation marks, for example "Ford Focus".
Google	Popular search engine.
Hits	Search results.
Instant Search box	Box at the top right of the *Internet Explorer 8* window that can be used to start a search on the Internet. In *Internet Explorer 9* the instant Search box is integrated in the Address bar.
Search engine	A program that is constantly busy indexing web pages. *Google* and *Bing* are search engines. You can use the search engine's web page to search for all the web pages that contain your search terms.
Search terms	A keyword or phrase that is typed into a search engine.
Wikipedia	A multilingual, web-based, free content encyclopedia project. *Wikipedia* is written collaboratively by volunteers, its articles can be edited by anyone with access to the website.

Source: Windows Help and Support

How does a search engine work?

Search engines are programs that are busy indexing web pages around the clock. This creates an enormous index of search terms. Search engines differ in the method they use to do this. That is why the results from different search engines are often very different. Some search engines index as many words as possible on a web page. Others only use search terms found in the titles of web pages.

There are also search engines that primarily use key words on web pages. These hidden key words are put in by the web page designer. Sometimes this feature is abused, and particular key words are used intentionally because these words are frequently typed into searches. This can be the reason why you sometimes see web pages in your search results that have very little to do with your search term.

Search engines work like a kind of robot and are therefore fairly limited. No editing or selection is performed on the pages. This limitation becomes particularly evident when you search for words that have multiple meanings. An editor would be able to separate the web pages based upon their content.

All the well-known search engine companies have a department where editing does take place, and hundreds of websites have been organized by subject or category.

There are also websites that specialize in this. These are called *directories* or *portals*.

Usually a website has to be submitted to a search engine in order to be included in its index. Websites that have not been submitted can not be found by the search engine. That might be a reason why you can not find the particular website you were looking for.

3.14 Tips

Tip

Using search engines

- First, get a lot of practice using a particular search engine such as *Google* and thoroughly investigate all its search options. You can find al lot of information in the search engine's Help pages.

- Once you have some experience, give other search engines a try.
  You will discover through experience which search engines you like best.

- Always begin with the most specific search possible. For example, if you want to find information about the *Epson Stylus Photo 1400* printer, then use this whole phrase as your search term. If you do not get enough results, then try *Epson Stylus*. As a last resort, type just the word *Epson*.

Tip

Google search tips

- Keep it simple: if you are looking for information on the city of Barcelona, try ***Barcelona***. But remember: this will get you millions of search results.

- Use multiple search terms: if you are looking for a hotel in Barcelona, you will get better results with ***hotel Barcelona*** than with either ***hotel*** or ***Barcelona***.

- *Google* only returns pages that include all of your search terms. To restrict a search further, just include more terms.

- *Google* searches are not case sensitive. All letters will be understood as lower case. For example, searches for ***Rembrandt Van Rijn*** and ***rembrandt van rijn*** will return the same results.

- To find pages that include either of two search terms, add an uppercase OR between the terms. For example, here is how to search for a hotel in either Barcelona or Rome: ***hotel Barcelona OR Rome***.

- When you place the tilde sign (~) immediately in front of your search term, *Google* will also search for synonyms of your search term. For example, a search for ***~milk*** will also produce results for ***dairy***.

Source: Google Search Tips

Tip

Using special symbols
You can also use various symbols in your search, such as **+**, **-**, **"**, *****

If you type: **+Jackson +Browne**
The search engine will search for web pages containing both *Jackson* **and** *Browne*.

If you type: **Jackson -Browne**
The search engine will search for web pages containing *Jackson* **but not** *Browne*.

If you type quotation marks around the words: **"Jackson Browne"**
The search engine will search for web pages containing the phrase *Jackson Browne*.

If you type a star ***** next to a word, for example: **Brown***
This means that any symbol(s) at all can come at the end of the word, and the search engine will find Brown, Browning, Brownies, Brownbag, etc.

If you search for **Jackson Brown***, then you might for example find sites for the singer Jackson Browne, but also for the author H. Jackson Brown.

Tip

Searching directly by a name
You do not always have to use a search engine to find a particular web address. Brand names and companies are generally easy to find. Usually, if you follow the brand name by .com, you will find the correct address.

For example, if you want to visit the website of the car manufacturer *Ford*, you can type www.ford.com in the Address bar.

Tip

Searching in the Address bar

In *Internet Explorer 9* searching with the Address bar is the standard way to search. In *Internet Explorer 8*, you can also search with the Address bar. You usually search for information based on a search term. For example, the word *highway*:

🖰 **Click the Address bar**

⌨ **Type:** highway

⌨ **Press** | Enter ⏎ |

First, *Internet Explorer* tries to open the website http://highway/:

When there is no such website, you are sent to the *Google* page:

The page contains various links to websites containing the word highway:

4. Internet, Your Source of Information

The Internet can be viewed as an enormous library containing all kinds of information: text, photos, drawings, video and music. The most amazing thing is that nearly everything on the Internet that you see on your screen can be saved to your computer's hard drive. Later on, you can use the information that you have stored, for example in your work or for a hobby.

You can copy texts and re-use or edit them in a text-editing program. You can open and edit photos with a photo-editing or drawing program. In this way, the Internet serves as an enormous source of information. In this chapter, you will learn the basic techniques for saving and re-using text and photos on your own computer.

In this chapter, you will learn how to:

- print a page
- select text
- copy and paste text
- copy and paste images
- save an image
- save a web page
- open a saved web page in *Internet Explorer*

4.1 Visiting the Practice Website

First, start *Internet Explorer*:

Do you have an external modem?
☞ **Turn on the modem**

☞ **Start *Internet Explorer*** 🐾**1**

☞ **Connect to the Internet** 🐾**3**

A connection is made to your ISP (Internet Service Provider) and you see the home page as it is set up on your computer:

Do you see a different home page?

☞ **Open the *Internet and E-mail for Seniors* practice website** 🐾**52**

There is a practice page for this chapter on the website. You can open it now:

☞ **Click**
   Information page

Now you see this information page with text and a photo which you can use for practice:

Do you want to disconnect from the Internet so you can receive calls?
☞ **Wait until the entire page has been loaded**

☞ **Disconnect from the Internet** 𝒢𝒢16

Now you can take all the time you would like to work through the rest of this chapter.

4.2 Printing a Page

It is not always easy to read a web page on the screen, particularly if it contains a lot of text.

If you have a printer, you can choose to print the page. You can read the printed version later on at your own pace.

☞ **First check if the printer is on**

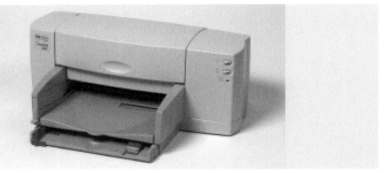

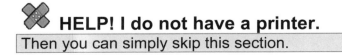 **HELP! I do not have a printer.**

Then you can simply skip this section.

Before you print the page, you can take a look at the Print Preview to see what the print will look like on letter-size paper:

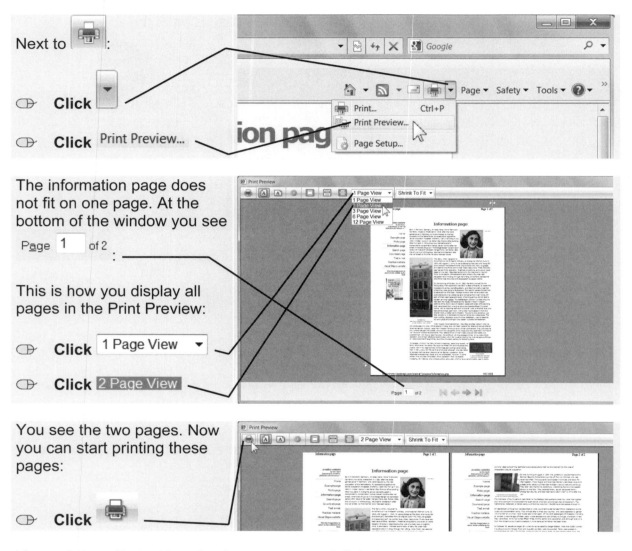

Next to 🖨 :

☞ **Click** ▼

☞ **Click** Print Preview...

The information page does not fit on one page. At the bottom of the window you see

Page `1` of 2 :

This is how you display all pages in the Print Preview:

☞ **Click** `1 Page View ▼`

☞ **Click** `2 Page View`

You see the two pages. Now you can start printing these pages:

☞ **Click** 🖨

Your printer will start to print the two pages. A little later, a document containing the text and photos from the information page will come out of your printer.

Now you can close the *Print Preview* window:

☞ **Close the *Print Preview* window** 𝒪𝒪³²

☼ Tip

Other buttons

The other buttons in the *Print Preview* window have the following functions:

Switch between printing the page vertically (*portrait*) or horizontally (*landscape*).

Open the *Page Setup* window.

Turn the *header* and *footer* options on or off.

Zoom the web page to fit the width of the preview window (*full width*), or zoom to fit the full web page (*full page*) in the preview window.

Adjust margins (only in 1 Page View ▼): drag the horizontal or vertical markers to change how the content fits on the printed page.

Stretch or shrink the page size by a percentage to fill the printed page. Increasing the print size to for example 150%, makes the text and images look larger on the print. However, you will need more pages to print the website.

4.3 Selecting Text

You can save a text you have read on the Internet on your computer and edit it later, perhaps using it in a text of your own. For example, you could copy information and use it in a club newsletter. To do this, you copy the text and paste it into another (text-editing) program.

In *Internet Explorer 8*, you first make sure the menu bar is displayed in the *Internet Explorer* window:

➥ Please note:

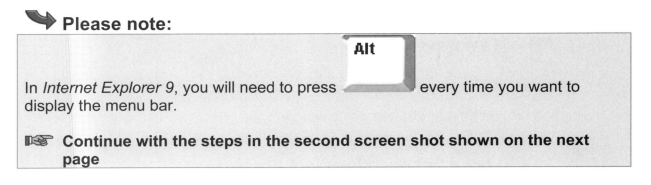

In *Internet Explorer 9*, you will need to press **Alt** every time you want to display the menu bar.

☞ **Continue with the steps in the second screen shot shown on the next page**

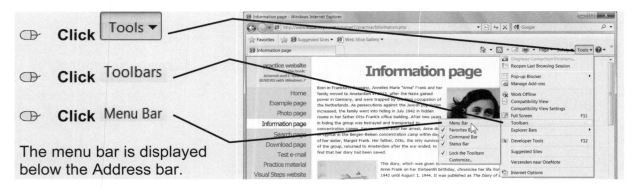

☞ **Click** Tools ▼

☞ **Click** Toolbars

☞ **Click** Menu Bar

The menu bar is displayed
below the Address bar.

For practice, you are going to copy a portion of text and paste it into the *WordPad* program. Before you can copy something, you have to *select* it first. In *Windows*, you do this by clicking and dragging the mouse.

✖ HELP! I do not know how to drag.

Read page 42 to find out how to drag.

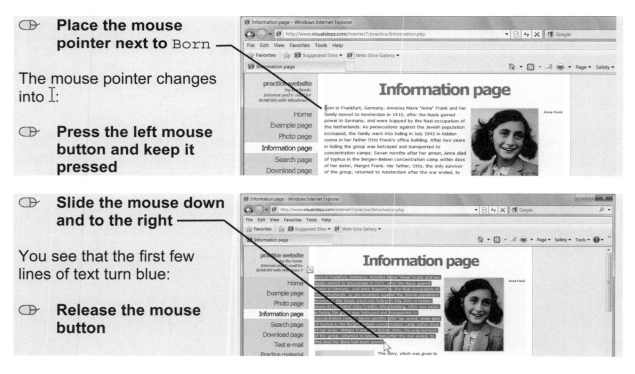

☞ **Place the mouse pointer next to** Born

The mouse pointer changes into I:

☞ **Press the left mouse button and keep it pressed**

☞ **Slide the mouse down and to the right**

You see that the first few lines of text turn blue:

☞ **Release the mouse button**

The blue indicates that the text has been selected. Now you can copy this text.

✖ HELP! I can not exactly select the text.

Having trouble selecting exactly the right text? It does not matter for this exercise. The important thing is that some part of the text has been selected.

4.4 Copying Text

Once the text has been selected, you can copy it:

In *Internet Explorer 9*:

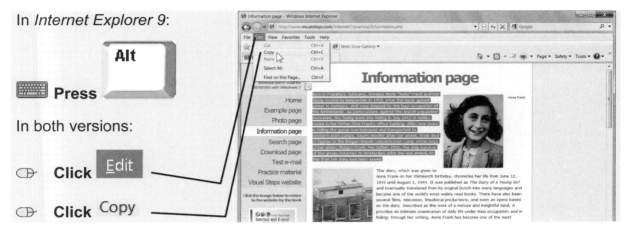

Press Alt

In both versions:

☞ **Click** Edit

☞ **Click** Copy

Although you did not see anything happen, the text has indeed been copied. Now you can paste it into another program. You can paste it into a text-editing program such as *WordPad* or *Microsoft Word*, an e-mail message, or a drawing program.

4.5 Pasting Text into WordPad

For practice, you are going to paste the copied text into the text editor *WordPad*. *WordPad* is a simple text-editing program that comes standard with *Windows*. This is how to open it:

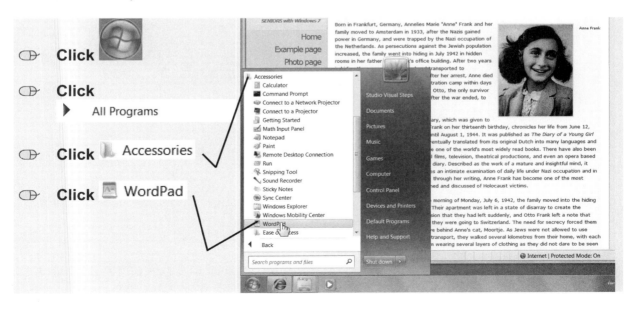

☞ **Click**

☞ **Click**
  ▶ All Programs

☞ **Click** Accessories

☞ **Click** WordPad

You see the *WordPad* window:

At the top left, you see a small blinking line. This is called the *cursor*.

The text will be pasted at the location of the cursor.

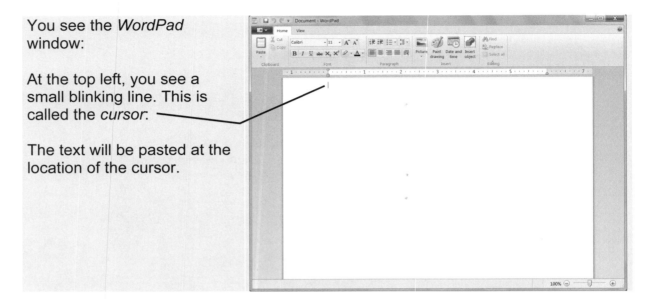

Now you can give the command to paste the text:

At the top left-hand side of the window:

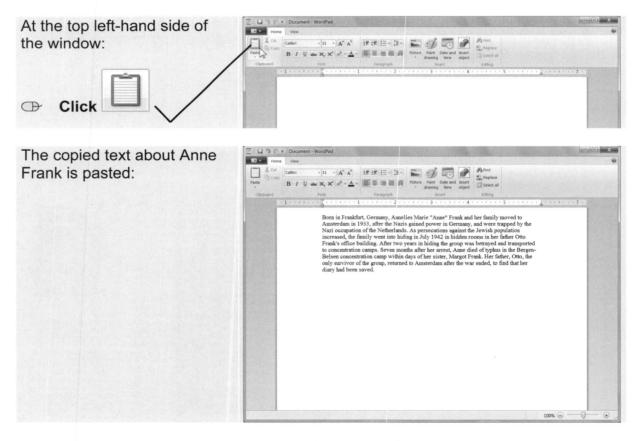

☞ **Click**

The copied text about Anne Frank is pasted:

> Born in Frankfurt, Germany, Annelies Marie "Anne" Frank and her family moved to Amsterdam in 1933, after the Nazis gained power in Germany, and were trapped by the Nazi occupation of the Netherlands. As persecutions against the Jewish population increased, the family went into hiding in July 1942 in hidden rooms in her father Otto Frank's office building. After two years in hiding the group was betrayed and transported to concentration camps. Seven months after her arrest, Anne died of typhus in the Bergen-Belsen concentration camp within days of her sister, Margot Frank. Her father, Otto, the only survivor of the group, returned to Amsterdam after the war ended, to find that her diary had been saved.

In this way, you can copy any text on the Internet and use it in another program. You can edit and save this text on your computer just like any other text.

You can also select the entire text all at once from a web page and then paste it. To see how, first minimize the *WordPad* window:

Click

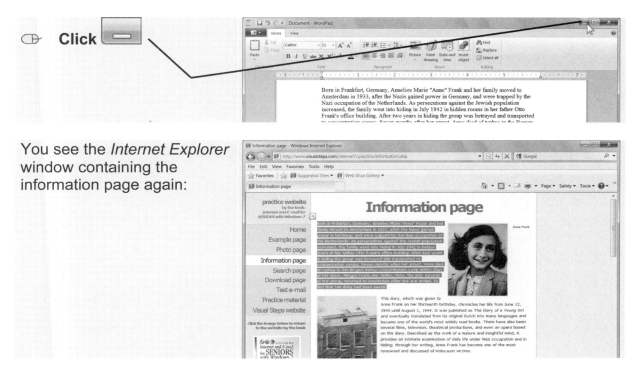

You see the *Internet Explorer* window containing the information page again:

It is not always practical to select a text by dragging the mouse. There is another method you can use.

4.6 Select All

You can select all the text and images on a web page with a single command. This is useful if you want to work quickly while you are surfing. Here is how you do it:

In *Internet Explorer 9*:

Alt

Press

In both versions:

Click Edit

Click Select All

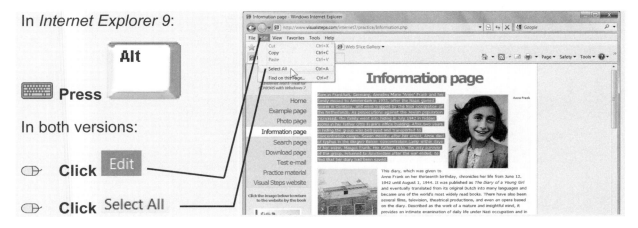

You see that not only all the text, but also the photos have been selected:

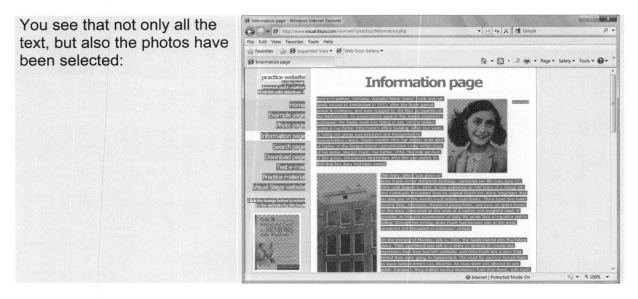

You can copy the text and pictures:

In *Internet Explorer 9*:

Press **Alt**

In both versions:

👆 Click **Edit**

👆 Click **Copy**

The entire page has been copied, and you can open the *WordPad* window again.

On the taskbar:

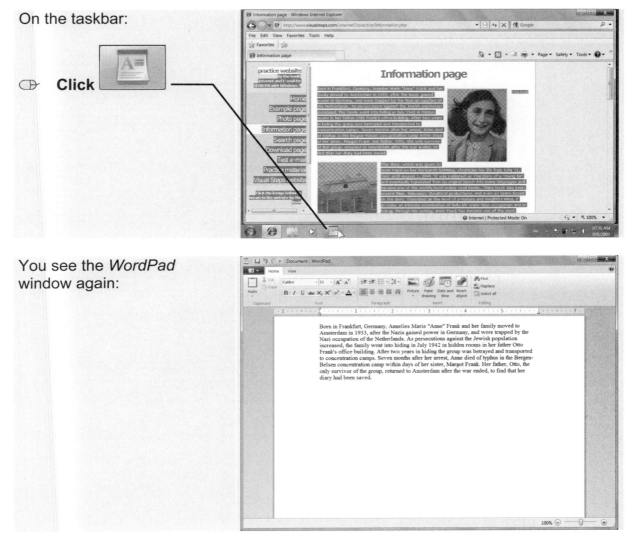

☞ **Click**

You see the *WordPad* window again:

Now you want to put the cursor (the blinking line) at the very top. The text will then be pasted there:

☞ **Click before the first line**

The cursor is blinking now on the left of the first line.

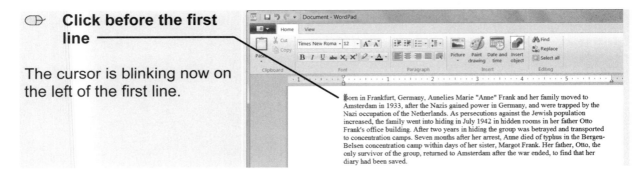

Now you can paste the text:

At the top left-hand side of
the window:

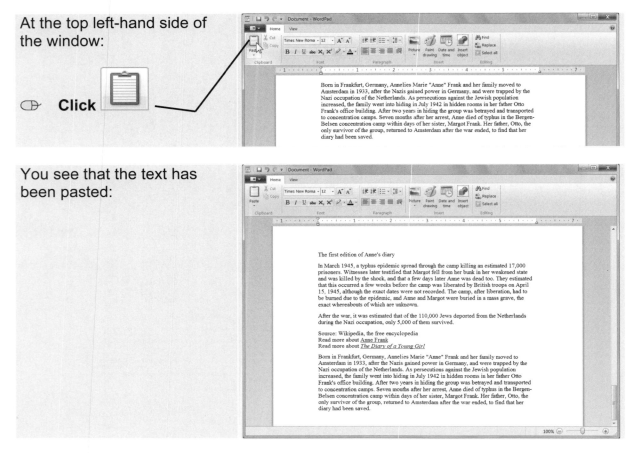

☞ **Click**

You see that the text has
been pasted:

![WordPad window showing pasted text about Anne Frank's diary]

The first edition of Anne's diary

In March 1945, a typhus epidemic spread through the camp killing an estimated 17,000 prisoners. Witnesses later testified that Margot fell from her bunk in her weakened state and was killed by the shock, and that a few days later Anne was dead too. They estimated that this occurred a few weeks before the camp was liberated by British troops on April 15, 1945, although the exact dates were not recorded. The camp, after liberation, had to be burned due to the epidemic, and Anne and Margot were buried in a mass grave, the exact whereabouts of which are unknown.

After the war, it was estimated that of the 110,000 Jews deported from the Netherlands during the Nazi occupation, only 5,000 of them survived.

Source: Wikipedia, the free encyclopedia
Read more about Anne Frank
Read more about *The Diary of a Young Girl*

Born in Frankfurt, Germany, Annelies Marie "Anne" Frank and her family moved to Amsterdam in 1933, after the Nazis gained power in Germany, and were trapped by the Nazi occupation of the Netherlands. As persecutions against the Jewish population increased, the family went into hiding in July 1942 in hidden rooms in her father Otto Frank's office building. After two years in hiding the group was betrayed and transported to concentration camps. Seven months after her arrest, Anne died of typhus in the Bergen-Belsen concentration camp within days of her sister, Margot Frank. Her father, Otto, the only survivor of the group, returned to Amsterdam after the war ended, to find that her diary had been saved.

🩹 HELP! I do not see any pictures.

The *WordPad* program does not display pictures.
If you paste this web page into a document in *Microsoft Word* or into an e-mail message in *Windows Live Mail*, it does work properly. The technique for doing this using one of these programs is exactly the same as described above.

4.7 Closing WordPad

Now you can close *WordPad*. You do not need to save the text. Here is how to close:

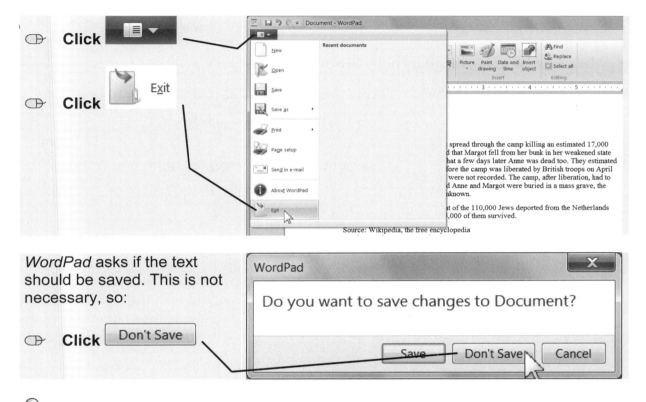

⊕ **Click** [icon]

⊕ **Click** Exit

WordPad asks if the text should be saved. This is not necessary, so:

⊕ **Click** Don't Save

💡 **Tip**

Text or image?
Some text on the Internet is in fact an image. For example, the text on the button Information page is an image. You can not copy the text on an image like this and paste it into a text-editing program or an e-mail program. You can, however, copy and paste the entire image. You will read how to do that later on in this chapter.

4.8 'Grabbing' Images from the Screen

You are bound to come across an interesting photo, image or drawing on the Internet that you want to save or even print. You can copy and save almost all the graphic material that appears on your screen, to use or print at a later time.

You can save an image by right-clicking it. Here is how you right-click:

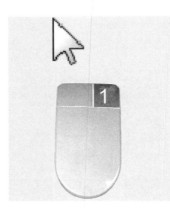

- point to something with the mouse pointer.

- press the right mouse button one time.

This mouse action is the same as regular clicking, except with the right mouse button instead of the left. The right mouse button has an entirely different function, however, as you will see.

☞ **Click in the text on the web page**

☞ **Use the scroll bar to scroll down to the second photo**

Now you can select the photo, like this:

☞ **Point to the photo**

While the pointer rests on the photo:

☞ **Right-click**

A menu with a list of various commands appears:

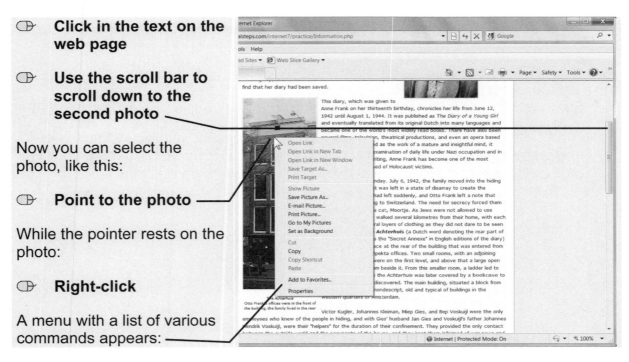

You can choose one of these commands. Use the left mouse button again to do that.

4.9 Copying an Image

First you are going to copy the image. Then you can use it in another program, such as a drawing program.

Click Copy

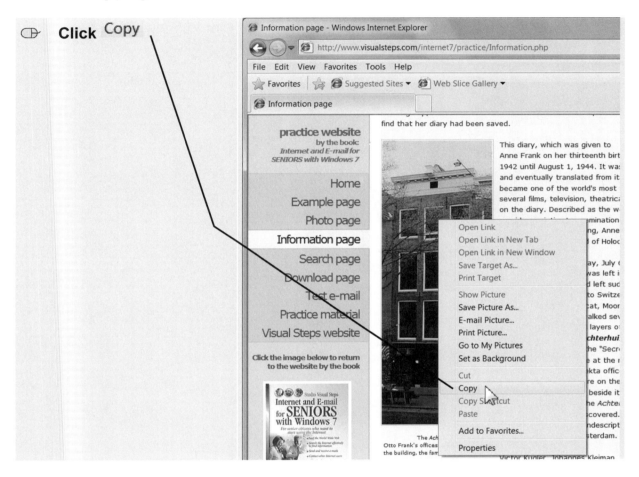

You did not see anything happen, but you can be certain that the image has indeed been copied.

4.10 Pasting an Image into Paint

You can paste the image not only into a text-editing program like *WordPad* or *Microsoft Word*, but also into a program for photo editing or a drawing program. For practice, you are going to paste the image into the drawing program *Paint*. *Paint* is a simple drawing program that comes standard with *Windows*.
Here is how you start this program:

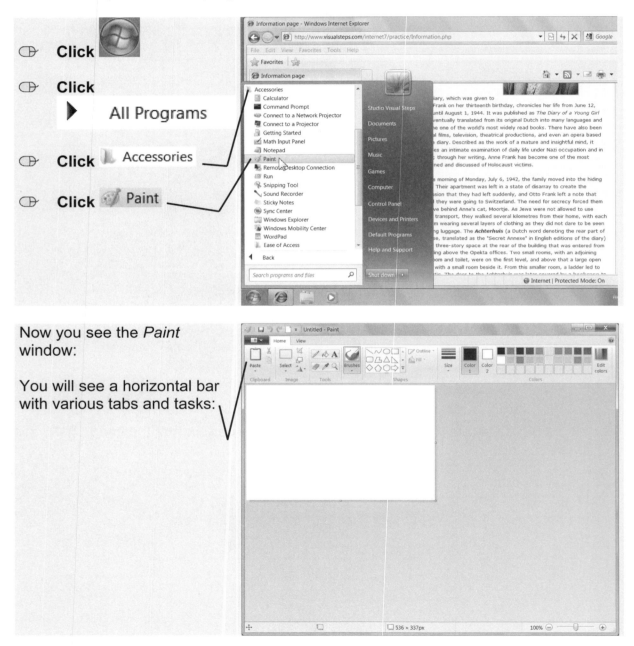

Now you see the *Paint* window:

You will see a horizontal bar with various tabs and tasks:

There is a large white surface on which you can draw. This is the piece of paper, so to speak. You can paste the image onto it.

At the top left-hand side of the window:

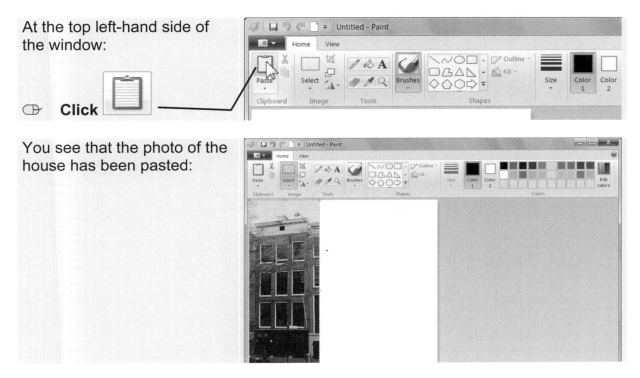

☞ **Click**

You see that the photo of the house has been pasted:

You can use *Paint* to edit, save, or print the photo.

Now you can close the *Paint* program. You do not need to save the photo:

☞ **Click**

☞ **Click** ⎯⎯ Exit

Paint asks if the photo should
be saved. This is not
necessary, so:

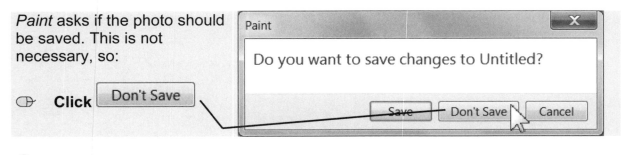

☞ **Click** Don't Save

☀ **Tip**

Paste in almost any program
You can use this method to paste an image into a *Microsoft Word* document or an
e-mail message in *Windows Live Mail*. In fact, you can paste it into a document in
almost any program.

4.11 Saving an Image

You can also save an image directly to your computer, without having to paste it into
a drawing program. Then you can use your favorite program at any time to open it.
This is how:

☞ **Right-click the photo
    of the house**

You see the menu again:

☞ **Click** Save Picture As...

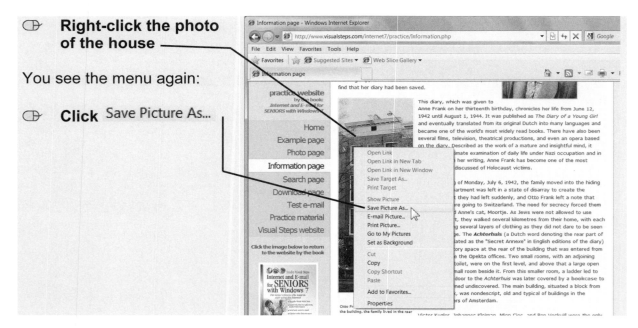

Now you see this window where you can specify the folder on your hard drive to be used for saving the photo:

The photo already has a name: *AnneFrankHouseAmsterdam*

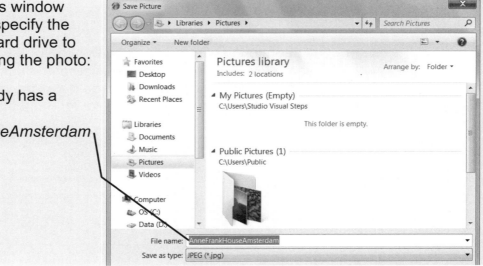

HELP! My window looks different.

If you do not see the folders on the left side of the window, then:

👉 **Click** ⊙ Browse Folders

You can give this photo a different name if you would like. For example, you can choose a name that tells you this is a photo.

Type: Photo House of Anne Frank

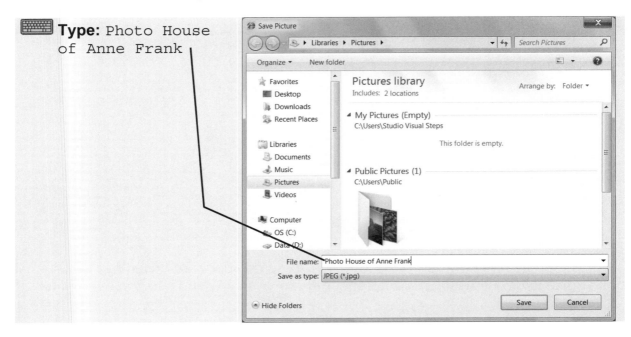

Now the photo has a name. Next you need to specify which folder on your hard drive is to be used for saving the photo.

4.12 Where to Save?

It is important to pay attention to where you save the photo. It is a good idea to always save to the same folder. That makes it easier to find things later and helps keep you from forgetting where things are. By default, images in *Windows 7* are saved in the *My Pictures* folder. You can find this folder in the *Pictures library*.

Here you see that the *Pictures library* has been opened:

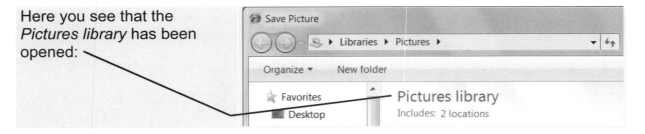

The *My Pictures* folder is intended for saving image files, for sample drawings or photos. You can save the photo Anne Frank's house in the *My Pictures* folder. The photo will automatically be stored in this folder

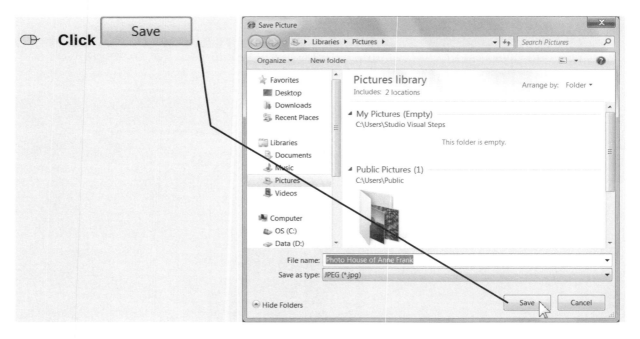

☞ **Click** Save

The photo has now been permanently stored on your hard drive. You can open it again later and use it in a different program, or even send it to someone in an e-mail.

4.13 Saving a Web page

You can also save an entire web page, including all its text and images. The page will be saved as a web page on your hard drive. You can open it again later in *Internet Explorer*. This can be useful, for example, if you find an interesting web page and want to look at it again later without having to connect to the Internet. Here is how you save a web page:

In *Internet Explorer 9*:

Press Alt

In both versions:

☞ **Click** File

☞ **Click** Save As...

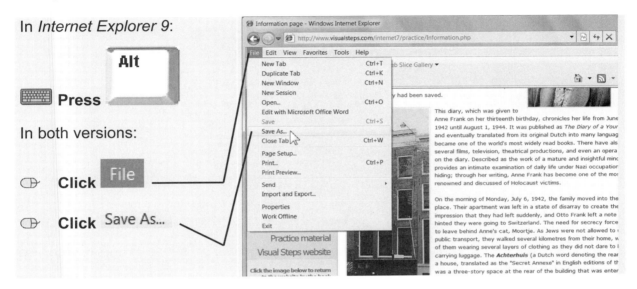

Instead of the *My Pictures* folder, save the web page in the *Documents library*. That is a folder in your *Personal folder* intended for saving all kinds of documents.

☞ **Click** Documents

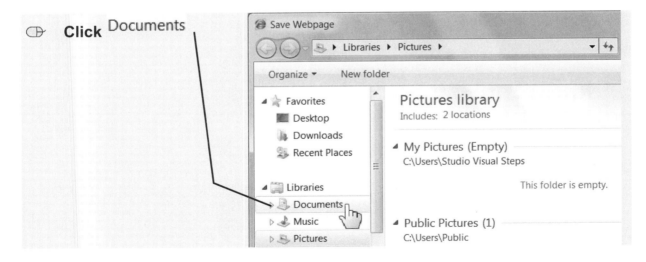

It is a good idea to choose a new name for the web page - one that describes the content better:

The filename is already blue which indicates that it has been selected. You can type the new filename right away:

Type: Information on Anne Frank

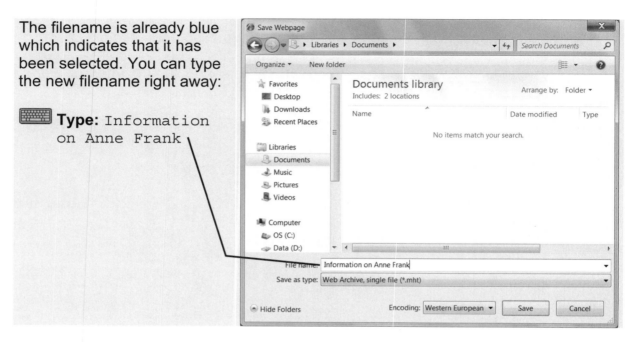

Now you need to make sure the entire web page will be saved. Then you can save the web page:

Next to Save as type: , make sure the setting is

Web Archive, single file (*.mht) .

If this is not the case, then:

Next to Save as type: .

Click ▼

Click

Web Archive, single file (*.mht)

Click   Save

The web page has now been saved to your hard drive in the *Documents library*. You can open the page again any time you like.

You can close *Internet Explorer* now. You do that by using a window button:

Click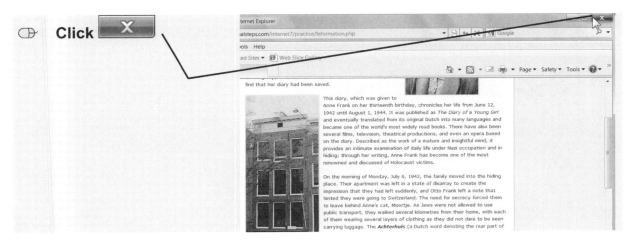

If you have a dial-up connection, you see the *Auto Disconnect* window:

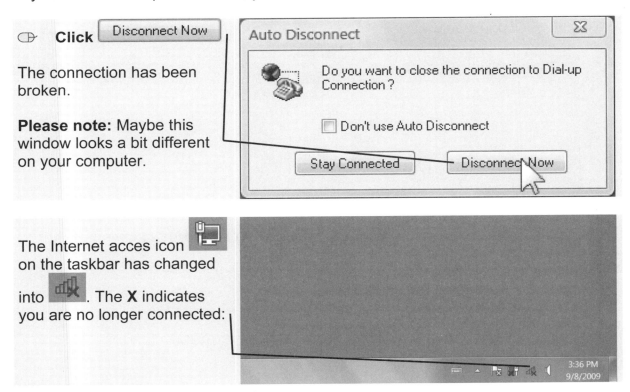

Click Disconnect Now

The connection has been broken.

Please note: Maybe this window looks a bit different on your computer.

The Internet acces icon on the taskbar has changed

into [icon]. The **X** indicates you are no longer connected:

If you have a broadband connection such as DSL or cable, you will not see the *Auto Disconnect* window. You will still see [icon] in the notification area on the far right side of the taskbar because you are continuously online.

In the following section, you will start the *Internet Explorer* program again.

4.14 Internet Explorer Offline

You are going to start *Internet Explorer* once more, but this time you do not need to connect to the Internet. This is called *working offline*.

☞ **Start *Internet Explorer* ✇¹**

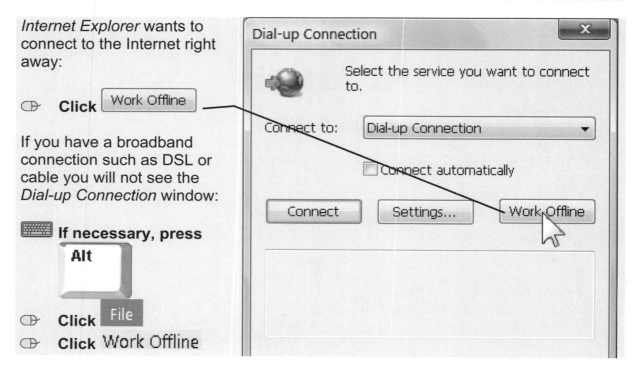

Internet Explorer wants to connect to the Internet right away:

☞ **Click** `Work Offline`

If you have a broadband connection such as DSL or cable you will not see the *Dial-up Connection* window:

⌨ **If necessary, press** `Alt`

☞ **Click** `File`
☞ **Click** `Work Offline`

When you are working offline, sometimes the home page will be read from memory ('cache'). It might seem like you are connected to the Internet but you are not.

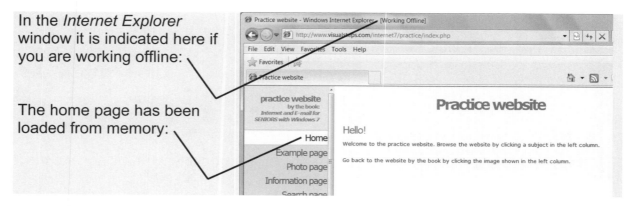

In the *Internet Explorer* window it is indicated here if you are working offline:

The home page has been loaded from memory:

Now that you have started *Internet Explorer* in offline mode you can open the saved page.

4.15 Opening the Web page

The web page can be opened from the *Documents library* like this:

In *Internet Explorer 9*:

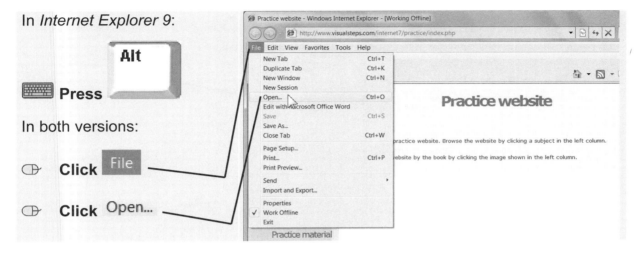

Press **Alt**

In both versions:

☞ **Click** File

☞ **Click** Open...

First you have to find the folder where you saved the web page. You do this by 'browsing' through the folders on your hard drive.

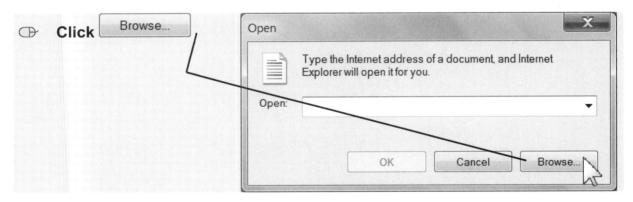

☞ **Click** Browse...

You see this window:

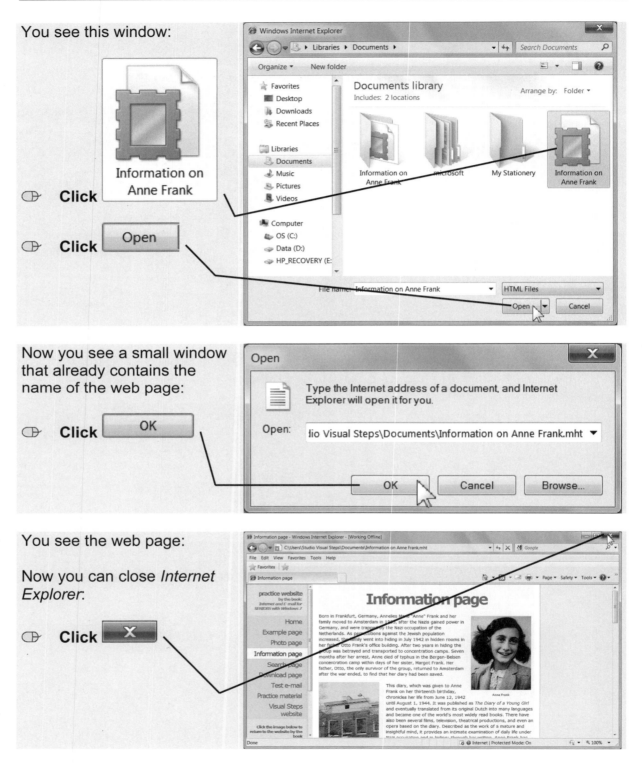

Click

Click **Open**

Now you see a small window that already contains the name of the web page:

Click **OK**

You see the web page:

Now you can close *Internet Explorer*:

Click **X**

You can practice what you have learned in the following exercises.

4.16 Exercises

Have you forgotten how to perform a particular action? Use the number beside the footsteps to look it up in the appendix *How Do I Do That Again?*

Exercise: Copying Text

In this exercise, you will practice copying text.
You do not need to open the information page on the Internet, because this web page has been saved to your computer.

☞ Start *Internet Explorer,* but stay offline. 👣²⁵

☞ Open the web page *Information on Anne Frank.* 👣²⁶

☞ Go to the last line of the text. 👣⁹

☞ Select the last line of the text. 👣²⁷

☞ Copy the text. 👣²⁸

☞ Minimize the *Internet Explorer* window. 👣¹¹

☞ Start *WordPad.* 👣²⁹

☞ Paste the text. 👣³⁰

☞ Close the *WordPad* window without saving the text. 👣³¹

Exercise: Saving an Image

In this exercise, you will practice saving an image.

☞ Open the *Internet Explorer* window on the taskbar. &⁄⁄12

☞ Right-click the photo of Anne Frank's Diary:

☞ Save the photo. &⁄⁄33

☞ Give the photo the name *Diary*. &⁄⁄34

☞ Close *Internet Explorer*. &⁄⁄2

Exercise: Saving a Page

☞ Start *Internet Explorer*. &⁄⁄1

☞ If necessary, connect to the Internet. &⁄⁄3

☞ Open the *Internet and E-mail for Seniors* practice website. &⁄⁄52

☞ Click Search page .

☞ Save this page. &⁄⁄53

☞ Close *Internet Explorer*. &⁄⁄2

☞ If necessary, disconnect from the Internet. &⁄⁄5

4.17 Background Information

Glossary

Cursor	A flashing vertical line that indicates where the next text that you type or paste will appear.
Footer	Text at the bottom of a printed web page.
Frame	An independent section on a web page. Each frame is actually a separate web page and can have its own scroll bars.
Grabbing	Popular term for copying images or text from a web page.
Header	Text at the top of a printed web page.
Orientation	The way your document is positioned on the paper. There are two orientation options: portrait and landscape. Portrait orients the page for vertical viewing, landscape orients the page for horizontal viewing.
Paint	*Paint* is a program used to draw, color, and edit pictures.
Personal folder	A folder containing your most frequently used folders (such as *My Documents*, *My Pictures*, *My Music*, *Favorites*, *Contacts*, and other folders that are specific to your user account). The *Personal folder* is labeled with the name you use to log on to your computer and is located at the top of the Start menu.
Print Preview	You can use Print Preview to see how a printed web page will look and to adjust page orientation, scaling, and margins.
Printer	Device that prints text and graphics from your computer onto paper.
Web Archive	A saved web page can be saved as a web archive. A web archive is saved in the Multipurpose Internet Mail Extension HTML (MHTML) format. Web archives can be recognized by the .MHT file extension. The .MHT file can be viewed using *Internet Explorer*.
WordPad	*WordPad* is a simple word processor that is included in *Windows*. A word processor is a computer program that you can use to create, edit, view, and print text documents.

Source: Windows Help and Support

Photos
You might be wondering how to get a photo onto a computer. There are different ways of doing this.

You can copy a printed photo with a *scanner*.

The photo is placed in the scanner, which is then closed. The computer then 'scans' the picture. This is also called *digitizing*.

It is also possible to scan photo negatives with a special kind of scanner, or to have a camera store place your photos directly onto a CD when you have them developed.

The newest method is to take photos without using a roll of film or photo paper. The photos you take are stored digitally from the start. You can do this using a *digital camera*.

The photos are stored in the camera on a small memory card. You can connect the camera to your computer with a cable when you want to transfer your photos to the PC.

If your computer is equipped with a card reader, you can remove the memory card from your digital camera and insert it into the card reader.

Scanner

Digital camera

Photo editing

Paint is a very simple drawing program that provides a few photo editing capabilities. Special photo editing programs contain many more features. In these programs, you can increase and decrease a photo's size, or crop it into a particular shape. You can also change the colors or sharpen the contrast. You have access to a complete digital darkroom.

Many programs have additional options for framing your photos or placing them in albums. Sometimes you can even create special web pages that you can upload to the Internet. In short, you can enjoy endless possibilities of using your computer with digital photography.

On the web page **www.visualsteps.com/info_downloads** you can download a free guide: *A Short Guide to Digital Photo Editing.* This useful guide gives you background information about photo editing, digital cameras and scanners. You do not necessarily need a digital camera for this interesting hobby, by the way. A scanner or a photo CD-ROM is enough. The free booklet is in PDF format. You can open this file and print it by using the free program *Adobe Reader.*

Free Short Guide to Digital Photo Editing - see www.visualsteps.com/info_downloads

Photo editing programs and the Internet
Photo editing programs are increasingly becoming specialized for Internet applications. Photos can be optimized for use on the Internet. Even with digital photos, the size, file type and color may have to be adjusted for the specific requirements of the Internet. Modern photo editing programs offer a variety of tools for making these kinds of technical modifications.

Easy photo editing and organizing in ArcSoft PhotoStudio

With the help of one of these programs you, too, can place your photos or photo albums on the Internet and share them with others. You can make a family album, for example, that is immediately accessible to anyone in your family around the world.

Some photo printing centers offer web space where you can put your photos online. Your photos are immediately available to family members all over the world. One useful option is that other people can order prints of your photos (if you specify that). This is often a paid service.

Pixels

Computer images (drawings or photos) are made out of dots. These dots are called *pixels*. If you zoom in on one of these photos, you will see a grid of colored dots. In computer terminology, this grid is called a *bitmap*:

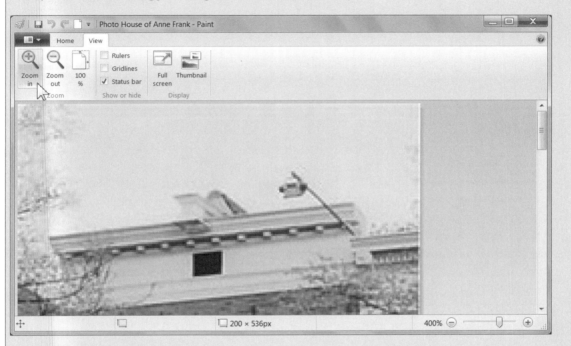

Each pixel can have a different color. The more colors that are used, the more information that can be stored in the photo. This is called the *color depth*. The more information that has to be saved, the larger the file. The standard files are called *bitmap files* and are denoted by the file extension *.bmp*.

The quality of a photo depends upon the number of pixels it contains. If the photo contains a lot of pixels, it will be sharp. As the number of pixels decreases, the photo becomes fuzzier. In addition, the quality is affected by the number of colors used. The more colors, the more realistic the photo. At present, sixteen million colors are the standard on a normal PC. For professional photos much larger numbers are used.

Color Depth	Number of Colors Possible	File Size BMP
1-bit	2 colors	59 KB
4-bit	16 colors	235 KB
8-bit	256 colors	470 KB
24-bit	millions of colors	1407 KB

- Continue reading on the next page -

BMP files with sizes like this are impractical for use on the Internet. They are too big and take far too long to load. This is why two file types have been developed that give good results, but still maintain a reasonable file size.

The first file type, *GIF,* is often used for colorful images like drawings. GIF files have the extension *.gif*. A photo with 256 colors and a file size of 470 KB in the BMP format needs only 3 KB when converted to GIF format.

The other file type, *JPEG*, is mainly used for photos and is recognizable by the extension *.jpg*.

Copyright
By copyright, we mean the rights of the creator of an original work. That work might be a book, an article, a composition, a painting or a CD recording. Someone who has created one of these things is entitled to call it his or her 'intellectual property'. It is obvious that this person also has the right to a reasonable compensation. That is why the law forbids copying another person's 'intellectual property'. The symbol © is often used to indicate that a work is protected by copyright. Even if there is no © symbol, the work may not be copied without permission.
This law clearly extends to the Internet. A good rule of thumb is to assume that nothing may be copied unless clearly stated otherwise, and under what conditions.
The Internet contains countless websites offering all kinds of material for free: images, photos, sounds, midi files (music), text, computer programs or complete music CDs.
On these websites, copying is permitted or even encouraged, sometimes on the condition that the source is identified - for example, if you copy a photo to put on your own website.
Sometimes website owners solicit material for which they do not own the copyright. In this case, both the offering and the copying are illegal activities strongly contested by the rightful copyright holders.

Making your own website
Most Internet Service Providers allow you to put your own website on the Internet. They give you a certain amount of space (in MB) on their hard drive for this.
Creating web pages is not all that terribly difficult, particularly if you use a special program. This kind of program is called a *web editor*.
Creating web pages is a lot like creating any kind of text. You write the text, add images and then add hyperlinks to your text. When your website is ready, you send the pages to your ISP's server. Your ISP gives you the web address where everyone can find your website.

The Internet keyboard

In recent years, the computer has been increasingly adapted for use with the Internet. One important component of this is the keyboard.

This keyboard has special Internet related buttons, which make it a snap to start your Internet browser, begin a search, go to your favorites or open your e-mail.

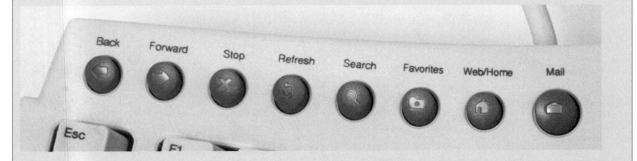

Here you see buttons for browsing forward and back, refreshing a page, searching on the Internet and opening your favorites. There is also a button for opening your home page. Another button opens your e-mail program.

4.18 Tips

💡 **Tip**

Zooming in
If you want to view the pixels in a photo in *Paint*, you will need to zoom in:

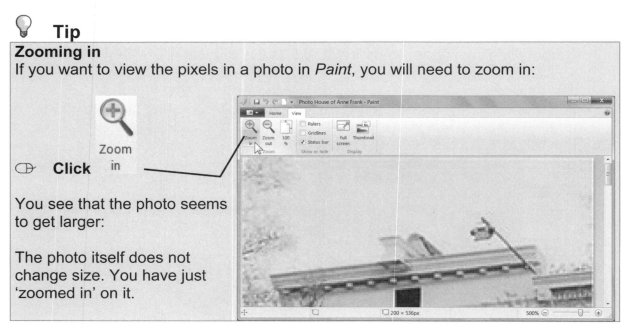

Zoom
in

☞ **Click**

You see that the photo seems
to get larger:

The photo itself does not
change size. You have just
'zoomed in' on it.

💡 **Tip**

Want to know more?
Would you like to know more about the *WordPad* program, for example: how to edit
and format text?
You can read about that in the books **Windows 7 for Seniors** and **More Windows
7 for Seniors**.
Have a look at **www.visualsteps.com/windows7** and
www.visualsteps.com/morewin7

5. E-mail, Your Electronic Mail

One of the most widely used Internet applications is electronic mail, or e-mail. E-mail uses no pen, paper, envelope or stamp. You type your message into the computer and it is sent via the Internet.

If you have an Internet service subscription, you will automatically be assigned an *e-mail address*. This e-mail address can be used to send and receive mail. Your *Internet Service Provider* (ISP) has a kind of post office, also called a *mail server*. Like with regular mail, this electronic post office handles all the daily mail traffic.

In order to send an e-mail to someone, the addressee must have an e-mail address of course. But it does not matter where that person lives. Sending an e-mail to someone in Australia takes the same amount of time and money as sending an e-mail to your next-door neighbor. There are no direct costs to you for sending an e-mail other than your Internet service subscription. There is also no limit on the number of messages you may send or receive.

E-mail is used a great deal by people who work with computers. It is fast: the message usually arrives at its destination within sixty seconds.

Windows 7 does not include a regular e-mail program. The manufacturer of *Windows 7*, *Microsoft*, provides a free e-mail program: *Windows Live Mail*.

You can use this program to simply and quickly send and receive electronic 'letters'. You will be using this program in this chapter.

In this chapter, you will learn how to:

- open *Windows Live Mail*
- create an e-mail message
- send and receive e-mail
- read e-mail

5.1 Opening Windows Live Mail

Windows 7 does not include a regular e-mail program. First, you need to download and install the *Windows Live Mail* program. You can read how to do this in *Appendix C Downloading and Installing Windows Live Mail* at the back of this book. If the program is already installed to your computer, you can open *Windows Live Mail*. Here is how you open the program *Windows Live Mail*:

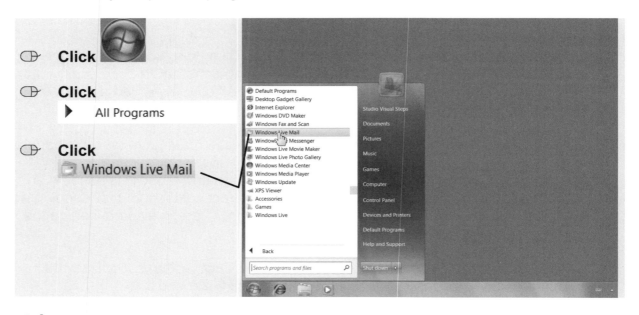

Click

Click
> All Programs

Click
Windows Live Mail

HELP! I do not see Windows Live Mail.

If you can not see Windows Live Mail , the program is not installed to your computer. In *Appendix C Downloading and Installing Windows Live Mail* at the back of this book, you will read how to download and install the *Windows Live Mail* program.

Windows Live Mail will immediately determine whether you are connected to the internet (*online*). If you are *offline*, you probably see a small window. You might want to work offline if you want to reduce the amount of time you spend online, either because your Internet Service Provider (ISP) charges you by the hour, or because you have only one phone line and you are not using a broadband connection.

Please note:

If you are using a broadband connection, such as cable or DSL, you will not see the following window. In that case, you can continue with the next step.

Possibly your e-mail account in *Windows Live Mail* has not yet been created. This is how you can activate your e-mail account.

 **Please note:**

If you already have an e-mail account, you can continue with *section 5.2 The E-mail Address*.

Now a wizard will be opened. In this wizard you will need to fill in data you have received from your Internet Service Provider. Such as your e-mail address, your password, and the name of the POP3-server and SMTP-server.

HELP! I want to use a webmail address.

Do you already have a webmail address from Hotmail or Gmail, for example? Then you need to define the settings for you e-mail account in a different way. Check the website that goes with this book **www.visualsteps.com/internet7** and you will find the information in *the Extra Appendix Setting up a Webmail Account in Windows Live Mail*.

Type your e-mail address

Type your password

Next to Display Name: :

Type a name

Click Next

Windows Live Mail

Add your email accounts

Email address:
name@provider.com
Get a Windows Live email address

Password:
••••••
☑ Remember this password

Display name for your sent messages:
Studio Visual Steps

☐ Manually configure server settings

Most email accounts work with Windows Live Mail including

Hotmail
Gmail
and many others.

Cancel   Next

HELP! I do not see the Add your e-mail accounts window.

If you do not see the *Add your e-mail accounts* window:

☞ **Click the** `Accounts` **tab**

☞ **Click** Email

HELP! I do not have this information.

Your Internet Service Provider should have given you these details. If you have not received this information, you should contact your ISP (Internet Service Provider).

⌨ **Type the name of the POP3-server**

⌨ **Type the name of the SMTP-server**

☞ **Click** Next

Now you have finished:

☞ **Click** | Finish |

> **Windows Live Mail**
>
> ## Your email account was added
>
> ✓   was added
>
> Add another email account
>
> | Finish |

🩹 HELP! I see a different message

If you see an error message, click | Cancel |. You will need to re-enter the account information. In the first window place a checkmark ☑ by Manually configure server settings. Enter the required information that you have received from your Internet provider.

You will see the *Windows live mail* window:

Here you will see the tabs:

On the left there is a folder list:

In the middle you will see a message list with headers:

In this example, no messages are yet received.

This is the Preview pane:

On the right you will see the Calendar:

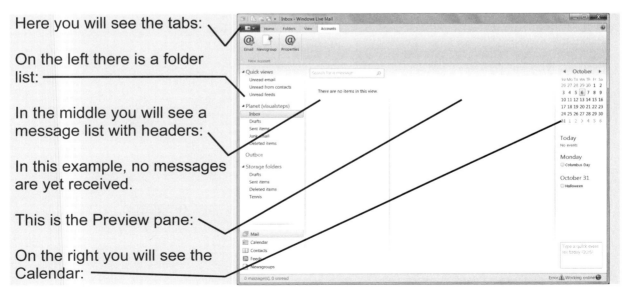

✖✖ HELP! My window looks entirely different.

When someone else already used the program, the window may look different. This does not matter. Just continue reading.

First, you will modify the layout of the window:

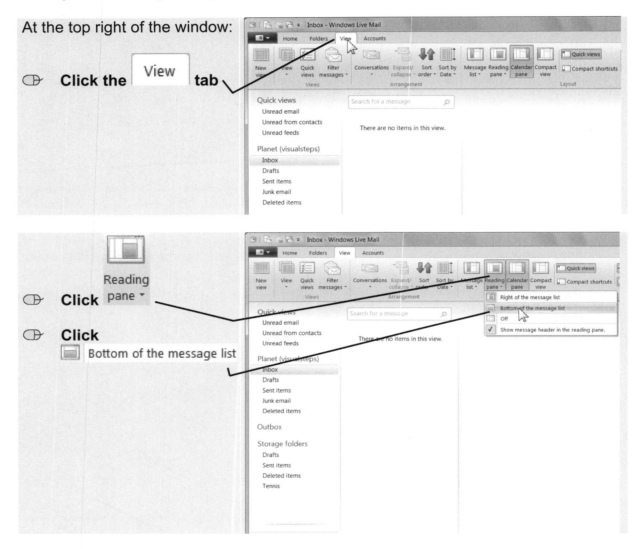

At the top right of the window:

☞ **Click the** View **tab**

☞ **Click** Reading pane ▾

☞ **Click** ▢ **Bottom of the message list**

In the next section you will learn how to send an e-mail message.

5.2 The E-mail Address

To practice, you will be sending a message to yourself. This is an excellent way to learn how to send e-mail. Since the message is sent straight to you, you will also learn how to receive e-mail. This is how to create a new e-mail message:

At the top left of the window:

☞ **Click the** Home **tab**

☞ **Click** Email message

Now you see the window *New Message* on top of the program window:

In this window you can create a new e-mail message:

The first thing to do is to address your message using an e-mail address. Every e-mail address consists of a number of words, with the familiar @ symbol somewhere in the middle. For example:

name@provider.com

The name of the addressee is located in front of the @. Behind it, the address usually contains the name of the Internet Service Provider from which you received the e-mail address.

 Please note:

E-mail addresses may not contain spaces.
This is why names or words are sometimes separated by a dot (.). These dots are extremely important. If you forget one in the address, your message will never arrive. Your mailman may understand what the sender means if the address is not completely correct. But a computer does not.

5.3 Creating an E-mail Message

The best way to test that your electronic mail works as it should is to send an e-mail message.

In the box next to To… :

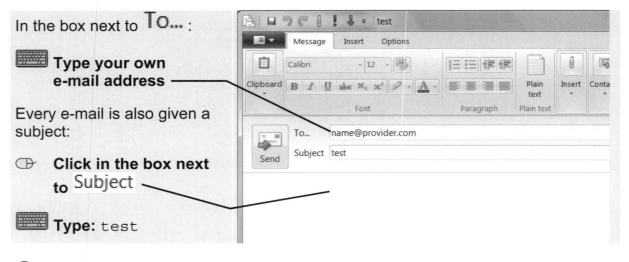

█ Type your own e-mail address

Every e-mail is also given a subject:

☞ **Click in the box next to Subject**

█ Type: test

💡 **Tip**

Entering more e-mail addresses
An e-mail can be sent to multiple recipients. If you want to send your e-mail to more than one e-mail address, you must type a semicolon (;) or comma between the addresses.

☞ **Click the main message window**

You can type the message here.

█ Type: This is a first e-mail as a test.

Writing a message in this window works just the same way as a text-editing program such as *WordPad*. To change font type, size, style, and to add effects such as color,

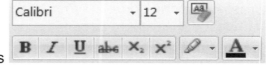

use the options ![formatting toolbar] just like in *WordPad*.

💡 Tip

Would you like to know more?
Would you like to know more about typing and formatting text in *Windows*?
Then read the Visual Steps book **Windows 7 for Seniors**.
See **www.visualsteps.com/windows7** for more information.

The most important keys for editing and correcting text are shown below.

💡 Tip

The keys for typing text

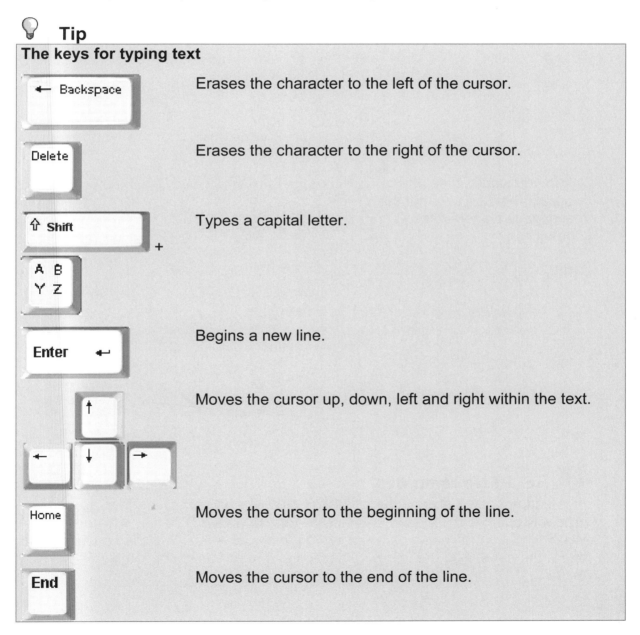

← Backspace	Erases the character to the left of the cursor.
Delete	Erases the character to the right of the cursor.
⇧ Shift + A B Y Z	Types a capital letter.
Enter ←	Begins a new line.
↑ ← ↓ →	Moves the cursor up, down, left and right within the text.
Home	Moves the cursor to the beginning of the line.
End	Moves the cursor to the end of the line.

5.4 Sending E-mail

When you have finished the e-mail, you can send it.

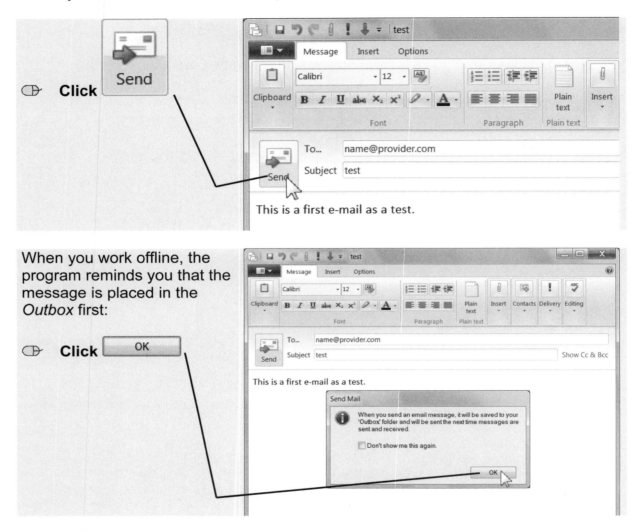

☞ **Click** Send

When you work offline, the program reminds you that the message is placed in the *Outbox* first:

☞ **Click** OK

✚ HELP! No reminder.

If you do not see the reminder about the *Outbox* on your screen then you are probably using a broadband connection, for example a DSL line. This means that *Windows Live Mail* has a different setting and your e-mail is mailed immediately. If this is the case, skip the following section and continue at *section 5.7 Reading an E-mail*.

5.5 The Outbox

When you work offline, all of the e-mails you write are collected in the *Outbox* first. Your message will not be sent until you connect to the Internet. This means that you can write as many e-mails as you want, and then send them all at one time.

Now you see the *Windows Live Mail* window again.

There is one message in the Outbox (1).

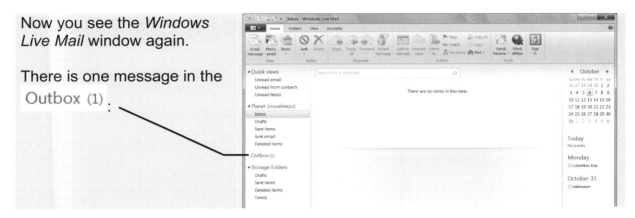

5.6 Sending and Receiving

Now you can manually send your message. The program will connect to the Internet to send it.

Sending and receiving manually is useful if you are using dial-up networking to connect to the Internet. In that case, be sure to check if your modem is ready before you try to connect.

🖝 **Make sure your modem is connected to the telephone line**

Do you have an external modem?
🖝 **If so, turn the modem on**

Do you have an internal modem?
🖝 **Then you do not need to do anything**

At the *Quick Access Toolbar*:

⟜ **Click**

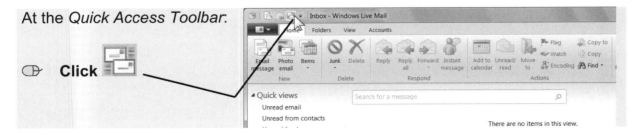

When you work offline, *Windows Live Mail* will tell you that you are still offline and asks whether you want to go online.

You need to go online to send a message, so:

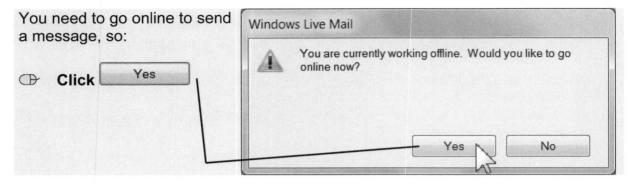

☞ **Click** Yes

If you are using dial-up networking to connect to the Internet, you will see a *Dial-up Connection* window. It probably looks like this one:

☞ **Click** Connect

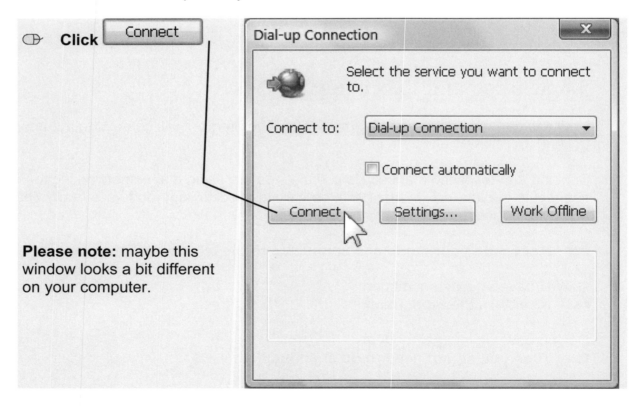

Please note: maybe this window looks a bit different on your computer.

At the bottom of the window:

⊕ **Click** [Dial]

Please note: maybe this window looks a bit different on your computer.

Connect Dial-up Connection 2	X

User name: kar008

Password: ●●●●●●●●●●●●●

☑ Save this user name and password for the following users:

⦿ Me only

○ Anyone who uses this computer

A connection is made to your ISP (Internet Service Provider). Next your e-mail message is sent. The program also automatically checks to see if you have any new e-mail messages.

HELP! I do not see these windows.

If you do not see this window it could mean that the program *Windows Live Mail* has different settings on your computer. Your program connects automatically and sends the message when you click the button .

☞ **Just continue reading**

You can follow this process as it proceeds in a window like this:

Windows Live Mail

Sending email using 'Planet (visualsteps)'...

Sending message 1 of 1...

[Hide] [Stop] [Details >>]

If everything went as it should, your test message was immediately sent to you. Then it is put in the *Inbox*.

5.7 Reading an E-mail

All e-mail messages you receive are placed in a separate folder called the *Inbox*.

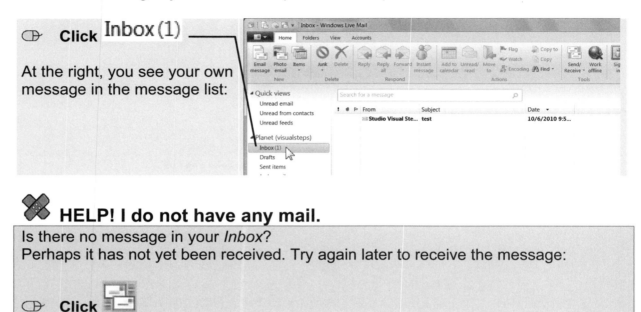

Click **Inbox (1)**

At the right, you see your own message in the message list:

🩹 HELP! I do not have any mail.

Is there no message in your *Inbox*?
Perhaps it has not yet been received. Try again later to receive the message:

Click

You can open the message in a new window and then read it:

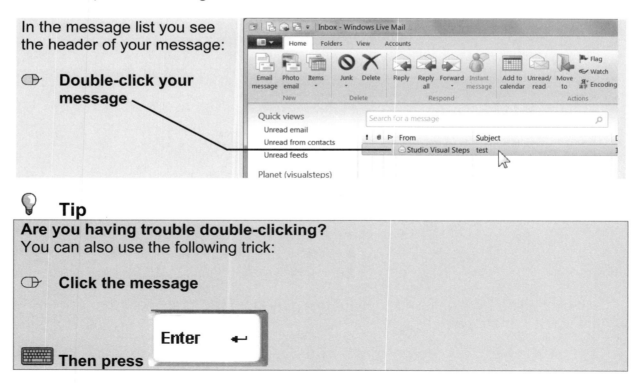

In the message list you see the header of your message:

Double-click your message

💡 Tip

Are you having trouble double-clicking?
You can also use the following trick:

Click the message

Then press Enter ↵

Tip

A better view
You can best read an e-mail if you temporarily maximize its window:

In the top right corner:

Click

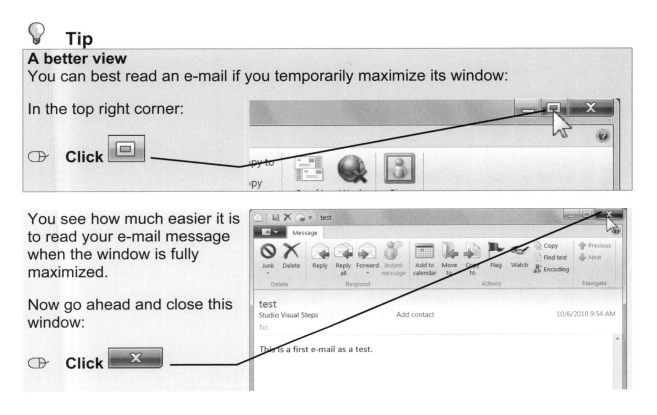

You see how much easier it is to read your e-mail message when the window is fully maximized.

Now go ahead and close this window:

Click

5.8 The Folders

Windows Live Mail has a sophisticated system of folders for organizing your e-mail messages. In addition to the *Inbox* and the *Outbox*, there are three other folders. *Windows Live Mail* saves all the e-mail messages you have sent in a separate folder called *Sent items*.
You can delete messages you do not want to keep. These will be stored in the *Deleted items* folder.
Last but not least, there is a folder for messages that are not yet finished. These are placed in the *Drafts* folder.

The Sent items folder contains copies of the e-mails you have sent:

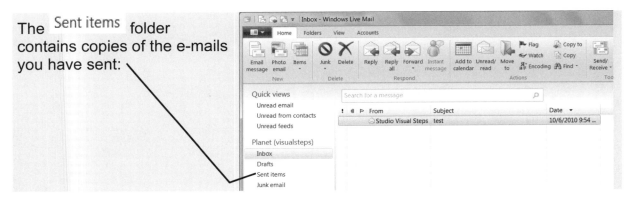

The message you just sent to yourself should be in there.

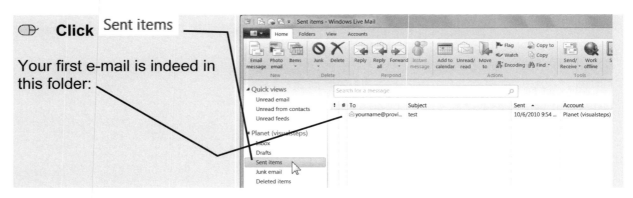

Click Sent items

Your first e-mail is indeed in this folder:

You can delete this e-mail message now.

5.9 Deleting E-mail Messages

Many people use the *Inbox* and *Sent items* folders as a kind of archive. All of your correspondence is stored neatly, and you can easily retrieve your e-mail messages. There is no limit on the number of e-mail messages you can store.
In practice however, you will want to regularly delete unnecessary messages to keep your folders from becoming too cluttered. You can delete the test message now.

Before you can delete an e-mail, you have to select it:

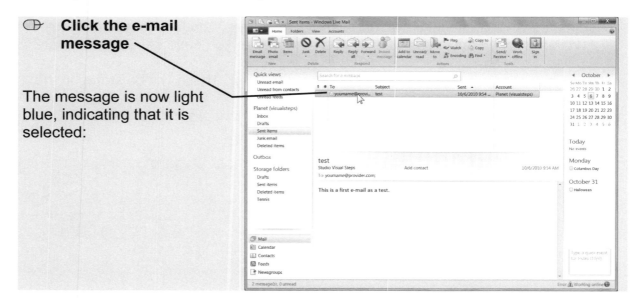

Click the e-mail message

The message is now light blue, indicating that it is selected:

Now you can tell *Windows Live Mail* to delete the message.

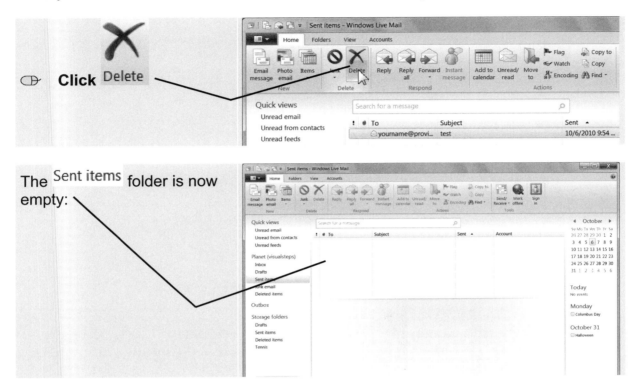

Click Delete

The Sent items folder is now empty:

A message that you have deleted in this manner, is not actually gone forever. *Windows Live Mail* saves all the e-mail messages you have deleted in a separate folder called *Deleted items*. This is actually a safety feature. You can retrieve a message out of this folder if you put it there by mistake. In the next step you will learn how to permanently delete the message.

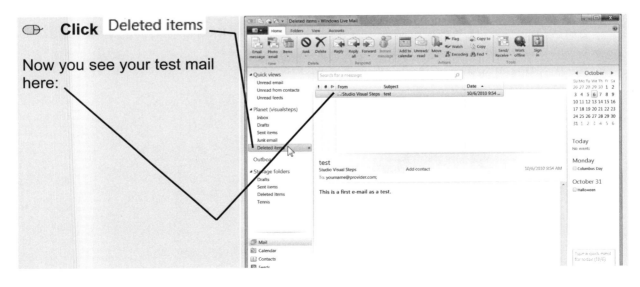

Click Deleted items

Now you see your test mail here:

When you are ready to permanently delete the e-mails you have thrown away, you can empty the Deleted items folder. This is how you do that:

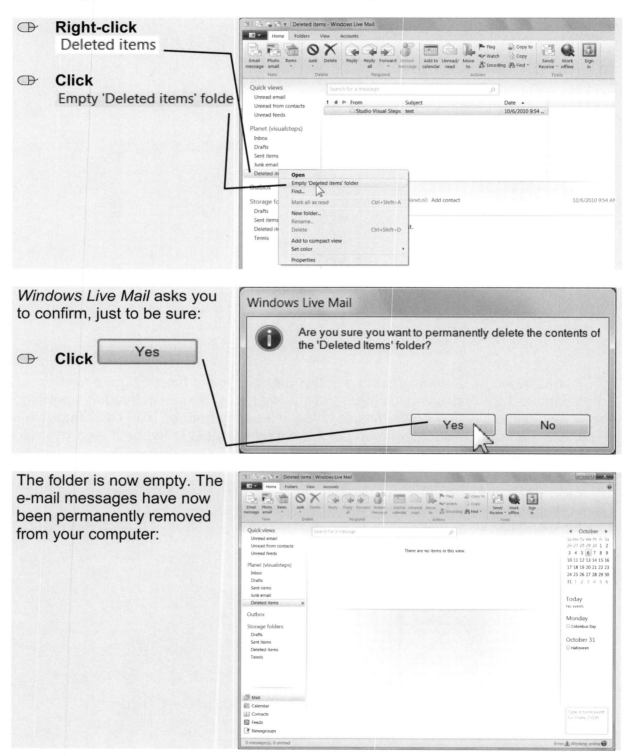

☞ **Right-click**
   Deleted items

☞ **Click**
   Empty 'Deleted items' folde

Windows Live Mail asks you to confirm, just to be sure:

☞ **Click** Yes

The folder is now empty. The e-mail messages have now been permanently removed from your computer:

5.10 A Second Test Message

In order to practice receiving, answering and forwarding e-mails, you can send a test message to a special e-mail address. You will get an automated e-mail reply back. First you create a new e-mail.

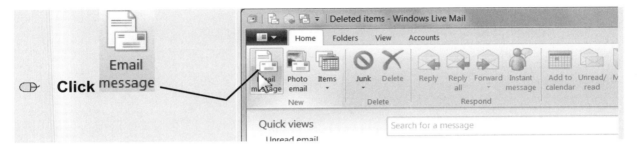

☞ **Click** Email message

The e-mail address for the test message is: **test@visualsteps.com**

Next to To...:

⌨ **Type:** test@visualsteps. com

Next to Subject:

⌨ **Type:** Test mail

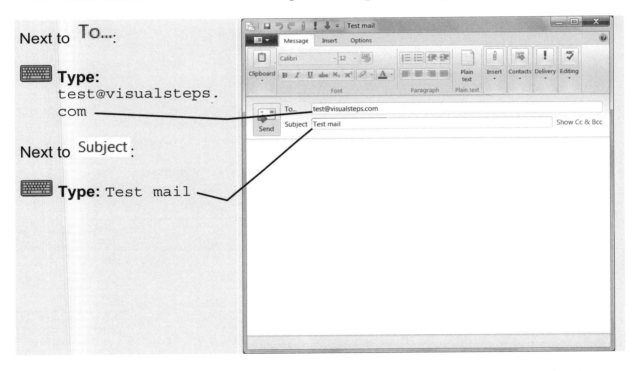

The test message is ready. You are not going to send this message immediately. Instead, you are going to save it in the Drafts folder first.

5.11 The Drafts Folder

Sometimes you do not want to send a message immediately, perhaps because you want to think about the content a little longer. In that case, you can save the e-mail in the Drafts folder.

Click 💾

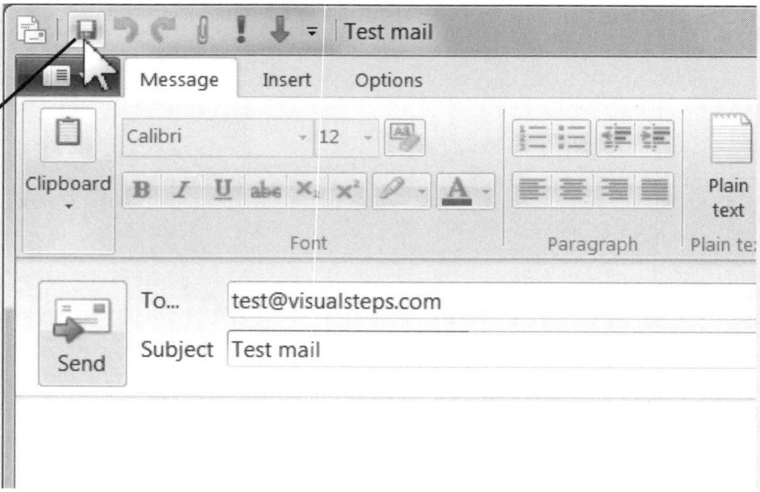

Windows Live Mail tells you the e-mail has been saved in Drafts.

Click OK

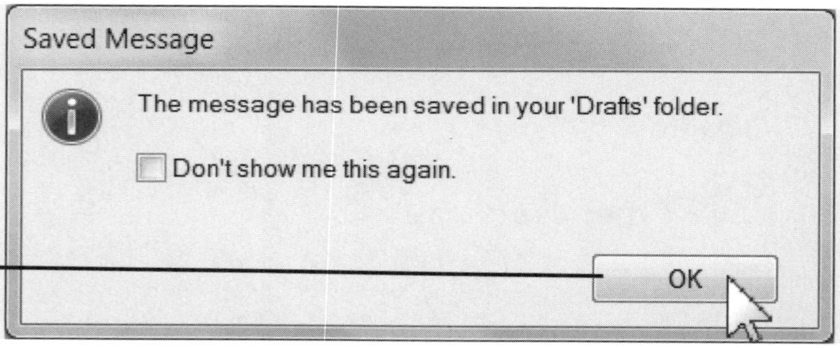

Now you can close the window containing the e-mail.

Click X

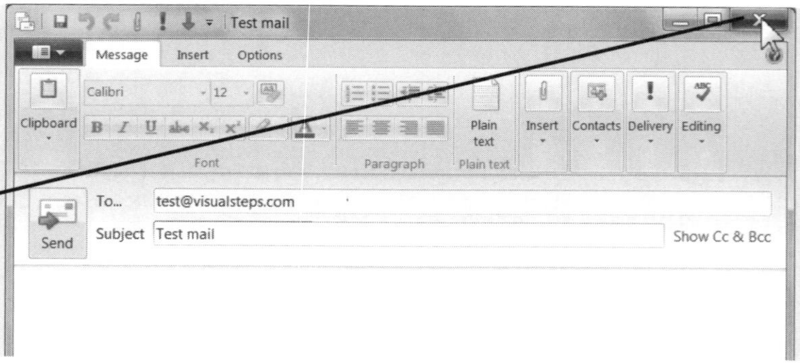

The number '1' is displayed in the word Drafts (1). That means there is one message in the folder:

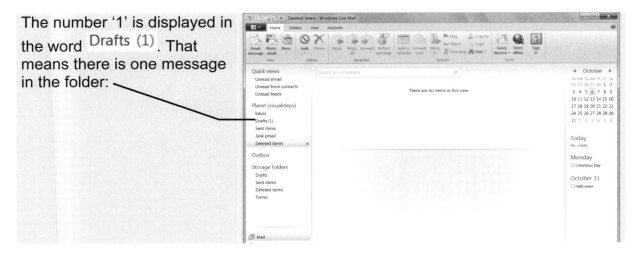

You can leave the message in this folder even if you close *Windows Live Mail*. Later on, you can simply open this message again and continue working on it:

👆 **Click** Drafts (1)

👆 **Double-click the message**

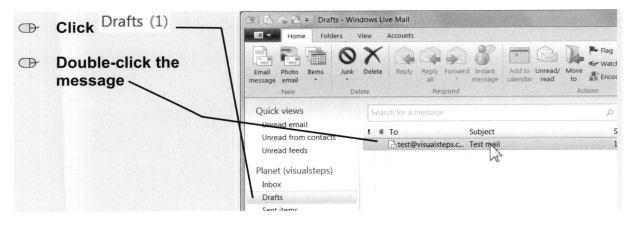

The message is opened. Now you can send it:

👆 **Click** Send

If you are working offline, the *Send Mail* window appears:

👆 **Click** OK

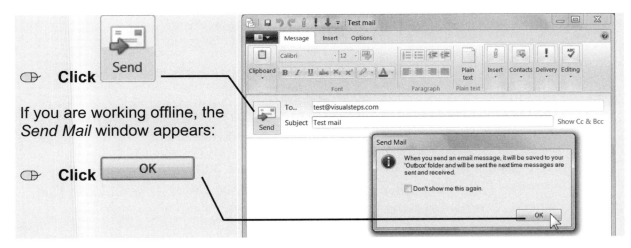

If you are using a broadband connection like DSL or cable, you are continuously online and your message is sent immediately. If you are working offline, or if your *Windows Live Mail* settings have been set up to do so, your message has been placed in the *Outbox*.

You can see this by the
number at the end
Outbox (1).

You can send your test
e-mail.

☞ **Click**

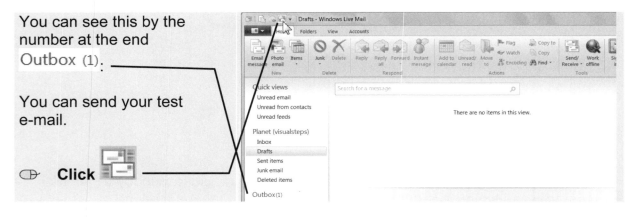

☞ **If necessary, connect to the Internet** 👣³

Your message is sent, and *Windows Live Mail* checks if you have received any mail.

👉 **Please note:**

It might take a little while before you receive a reply to your test mail.
Wait about fifteen minutes and try again:

☞ **Click**

HELP! I see a message about junk mail.

Do you see this window?

☞ **Click** [Close]

Windows Live Mail   X

Windows Live Mail has downloaded a message that appears to be Phishing
E-mail.

What is phishing?

☐ Please do not show me this dialog again

[Phishing E-mail Options...] → [Close]

This message means that the response to your test mail has been moved to the
Junk e-mail folder. *Windows Live Mail* automatically identifies what looks like
unsolicited commercial e-mail messages and moves them to this folder.

- Continue reading on the next page -

You can open the *Junk e-mail* folder:

☞ **Click** Junk email (1)

The folder is opened and you see the message:

It is very easy to move a
message from the *Junk
e-mail* folder to your *Inbox*:

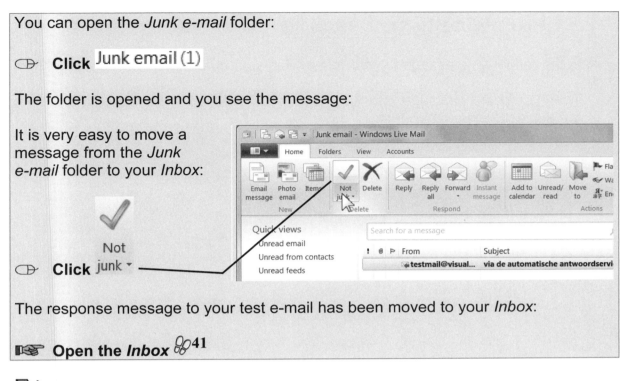

☞ **Click** junk ▾

The response message to your test e-mail has been moved to your *Inbox*:

☞ **Open the *Inbox*** 👣41

➥ Please note:

Windows Live Mail unfortunately does not see the difference at times between a harmless test e-mail and unwanted commercial e-mail (also called *spam*). E-mail from your friends or family could also end up in the folder Junk e-mail .

Check this folder regularly to make sure you do not miss any e-mails that you do want to receive.

💡 Tip

Read more about the Junk Mail Filter
In *Bonus Online Chapter 10 Security and Privacy* on the website that goes with this book you can read more about the *Junk Mail Filter* and how to customize the settings for this filter.

5.12 Replying to an E-mail

Is the response message to your test mail in your *Inbox*?

Then you see a message with the subject *Response to test e-mail*:

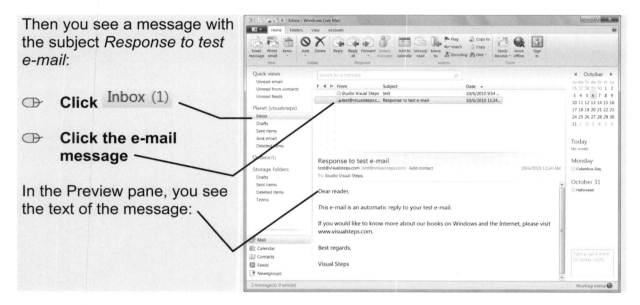

☞ **Click** Inbox (1)

☞ **Click the e-mail message**

In the Preview pane, you see the text of the message:

If you have received an e-mail, you do not have to type in the e-mail address again in order to reply to it. *Windows Live Mail* has various buttons for replying to this e-mail. There is a toolbar for this, containing the following buttons:

Reply	**Reply** Reply to sender, the 'to' portion already contains the correct e-mail address.
Reply all	**Reply All** An e-mail message can be sent to more than one person. This button is used to send a reply to everyone to whom the original e-mail was addressed. The original e-mail message is included.
Forward	**Forward** A new e-mail is made from the original message that can be sent to someone else. The original e-mail message and any attachments are included.

In most cases, you will just want to reply to a message. Give it a try:

In the top left corner:

☞ **Click** Reply

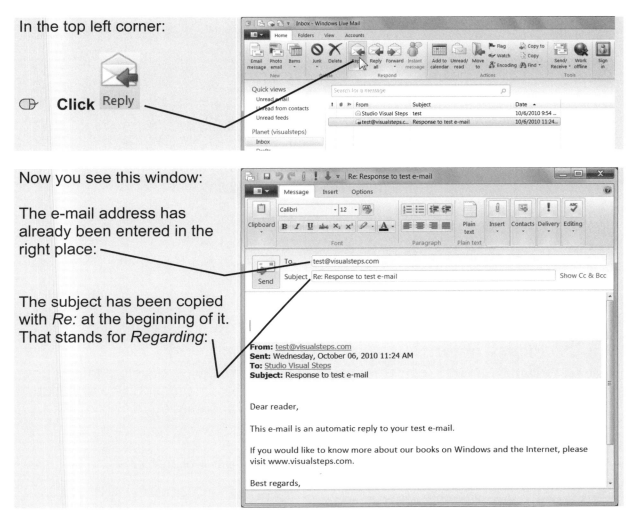

Now you see this window:

The e-mail address has already been entered in the right place:

The subject has been copied with *Re:* at the beginning of it. That stands for *Regarding*:

The text of the original message is automatically included in the reply message. This is very useful. The person to whom you are replying can immediately see what the message was about. On the other hand, the message just gets longer and longer in an extended correspondence.

💡 **Tip**

Would you prefer the original message not be included in the reply?
You can prevent its inclusion by:
- creating a new message instead of using the *Reply* button
- setting up *Windows Live Mail* differently; see *section 5.15 Send Options*.

You can type your reply at the top of the message:

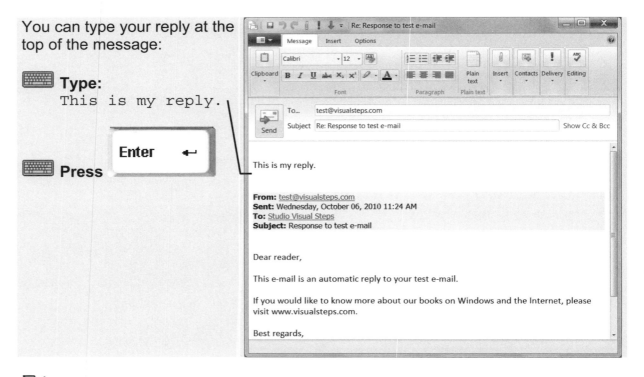

⌨ **Type:**
This is my reply.

⌨ **Press** Enter ⏎

Please note:

You will only get one reply a week to e-mail you send to **test@visualsteps.com**. The reply message is automatically sent by our ISP's computer. The limitation to one message per week has been made so that two computers do not become overwhelmed sending automated messages back and forth.

Now you can send this message, but you will not get a reply to it.

☞ **Send the message to the *Outbox* 🦶³⁷**

If you are working offline:

☞ **Send and receive your e-mail 🦶³⁹**

☞ **If necessary, connect to the Internet 🦶³**

5.13 Optimizing Your Windows Live Mail Settings

You can adjust various things in *Windows Live Mail* such as:

- your mail delivery
- the way in which your e-mail messages are sent
- your e-mail account information

5.14 Mail Delivery

Windows Live Mail can be set up in one of two ways:

- Automatic connection - It connects automatically to the Internet and sends and receives mail when it opens.
- Manual connection - It does not connect automatically to the Internet. You must manually give the command to send and receive.

It is a matter of personal preference which setting you decide to use.

You can adjust the settings as follows:

At the top right-hand side of the window:

☞ **Click** [icon]

☞ **Click** [Options]

☞ **Click** [Mail...]

Now you see this window with a large number of settings:

See if the box for
Send and receive messages at startup
has been checked:

Do you want to send and receive mail immediately at startup?

☞ **Click a check mark for**
Send and receive messages a

If you do not want to automatically connect to the Internet when it opens:

☞ **Make sure this box is not checked**

Options

Spelling		Connection		Advanced	
General	Read	Receipts	Send	Compose	Signatures

General

☑ Notify me if there are any new newsgroups
☐ Automatically log on to Windows Live Messenger
☐ Help us improve Windows Live programs by allowing Microsoft to collect information about your system, and how you use our software. This data will not be used to personally identify you.

Learn more

Send / Receive Messages

☑ Play sound when new messages arrive
☑ Send and receive messages at startup
☑ Check for new messages every [30] ⏶⏷ minute(s)
   If my computer is not connected at this time:
   [Do not connect ▼]

Default Messaging Programs

This application is the default Mail handler [Make Default]
This application is NOT the default News handler [Make Default]

[OK] [Cancel] [Apply]

💡 **Tip**

Automatically check your e-mail
There is also a setting in *Windows Live Mail* to determine how often you want to automatically connect to the Internet and check your e-mail.

You can turn this on by checking this box:

Here you can set the number of minutes:

Here you can specify what should happen if you are not already connected:

Send / Receive Messages

☑ Play sound when new messages arrive
☑ Send and receive messages at startup
☑ Check for new messages every [30] ⏶⏷ minute(s)
   If my computer is not connected at this time:

[Do not connect ▼]
Do not connect
Connect only when not working offline
Connect even when working offline

Default Messa
This application is NOT the default News handler [Make Default]
[Make Default]

5.15 Send Options

Windows Live Mail has several settings for answering your e-mail. You can view these as follows:

Click the [Send] **tab**

You see several check boxes:

Not all these settings are equally important. They are often a matter of personal preference. For that reason, we are only going to discuss the most important ones here:

- sending your mail immediately, instead of putting it in the *Outbox* first
- not including the original message in your replies

You can try out all the other options if you would like. These kinds of changes are easy to undo.

5.16 No Outbox

You can choose not to use the *Outbox*. When you have written an e-mail message and you click the *Send* button, you will connect automatically to the Internet. This does however, have a slight disadvantage. You can not write all your e-mail messages first and then send them all at the same time.

Do you want to send your e-mail immediately?

☞ **Click a check mark for**
Send messages immediately

If you do not want to do that:

☞ **Make sure the box is not checked**

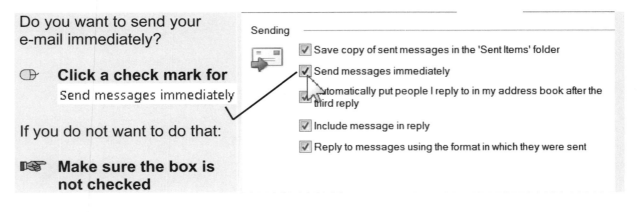

5.17 Your Reply

You can choose to include the original message in your reply to an e-mail.

You do this using the option Include message in reply :

Do you want to include the original message in your reply?

☞ **Click a check mark for**
Include message in reply

Do you not want to include the original message in your reply?

☞ **Make sure this box is not checked**

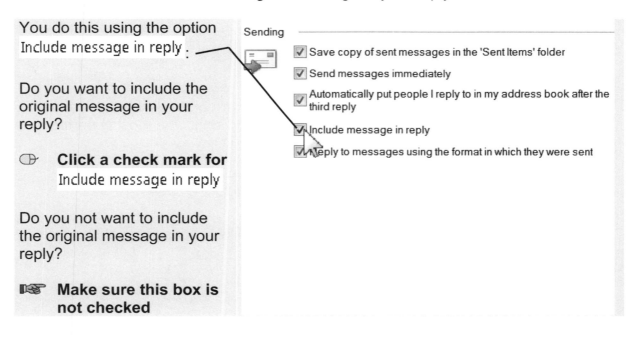

If you do not check this box, you will begin with an empty message and the original message will not be shown.

You can save the settings and then close the window.

☞ **Click** OK

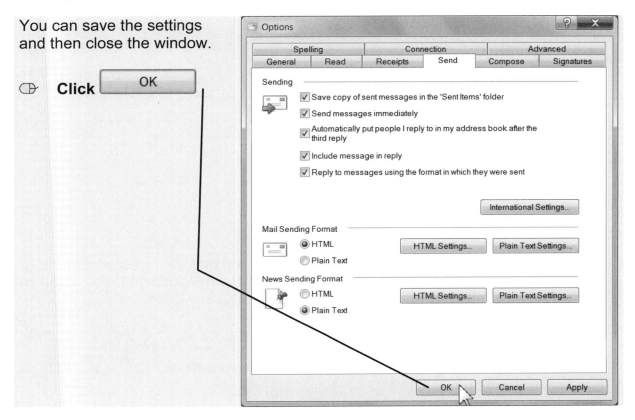

5.18 Checking Your E-mail Account

By *e-mail account*, we mean your mailbox at your ISP. It is a good idea to check the settings of your e-mail account information from time to time.
Here is how you do it:

☞ **Click** ▤ ▼

☞ **Click** Options

☞ **Click** @ Email accounts...

You see this window with the name(s) of your e-mail account(s):

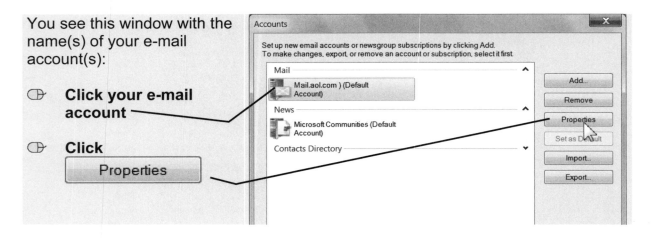

☞ **Click your e-mail account**

☞ **Click**

Properties

5.19 Checking Your Name

When you were setting up your e-mail account, you probably entered a name. That name is used as the name of the sender for each e-mail you send. You might want to change or edit this name. You can do that in the window below:

☞ **Check your name**

If you are not satisfied, you can change the name.

If you have multiple e-mail addresses, you can also use one of these other addresses as your reply e-mail address.

You can use this box:

At the bottom of the window:

☞ **Click** OK

Planet (visualsteps) Properties

General | Servers | Security | Advanced

Mail Account

Type the name by which you would like to refer to these servers. For example: "Work" or "Windows Live Hotmail".

Planet (visualsteps)

User Information

Name: Studio Visual Steps

Organization:

E-mail address: name@provider.com

Reply address:

☐ Include this account when receiving mail or synchronizing

☞ **Close the *Internet Accounts* window** ₰₰³²

☞ **Close *Windows Live Mail*** ₰₰⁴³

In the following exercises, you can practice sending and receiving e-mails.

5.20 Exercises

Have you forgotten how to perform a particular action? Use the number beside the footsteps to look it up in the appendix *How Do I Do That Again?*

Exercise: Creating an E-mail

In this exercise, you are going to write a new e-mail message.

☞ Start *Windows Live Mail.* $\mathcal{B}^{35}$

☞ Create a new e-mail message addressed to yourself. $\mathcal{B}^{36}$

☞ Send it. $\mathcal{B}^{37}$

☞ Check if your e-mail is in the *Outbox.* $\mathcal{B}^{38}$

☞ Send and receive your e-mail. $\mathcal{B}^{39}$

☞ Check if you have received e-mail in the *Inbox.* $\mathcal{B}^{41}$

☞ Read your e-mail message. $\mathcal{B}^{42}$

☞ Close *Windows Live Mail.* $\mathcal{B}^{43}$

Exercise: Do You Have Mail?

In this exercise, you are just going to check if you have any new e-mail messages.

☞ Start *Windows Live Mail.* $\mathcal{B}^{35}$

☞ Send and receive your e-mail. $\mathcal{B}^{39}$

☞ Check if you have received e-mail in the *Inbox.* $\mathcal{B}^{41}$

☞ Close *Windows Live Mail.* $\mathcal{B}^{43}$

Exercise: Deleting an E-mail

☞ Start *Windows Live Mail*. $\theta\!\theta^{35}$

☞ Send and receive your e-mail. $\theta\!\theta^{39}$

☞ Look in the *Inbox*. $\theta\!\theta^{41}$

☞ Delete your test e-mail. $\theta\!\theta^{44}$

☞ Close *Windows Live Mail*. $\theta\!\theta^{43}$

Exercise: E-mail in the Drafts Folder

☞ Start *Windows Live Mail*. $\theta\!\theta^{35}$

☞ Create a new e-mail message addressed to yourself. $\theta\!\theta^{36}$

☞ Save it. $\theta\!\theta^{45}$

☞ Close the window containing the new e-mail. $\theta\!\theta^{32}$

☞ Check if your e-mail is in the *Drafts* folder. $\theta\!\theta^{46}$

☞ Delete your new e-mail. $\theta\!\theta^{44}$

☞ Close *Windows Live Mail*. $\theta\!\theta^{43}$

5.21 Background Information

Glossary

Deleted items	Deleted e-mails are moved to the *Deleted items* folder. To permanently remove a deleted item from your computer: delete the message in the *Deleted items* folder.
Drafts	An e-mail that you write and save instead of sending it right away, is placed in the *Drafts* folder.
DSL	A type of high-speed Internet connection using existing copper telephone wires. Also referred to as a broadband connection.
E-mail	Short for electronic mail. Messages sent via the Internet.
E-mail account	The server name, user name, password, and e-mail address used by *Windows Live Mail* to connect to an e-mail service. You create the e-mail account by using information provided by your Internet Service Provider (ISP).
E-mail header	Information included at the top of an e-mail message: name of the sender and recipient, subject, date, and other information.
Inbox	The *Inbox* is where all of the e-mail messages that you receive are placed.
ISP	Internet Service Provider. A company that provides Internet access. An ISP provides a telephone number, a user name, a password, and other connection information so that users can access the Internet through the ISP's computers.
Junk e-mail	Unsolicited commercial e-mail, also known as spam.
Junk e-mail folder	*Windows Live Mail* filters obvious unsolicited commercial e-mail messages and moves them to a special folder called *Junk e-mail*.
Message list	List of messages in various folders in *Windows Live Mail*.
Outbox	When you manually send e-mail and you finish writing a message and click the Send button, the message will be placed in your *Outbox* folder. Messages in the *Outbox* folder will be sent when you click the Send/Receive button.

- Continue reading on the next page -

Preview pane	Here you can view the message's contents without opening the message in a separate window. To view an e-mail message in the Preview pane, click the message in the message list.
Sent items	A copy of every message you send is saved in the *Sent items* folder, just in case you need it later.
Spam	Unsolicited commercial e-mail, also known as junk e-mail.

Source: Windows Help and Support

The parts of the Windows Live Mail window
You can display or hide the following parts of the window.

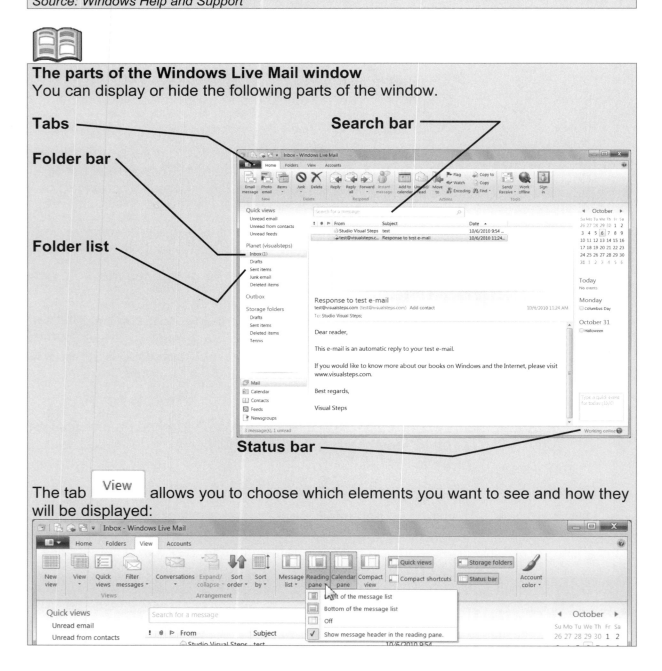

The tab View allows you to choose which elements you want to see and how they will be displayed:

How does e-mail work?

All e-mail messages are delivered to a *mail server*. This is a computer at your ISP (Internet Service Provider) that is dedicated to processing electronic mail.

If you have written to someone and the e-mail has been sent, then it is transported by your ISP's mail server until - after passing through a number of intermediate stations - it reaches the mail server at the addressee's ISP and is stored there.

It works the same way in reverse. E-mail for you is saved on your ISP's mail server until you pick it up with *Windows Live Mail*.

Netiquette

The word *netiquette* is an abbreviation of the phrase '*Internet etiquette*'. It denotes a collection of rules that people who use e-mail are advised to follow. It is particularly advisable for *newbies* (beginners on the digital highway) to take note of netiquette.

For effective communication, follow these guidelines:

- Be careful with humor and emotion. E-mail does not convey emotion well, so the recipient might not understand your intended tone. Sarcastic humor is particularly risky because the recipient might interpret it literally and take offense.

- Think before you send. Writing and sending an e-mail message is fast and easy. Make sure you have thought out your message first, and avoid writing when you are angry. Once you send the message, you can not get it back.

- Use a clear and concise subject line. Summarize the contents of the message in a few words. People who receive a large amount of e-mail can use the subject to prioritize the message.

- Keep messages short. Although an e-mail message can be of any length, e-mail is designed for quick communication. Many people do not have the time or patience to read more than a few sections.

- Avoid using ALL CAPITAL LETTERS. Many people perceive sentences written in all uppercase letters as 'yelling' and find it annoying or offensive.

- Be careful with sensitive or confidential information. The addressee might share his or her computer and e-mail program with other persons. Any recipient can forward your message to others, either intentionally or accidentally.

Unwelcome e-mails and spam
There are two kinds of unwelcome e-mails that you may receive.

The first are e-mails from businesses you know that are trying to sell you something. This can happen, for example, after you e-mailed them asking for information about a product or ordered something from them before. By doing that, you could have ended up on their mailing list.

The second group of e-mails seems to 'fall out of nowhere' and you have no idea how such a company has gotten your e-mail address. This type of unsolicited commercial e-mail is called *spam*. There is a thriving trade in e-mail addresses, and you may have ended up on such a list. Usually, these spam e-mails offer things like cheap medication, university degrees, stock advice and 'get rich quick' -schemes.

What can you do?
- If the e-mails come from a company you know, you can follow the instructions in the e-mail to unsubscribe from their mailing list. This can be done by clicking a link, or by sending an e-mail with a subject or text consisting of a particular sentence or command. This command is processed by a computer without any human intervention. There is often no other way to unsubscribe.

- But be careful: never respond to a spam e-mail and never click on an unsubscribe-link in such an e-mail. Also: never order something that is offered in an spam e-mail. By doing any of these things, you confirm to the company that your e-mail address is a real address. The only result will be that you are flooded with ten times as much spam.

- If you can not stop the messages by the above method, you can think about filtering them out. Most ISPs offer spam filters that stop spam at their mail server, even before it enters you mailbox. Some ISPs allow you to change the settings for the spam filter.

- *Windows Live Mail* includes a *Junk E-mail Filter* that analyzes the content of messages sent to you and moves suspicious messages to the special *Junk e-mail* folder, where you can view or delete them at any time.

- Some antivirus programs contain a spam filter. Consult the program's *Help* function to find out how to install this spam filter.

5.22 Tips

💡 **Tip**

Larger text
If you have trouble reading e-mail messages, you can increase the text size.

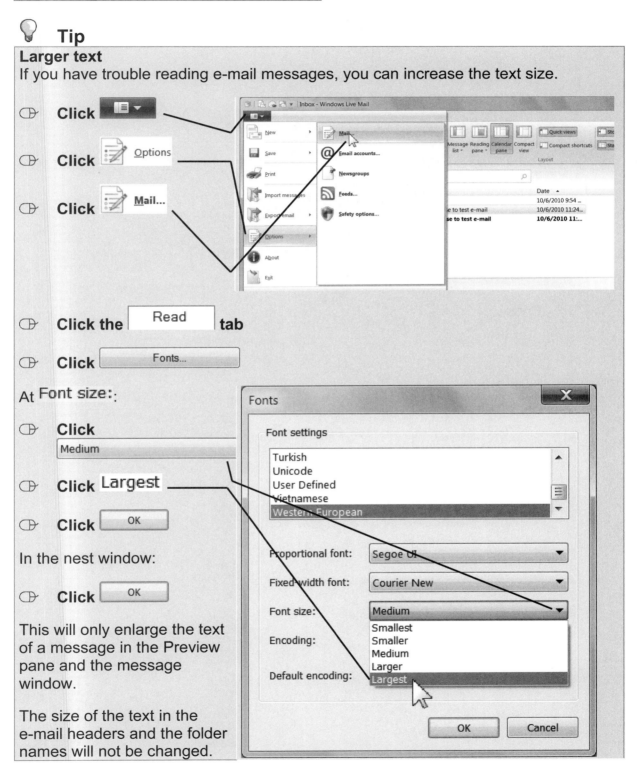

⟊ **Click** [▤ ▼]

⟊ **Click** 📝 Options

⟊ **Click** 📝 Mail...

⟊ **Click the** [Read] **tab**

⟊ **Click** [Fonts...]

At Font size::

⟊ **Click** [Medium]

⟊ **Click** Largest

⟊ **Click** [OK]

In the nest window:

⟊ **Click** [OK]

This will only enlarge the text of a message in the Preview pane and the message window.

The size of the text in the e-mail headers and the folder names will not be changed.

Tip

Printing an e-mail
If you want to print an e-mail message:

○► **Click**

○► **Click** Print

Tip

Do you want to avoid seeing this window again?
You see this window every time you send a new e-mail message:

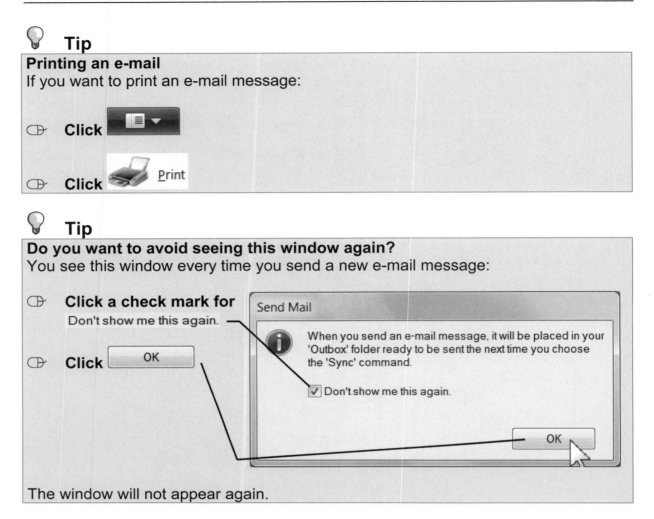

○► **Click a check mark for**
Don't show me this again.

○► **Click** OK

The window will not appear again.

6. Addresses, E-mails and Attachments

In the 1970s, people thought the computer would come to occupy such a central position that a paperless society would arise. All information would be read on (portable) monitors. Paper would become superfluous. In reality, things have turned out differently. In fact, more paper than ever is being used. After all, it is very easy to print out an e-mail message, and people do it quite often.

Nonetheless, the rise of the Internet has contributed to a change in communication. E-mail is replacing the function of the telephone, the letter and the fax. This is in part a result of the fact that, not only short messages but all kinds of other information can be sent by e-mail, such as photographs or drawings.

The speed of communication has also increased dramatically. An e-mail can arrive within seconds. A photo can be sent within seconds. Extensive exchange of e-mails also occurs in work environments. The increase in e-mail usage has led to an increased importance of its management. The computer is being used more and more as an archive for our correspondence.

In this chapter, you will learn how to organize your e-mail messages. You will also learn how to save your e-mail addresses in your *Windows Live Contacts* folder, and how to keep them organized so you can quickly retrieve them. You will learn how to send an attachment with an e-mail message. This will enable you to exchange photos with family and friends, wherever in the world they may be.

In this chapter, you will learn:

- how to add information to a contact
- how to add a new contact
- what happens with a bad e-mail address
- how to use a signature in your e-mails
- how to sort your e-mails
- how to search within your e-mails
- how to send, view, open and save an attachment

6.1 Opening Windows Live Mail

First, open the program *Windows Live Mail*:

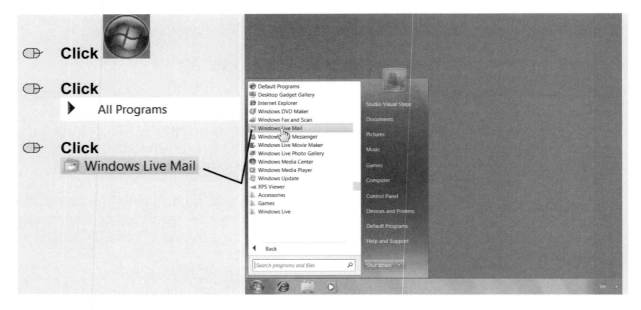

In this chapter, *Windows Live Mail* does not need to connect to the Internet right away.

Of course, you can check your e-mail if you would like.

You see the *Windows Live Mail* window:

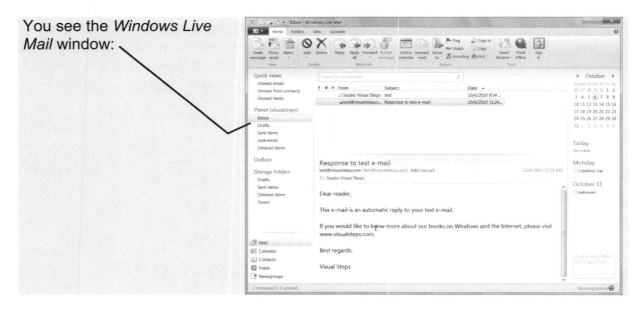

6.2 Adding a Contact

This is how you add the sender's address to your contacts, from an e-mail you have received.

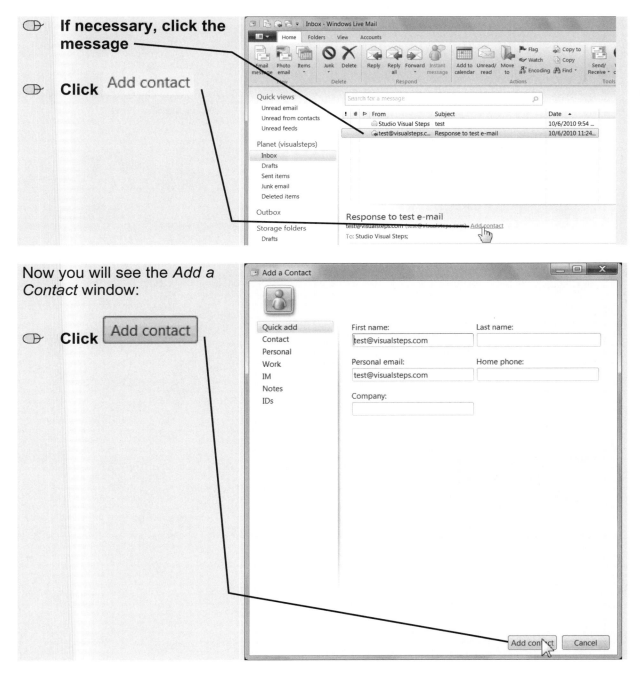

☞ **If necessary, click the message**

☞ **Click** Add contact

Now you will see the *Add a Contact* window:

☞ **Click** Add contact

The contact has been added. Now you will add extra information to this contact.

6.3 Adding Information to a Contact

Each listing in your *Windows Live Contacts* folder contains at least an e-mail address. More information such as name, address or telephone number can be added.

You can open and edit the e-mail address information as follows:

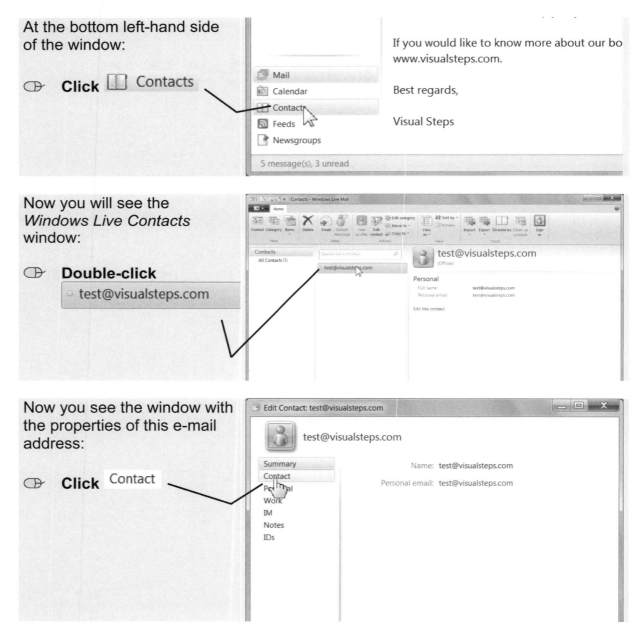

At the bottom left-hand side of the window:

☞ **Click** Contacts

Now you will see the *Windows Live Contacts* window:

☞ **Double-click**

□ test@visualsteps.com

Now you see the window with the properties of this e-mail address:

☞ **Click** Contact

The name has already been filled in by the program, but is not right in this case. You can fix that yourself.

First erase the first name:

⌨ **Keep depressed, until the text has been removed**

Now you can change the last name.

🖰 **Click the box under** Last name:

⌨ **Type:** Test e-mail

You can see that the e-mail address has been filled in correctly:

🖰 **Click** Save

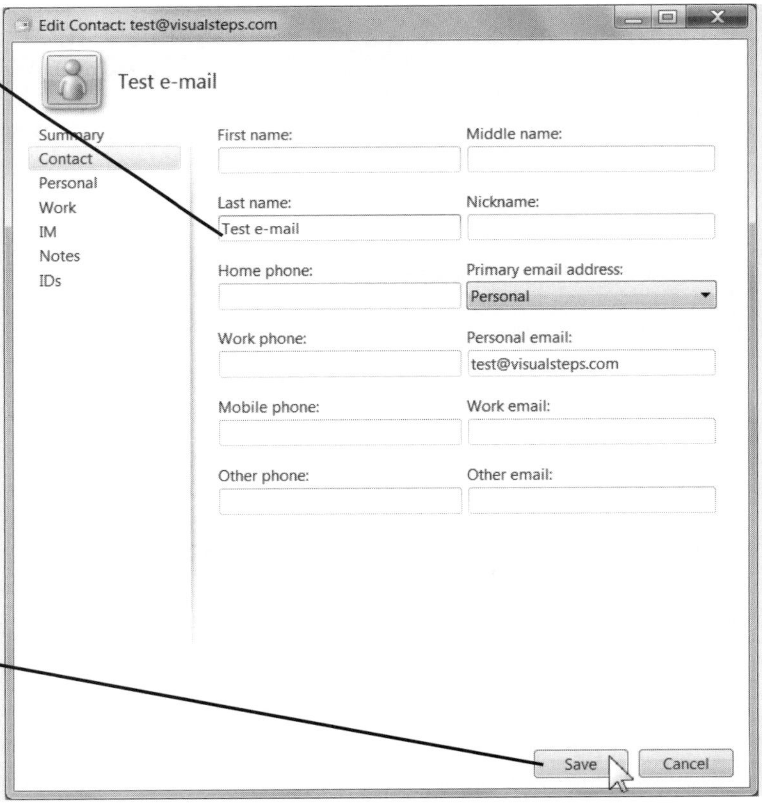

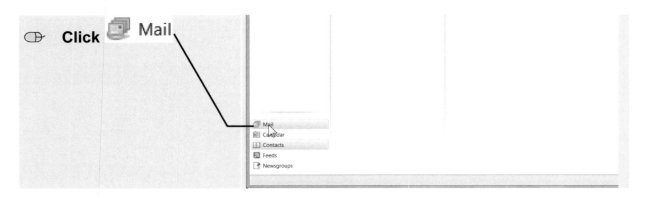

In this example, you have given the e-mail address a made-up last name (*Test e-mail*), but in general this will be the name of an existing person or organization.

6.4 Using an Address

Now that the e-mail address has been saved in the *Windows Live Contacts* folder, you can easily use it to create a new e-mail message:

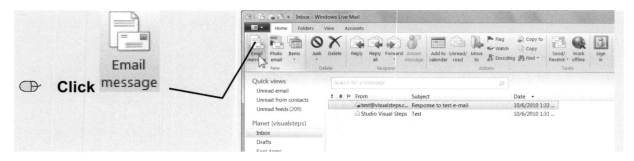

Here is how you choose an address from the *Windows Live Contacts* folder:

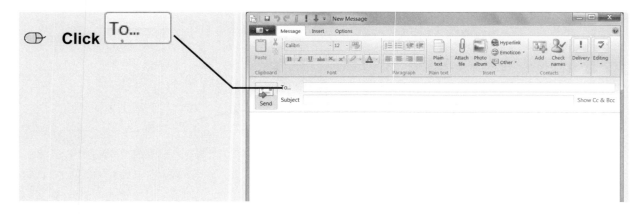

Now you see this window:

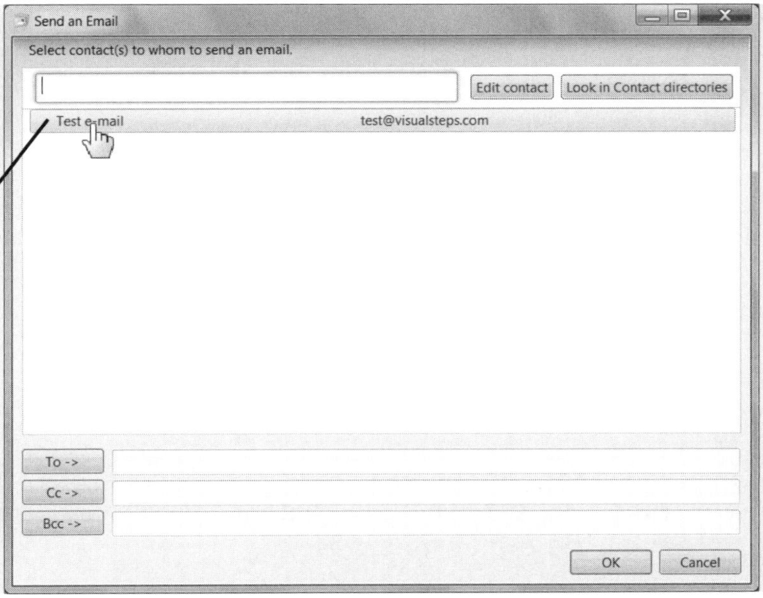

First choose a name from the list:

⟐ **Click** Test e-mail

Then you can add the address:

⟐ **Click** To ->

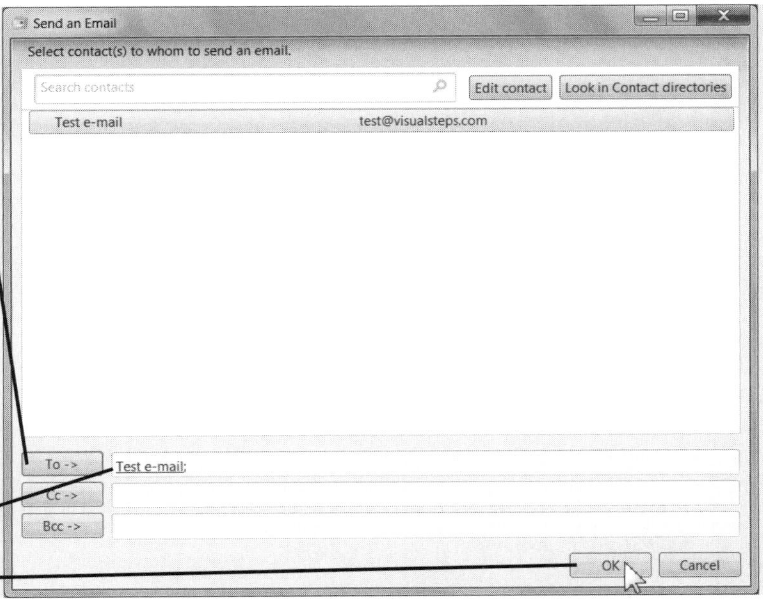

The name has been added:

⟐ **Click** OK

💡 **Tip**

Multiple addresses?
You can also use this window to send the same e-mail to multiple addresses. You do this by selecting the names, and clicking the To -> button.

You see that the name has been entered next to To…:

You do not actually have to send this e-mail. You can close the window without saving the e-mail message:

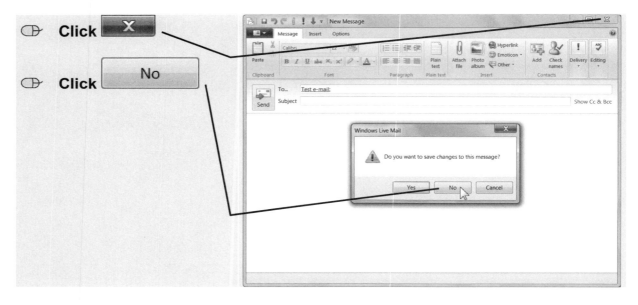

Click X

Click No

Now you have seen how you can use an e-mail address from the *Windows Live Contacts* folder.

You can add an e-mail address to the *Windows Live Contacts* folder at any time.

6.5 Adding a New E-mail Address

You can manually add the e-mail addresses of your family, friends and acquaintances to the *Windows Live Contacts* folder. This is how:

At the bottom left-hand side of the window:

☞ **Click** Contacts

Once the *Windows Live Contacts* folder is opened, you can add a new contact:

☞ **Click** Contact

You see this window again for entering the name and e-mail address:

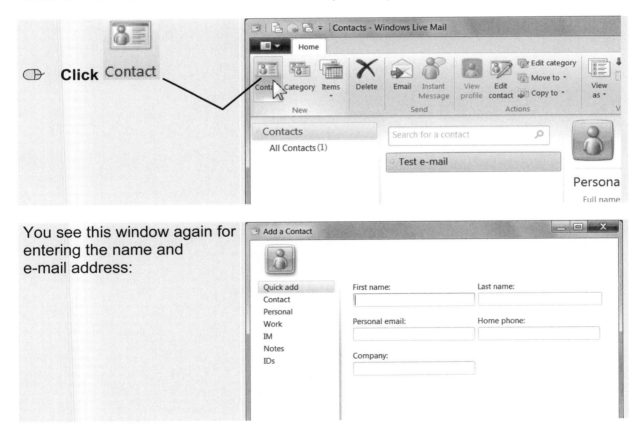

6.6 A Wrong E-mail Address

There is a good chance that once in a while you will use a wrong e-mail address. People frequently change their Internet Service Provider, and ISPs themselves go out of business or change their names. Furthermore, you can always make a typing error. A single letter or dot in the wrong place means the e-mail will never arrive. It is a good exercise to send an e-mail to a wrong address and see what happens:

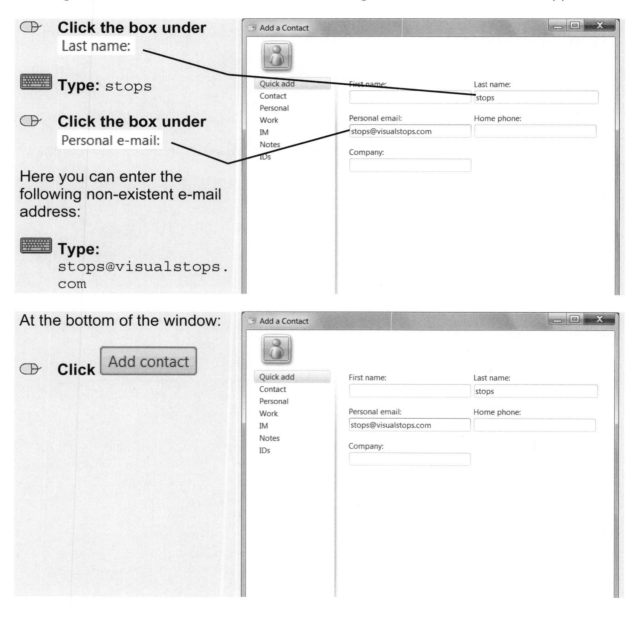

Click the box under Last name:

Type: stops

Click the box under Personal e-mail:

Here you can enter the following non-existent e-mail address:

Type: stops@visualstops. com

At the bottom of the window:

Click Add contact

The name has been added to your *Windows Live Contacts* folder, now you can close it:

☞ **Click** 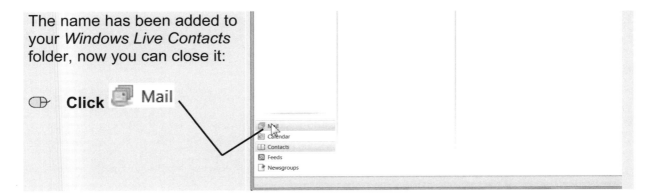 **Mail**

You can create a test mail and send it to the wrong address **stops@visualstops.com**. Then you can see what happens:

☞ **Create a new message** 🐾³⁶

☞ **Choose from the *Windows Live Contacts* folder:** stops

(stops@visualstops.com) 🐾⁵⁴

⌨ **Type for the subject:** Wrong address

⌨ **Type for the body:** This is an e-mail to a wrong address.

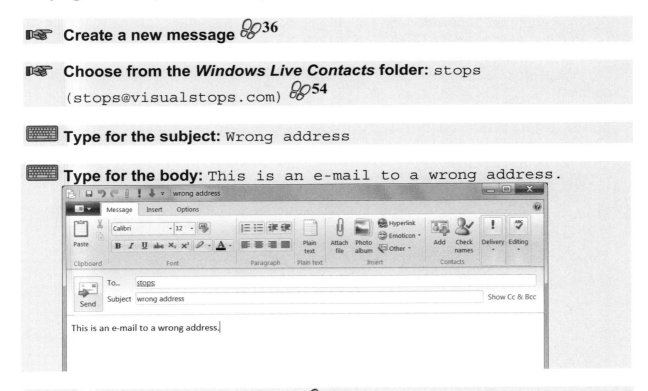

☞ **Send your e-mail to the *Outbox*** 🐾³⁷

☞ **Send and receive your e-mail** 🐾³⁹

☞ **If necessary, connect to the Internet** 🐾³

After a while, you will automatically receive a message about this wrongly addressed e-mail. This occurs quickly with some ISPs, and takes a bit longer with others.

☞ **Check your mail later in the *Inbox*** 𝄞**39**

HELP! I did not receive any mail.

Is there no message in your Inbox?
Maybe it has not been received yet. Try again later. If necessary, continue on with the next section and check again tomorrow.

☞ **Check your received e-mail again later** 𝄞**39**

Once you have received mail, you should have an automatic message from a *Mail Administrator* or a *Mail Delivery Subsystem*.

For example, a message like this:

The technical terms describe what went wrong during delivery. In this case, the destination e-mail system was unkown or invalid:

You can close the message:

☞ **Click** ❎

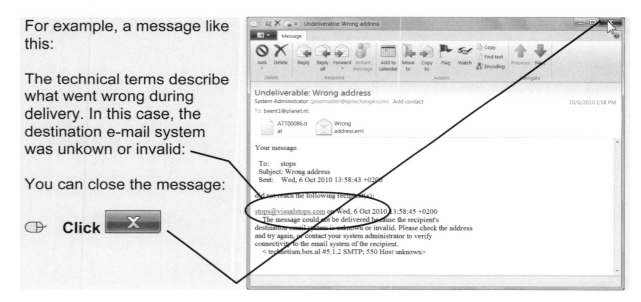

When you get this kind of error message, check in the *Sent items* folder to see if the e-mail address you used is correct. Check:

- Are there any spaces in the e-mail address?
- Are all the dots in the right places?
- Is there a typing error in the e-mail address?

Tip

Type it over?
You do not have to retype an e-mail that has been addressed incorrectly. You can select the text and copy it. Then you can paste it into a new message, and send this to the right e-mail address.

6.7 Your Signature

In some cases, e-mail will replace your regular correspondence. Just as in every letter, your full name and address information should appear in these messages. You do not have to type these in with every new message. You only have to type them once, into a 'signature'. Here is how you create a signature:

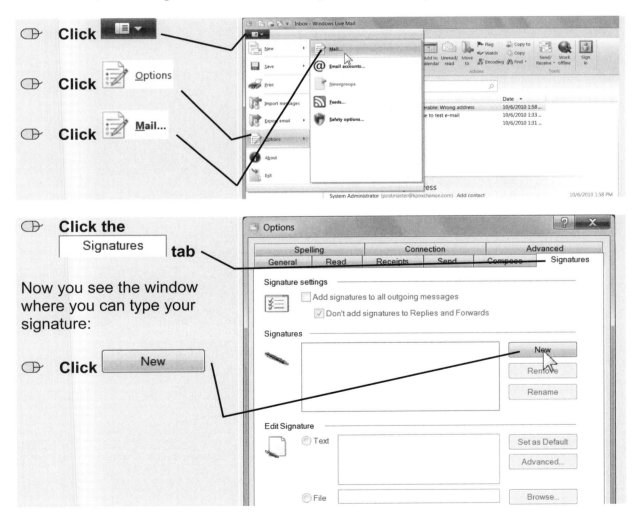

☞ **Click** ▣▾

☞ **Click** 📝 Options

☞ **Click** 📝 Mail...

☞ **Click the** Signatures **tab**

Now you see the window where you can type your signature:

☞ **Click** New

In *Windows Live Mail*, you can create and save multiple signatures.

You see that Signature #1 has been created:

In the box next to ⊙ Text you can type your information:

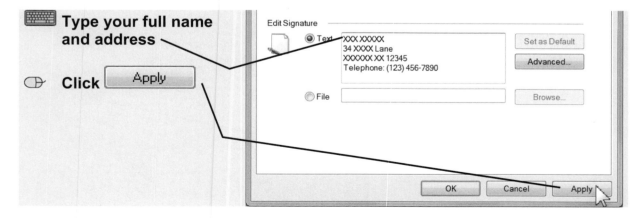

The signature does not look like a signature you would write with a pen. This signature consists solely of text and contains your address. Now you can type your information:

⌨ **Type your full name and address**

🖰 **Click** [Apply]

You can also decide whether you want the signature to appear automatically at the bottom of every new e-mail.

You do this by checking this box: ―――――――

If you would rather add your signature manually make sure the box is not checked.

In this example, you will add the signature manually:

☞   **Click** [OK]

Now you can add your signature to any e-mail message. First, create a new e-mail message.

☞ **Create a new e-mail message** ⦿⦿**36**

☞   **Click the body of the message** ―――――

You can add the signature at the location of the cursor.

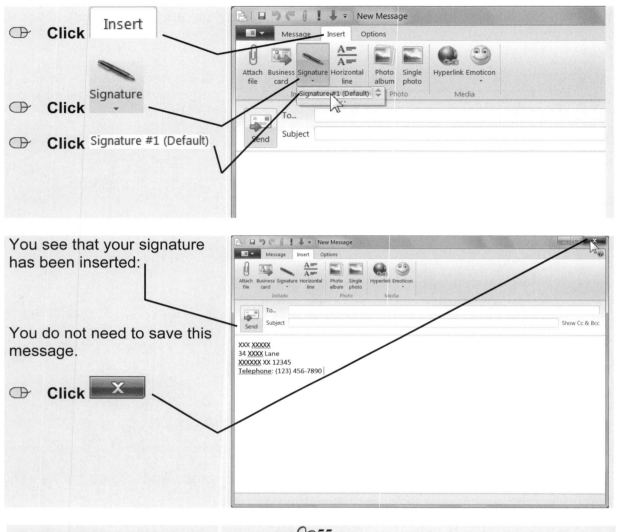

👆 **Click** Insert

👆 **Click** Signature ▾

👆 **Click** Signature #1 (Default)

You see that your signature has been inserted:

You do not need to save this message.

👆 **Click** ✖

☞ **Do not save the e-mail message** 👣⁵⁵

6.8 The Inbox, Your Archive

All the messages you receive are saved in the *Inbox*. You will notice that your *Inbox* soon begins to function as an archive. Especially if you do a lot of e-mailing, the number of e-mails will grow quickly and it will become more and more difficult to find a particular message. There are two ways you can find an e-mail. You can *sort* the list of e-mails, or you can *search* through the messages.

6.9 Sorting E-mails

Your e-mail messages are usually sorted by date received.
You can sort them differently, however, such as by the sender's name. Here is how you do that:

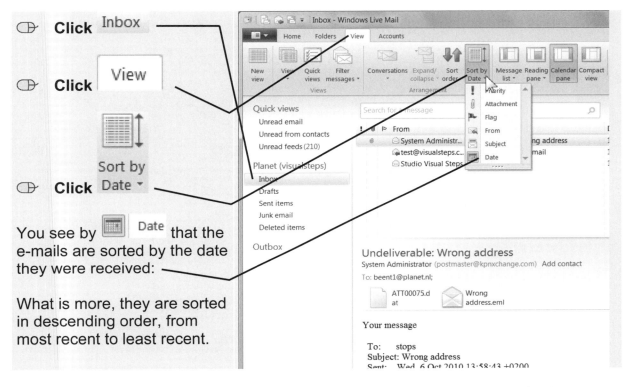

☞ **Click** Inbox

☞ **Click** View

☞ **Click** Sort by Date

You see by ▦ Date that the e-mails are sorted by the date they were received:

What is more, they are sorted in descending order, from most recent to least recent.

Now you can sort them by the sender's name. The name is in the *From* field:

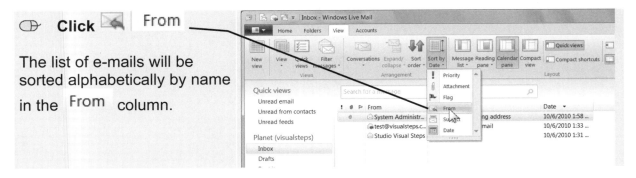

☞ **Click** ✉ From

The list of e-mails will be sorted alphabetically by name in the From column.

If your e-mails are sorted alphabetically by the sender, it is easier to find an e-mail from a particular person. All e-mails from the same person will be together.

➥ **Please note:**

Did you choose a different sorting method?
Windows Live Mail stores this setting, and uses it the next time you open the program.

The default setting is to sort on date received, with the most recently received e-mails at the top. That is quite useful, so you can restore the old setting:

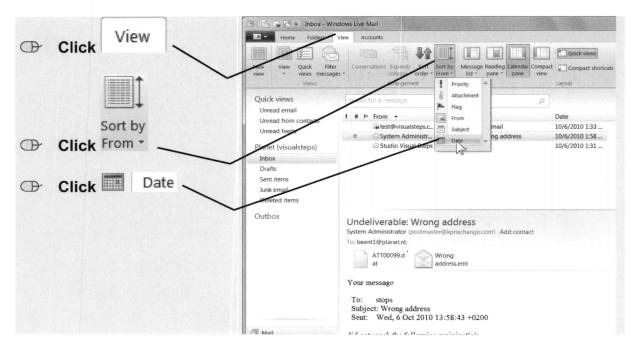

The e-mails will again be sorted by date received.

6.10 Searching Your E-mails

Windows Live Mail has an extensive search function that you can use to search through your e-mails. Here is how you start:

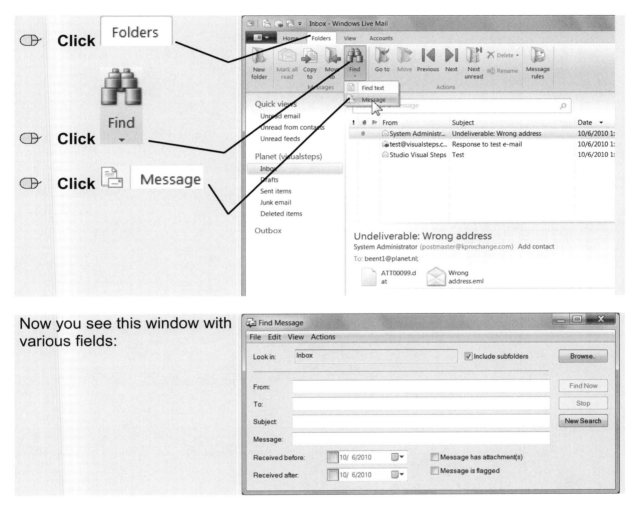

Now you see this window with various fields:

You can search every part of an e-mail message: *From*, *To*, the *Subject* or within the body of the *Message* itself. In addition, you can refine the search, such as specifying the date of receipt.

If you know what the content of the e-mail message is, you can search for it by using a search term. For example, you can use the word 'Internet'. That word should be in a test mail you received earlier.

Next to Message: :

☞ **Click the box**

⌨ **Type:** Internet

☞ **Click** Find Now

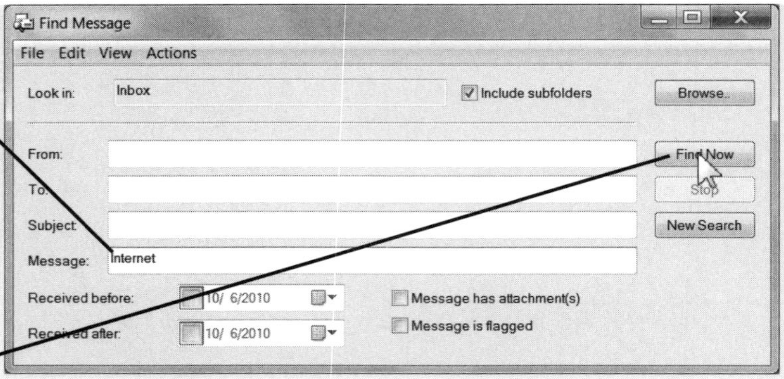

At the bottom of the window, you see the e-mails in which the word "Internet" appears:

To view one of these e-mails:

☞ **Double-click the e-mail header**

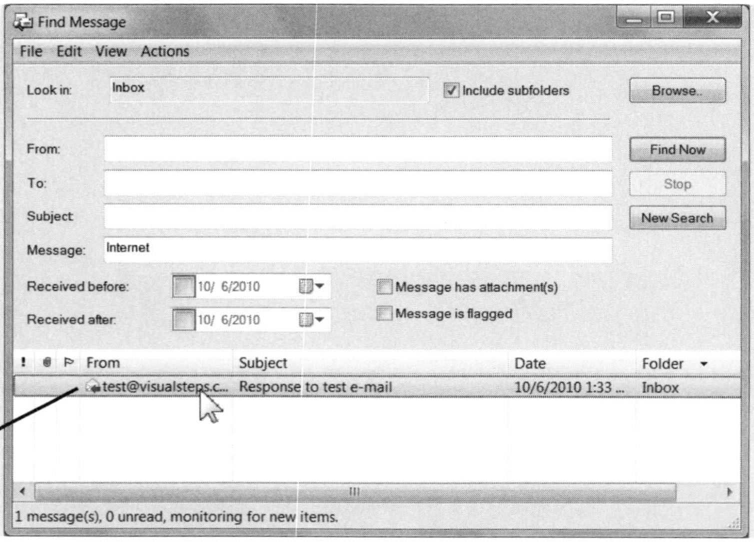

🩹 HELP! I do not see any e-mails.

If you do not see any e-mails in the above window, then you may not have received the test mail in the previous chapter.

☞ **Just continue reading**

The message opens and you can read it. The word 'Internet' appears somewhere in this message.

When you are finished, you can close the message window:

☞ **Click** X

You can also close the *Find Message* window:

☞ **Click** X

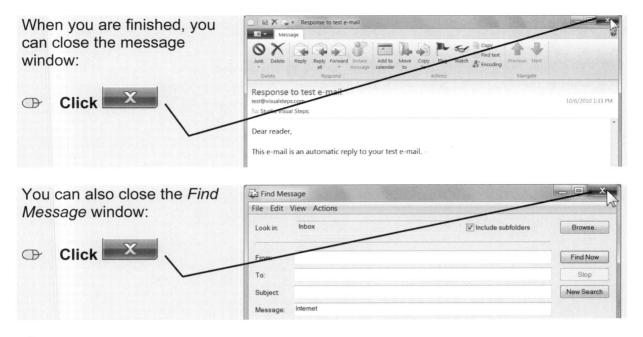

💡 **Tip**

Quick search using the search box
In the top right corner of the *Windows Live Mail* window you see the search box:

> Search for a message

Using this search box you can search an entire folder for a particular search term. When you type a search term in the search box, not only the body of the messages, but also the e-mail headers and the names of senders and addressees are searched.

☞ **Click the folder you want to search**

☞ **Click the search box**

⌨ **Type your search term**

While you type, the message list is filtered so that it only shows messages containing your search term:

6.11 Including an Attachment

The nice thing about e-mail messages is that you can send all kinds of things along with them. You can add a photo, a drawing, or another document. Something that you want to send with an e-mail message is called an *attachment*.

You can practice sending an attachment by sending another e-mail to yourself.

☞ **Create a new e-mail** ✇³⁶

In the box next to To… :

⌨ **Type your own e-mail address**

Every e-mail message should contain a subject.

Next to Subject: :

🖱 **Click the box**

⌨ **Type:** Test with attachment

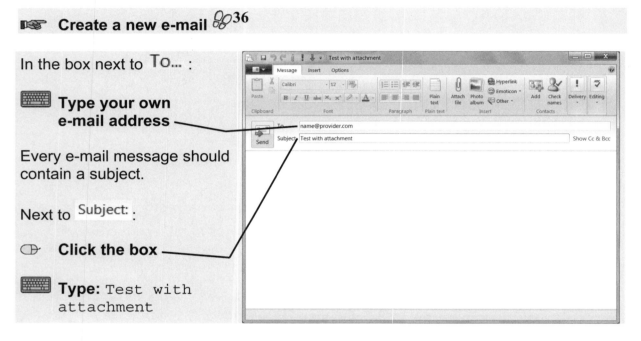

Now you can add the attachment: in this case, one of the sample pictures that comes with *Windows 7*. To do that, you use the **Attach file** button:

🖱 **Click the body of the message**

⌨ **Type:** Here is a nice picture!

🖱 **Click Attach file**

Now you see this folder window. By default, the *My Documents* folder will be opened.

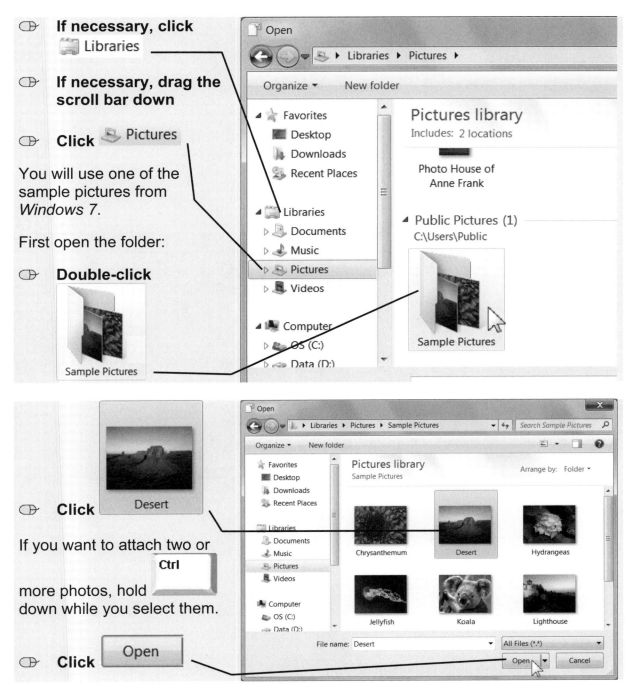

☞ **If necessary, click** 🗂 Libraries

☞ **If necessary, drag the scroll bar down**

☞ **Click** 🖼 Pictures

You will use one of the sample pictures from *Windows 7*.

First open the folder:

☞ **Double-click**

Sample Pictures

☞ **Click** Desert

If you want to attach two or more photos, hold **Ctrl** down while you select them.

☞ **Click** Open

The attachment is added to your message: —

The size of the attachment is shown: (826 KB)

: 🖼 Desert.jpg (826 KB)

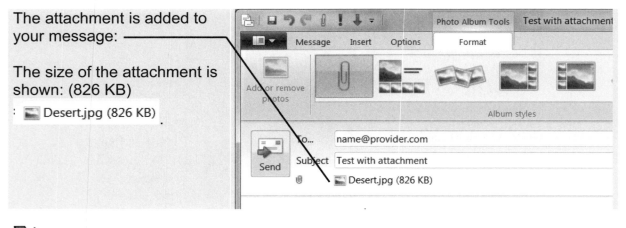

🏹 Please note:

Sending an e-mail with an attachment takes more time than sending and receiving a "bare" e-mail message, especially if you or the addressee are using dial-up networking to connect to the Internet. Sending pictures takes a particularly long time. You may decide for yourself whether or not you really want to send this message.

If you do not want to send it:

☞ Close the message window

The program will ask whether you want to save the changes:

☞ **Click** [No]

☞ **Click** [Send]

If your message is placed in the *Outbox*, you can send it now manually. If your mail is sent immediately, you do not have to send it manually.

☞ Send and receive your e-mail 👣³⁹

🏹 Please note:

Sending this e-mail will take some time if you are using dial-up networking.

6.12 Opening an Attachment

Once your e-mail is sent, it should arrive very quickly. You can see this in the *Inbox*:

☞   **If necessary, click**
Inbox (1)

☞   **Click the message**
     with the attachment

Here you see the preview of
your own message:

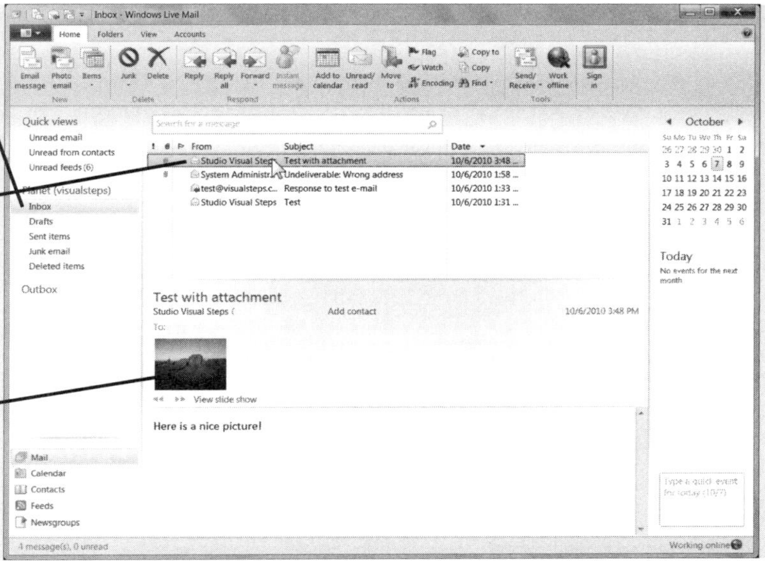

![A screenshot of the Windows Live Mail Inbox window.]

HELP! I do not have any mail.

Is there no new message in your Inbox?
Perhaps it has not yet been received. Try again later:

☞   **Click**

In one of the first columns in
the message list, a small

paper clip   indicates that
an attachment has been
included:

☞   **Double-click your new**
     message

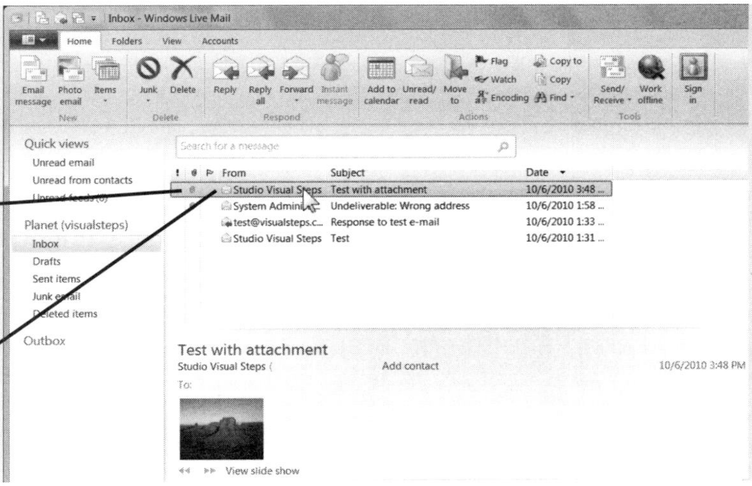

💡 **Tip**

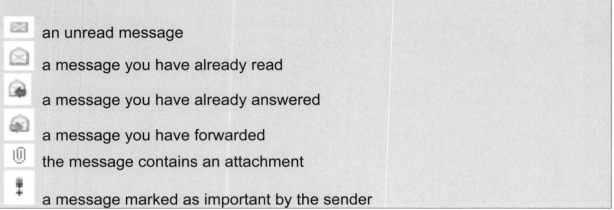

In *Windows Live Mail*, there is an icon next to every e-mail. Here is what they represent:

an unread message

a message you have already read

a message you have already answered

a message you have forwarded

the message contains an attachment

a message marked as important by the sender

You see your message in a separate window:

☞ **Double-click the photo**

The default program to view the picture is called *Windows Photo Viewer. Windows Photo Viewer* is a tool included with *Windows 7* that you can use to view, share, and print your digital pictures. If your computer is set up differently, the picture may be shown in another program.

After you have seen the
picture, you can close the
program window:

☞ **Click** [X]

You see the message window again.

6.13 Saving an Attachment

After you have saved an attachment such as a photo, you can use it again in various ways. For example, you can open it in a program like *Paint* or another photo editing program. There you can edit and change the photo. Maybe you want to use the photo in a club newsletter you have written in *WordPad* or *Microsoft Word*. You can also send the photo by e-mail to someone else.

An e-mail can contain various attachments. The easiest way to save attachments is as follows:

☞ **Click** [▤ ▼]

☞ **Click** [💾] Save

☞ **Click** [💾] Save attachments

Now you see this window:

Here you see the name of the attachment:

If there are more attachments in the e-mail, they will also be listed here.

In this field you can specify where the attachment should be saved:

In this case, it is not necessary to save the photo; after all, it is already on your hard drive.

☞ **Click** Cancel

You see your e-mail message again:

☞ **Click** X

☞ **Close** *Windows Live Mail* ℰ℘43

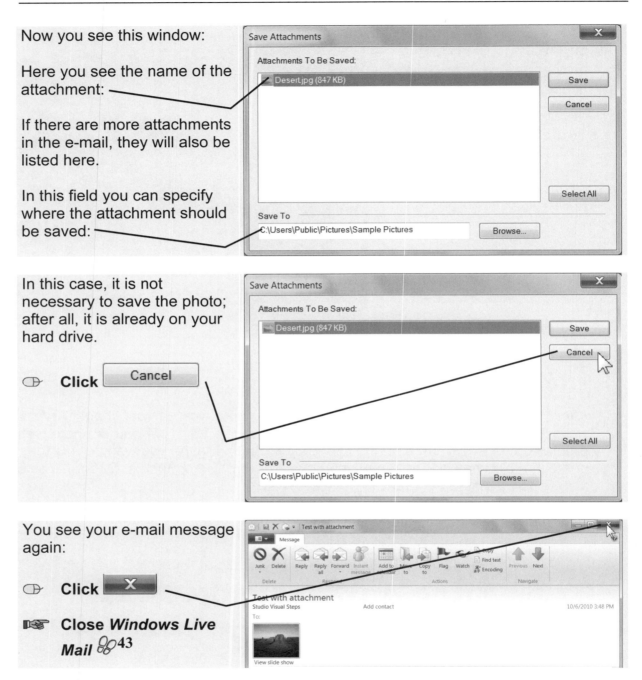

Now you have seen how you can send an attachment through e-mail, and how to save an attachment you have received. The following exercises will help you master what you have just learned.

6.14 Exercises

🐾

Have you forgotten how to do something? Use the number beside the footsteps to look it up in the appendix *How Do I Do That Again?*

Exercise: Sending an Attachment

In this exercise, you will practice writing a new e-mail message with an attachment.

☞ Start *Windows Live Mail*. 🐾³⁵

☞ Create a new e-mail message addressed to yourself. 🐾³⁶

☞ Add the photo of Anne Frank's house (from Chapter 4) as an attachment. 🐾⁴⁰

☞ Send the e-mail message to the *Outbox*. 🐾³⁷

☞ Send and receive your e-mail. 🐾³⁹

Exercise: Viewing an Attachment

☞ Check your mail. 🐾³⁹

☞ See if you have new mail in your *Inbox*. 🐾⁴¹

☞ Open your e-mail message. 🐾⁴²

☞ View the attachment. 🐾⁵⁷

☞ Close *Windows Photo Viewer*. 🐾³²

☞ Close the e-mail message window. 🐾³²

☞ Close *Windows Live Mail*. 🐾³²

6.15 Background Information

Glossary

Attachment	Documents, images, and other files can be sent as attachments to an e-mail message. Messages that contain attachments are indicated by a paper clip icon in the attachment column of the message list. For security reasons many e-mail programs (including *Windows Live Mail*) prevent recipients from opening executable file attachments, such as those with .exe, .bat and .inf file name extensions.
Contacts folder	You can use *Windows Live Mail* to keep track of people and organizations by creating contacts for them in your *Windows Live Contacts* folder. Each contact contains the information for one person or organization: name, address, telephone number and e-mail address.
Search box	*Windows Live Mail* includes the search box, which makes it easy to find specific e-mail messages. Using the search box, you can quickly filter your message list so that it only shows messages containing specific words, characters, or e-mail addresses.
Signature	A signature can contain your name, e-mail address, phone number, and any other information that you want to include at the bottom of your e-mail messages.
Virus	A piece of code or program designed to cause damage to a computer system (by erasing or corrupting data) or annoying users (by printing messages or altering what is displayed on the computer screen).

Source: Windows Help and Support

Risks involved in opening attachments

Opening an attachment received with an e-mail could possibly infect your computer with a computer virus. A computer virus is a very small program that can copy itself to another computer. Once present on a computer system, it can do a lot of damage. Not all viruses are equally dangerous. Because the virus arrives together with another file, you can not tell without using a special program whether or not you have been infected.

If an e-mail with an attachment was sent by someone with whom you frequently correspond, the risks are smaller than if it comes from someone you do not know. Nonetheless, caution is always advisable.

☞ **Never open an attachment if you are suspicious.**
   If necessary, send your acquaintance an e-mail requesting clarification.

☞ **If you are suspicious of an unknown sender. Delete the e-mail and its attachment immediately without opening.**
   If the attachment did not contain a virus, that is too bad, but the sender should have been more clear about his subject. In situations like these, the sender can always send the e-mail again.

☞ **If you receive a 'strange' e-mail from a known sender. Delete the e-mail without opening it.**
   If necessary, ask for clarification from the sender.

☞ **Do not forget to empty the *Deleted items* folder.**
   Only then is the e-mail permanently deleted from your computer.

Viruses like the infamous 'I love you' virus not only do great damage, but also read your entire *Windows Live Contacts* folder and send an e-mail containing a copy of themselves to all the contacts inside. This is also the reason why you can not always trust e-mail from people you know.

In any event, if you regularly use the Internet be sure you use a good antivirus software. This software will give a warning in most cases before the virus can do its work. It is very important that you keep this software up-to-date. Consult the software's documentation for this.

In *Bonus Online Chapter 10 Security and Privacy* on the website that goes with this book can read more about viruses and antivirus software.

The smaller, the faster
On the Internet, there is one golden rule: the smaller the message is, the faster it is sent. The same applies to attachments. If you send a small attachment, such as a small photograph, the transmission will only take a few seconds. If you send a larger drawing, it will take more time and the telephone line will be used longer.

Along with the name of an attachment, such as a text or a picture, its size is always shown, expressed in MB or KB.

The size of a file is always indicated in KB or MB. These are units of measurements, just like pounds and ounces.

A **Kilobyte** is (about) one thousand bytes.
This means that: 20 Kilobytes is 20,000 bytes. The abbreviation of kilobyte is **KB**.

A **Megabyte** is (about) one thousand kilobytes.
This means that one Megabyte is (about) one million (one thousand times one thousand) bytes. The abbreviation of megabyte is **MB**.

How long does it take to send or receive something?
The speed at which something can be sent or received depends on a number or things, including the speed of your modem, the type of connection and how busy it is on the Internet. If for example, you are using dial-up networking to connect to the Internet, you can receive 6 KB per second with a regular modem. This translates into 360 KB or 0.36 MB per minute.

A message that consists of 16 KB will take about three seconds. The size of the picture attachment you used in this chapter, is 826 KB. It takes about 38 seconds to send or receive. An attachment that is 1.73 MB in size will take about three minutes. As you see, this is quite a long time. Your ISP may also have a limit on the amount of data you can receive in an e-mail. If the limit is exceeded the e-mail will not arrive. Try sending larger pictures, for example, in separate e-mails.

You can send different types of files with an e-mail message. You can even send sounds or video clips. But be careful: sound and video files are also usually quite large. It may take a very long time to send or receive files of this type. However, when you are using a broadband connection, for example a DSL line, this will not be a problem. This type of service offers high speed connection to the Internet.

A faster modem: internal or external?

Do you have an older computer and a dial-up Internet connection that requires you to connect manually? Are you dissatisfied with the speed of your internet connection? You might want to consider buying a faster modem.

The fastest modem available which uses the regular telephone line is a modem with a speed of 56K. You can choose either an internal or an external modem:

Internal modem   *External modem*

An external modem has certain advantages:
- You can connect the modem easily. The computer does not have to be opened in order to install the modem, so you do not need a computer mechanic.
- An external modem has little lights that let you see what is happening on the telephone line. This is useful when the connection is not functioning properly.
- You can easily connect an external modem to a different computer.

But there are also disadvantages:
- An external modem is more expensive.
- The modem has more cables and often a separate power supply which has to be plugged into an outlet.
- You always have to turn the modem on.

If you want a really fast connection, you will have to switch to DSL or cable Internet. You need a special kind of modem for that. Your ISP can give you more information.

6.16 Tips

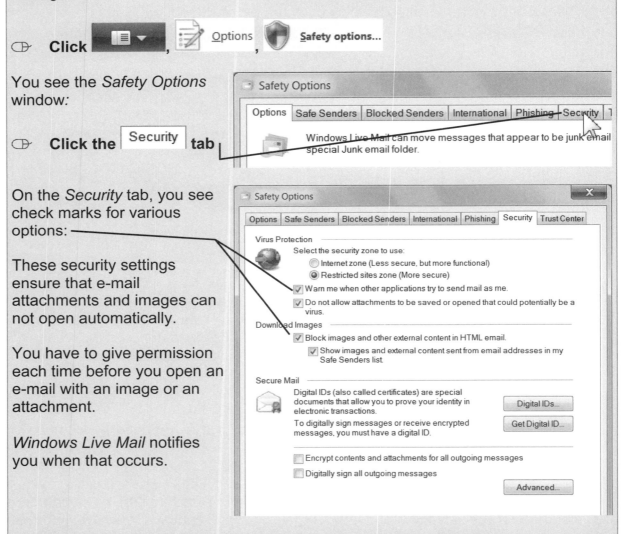

Tip

Security settings in Windows Live Mail
Windows Live Mail has various security settings. You can take a look at these settings:

☞ **Click** [icon] , [Options] , [Safety options...]

You see the *Safety Options* window:

☞ **Click the** [Security] **tab**

On the *Security* tab, you see check marks for various options:

These security settings ensure that e-mail attachments and images can not open automatically.

You have to give permission each time before you open an e-mail with an image or an attachment.

Windows Live Mail notifies you when that occurs.

It is advisable to leave the security settings on this page just as they are. That keeps you in control of any undesirable e-mails.

Check whether you trust the content or attachment on a per e-mail basis. If you have any doubts, ask the sender for clarification about the e-mail, or delete it without opening. Do not forget to empty the *Deleted items* folder afterward.

⚲ Tip

Zipping and unzipping

When you send an attachment, you should consider the size of the file. Files containing only text are relatively small. Photos are much larger, and it takes longer to download them. Because this download time can be frustrating, programs have been developed that can shrink files. This technique is called *compressing* or *zipping*.

A compression program takes all the 'extra air', so to speak, out of a file, making it smaller. This way, a photo (*bitmap*) with a size of 1400 KB (or 1.4 MB) can be reduced to 23 KB, a reduction of 98%. In order to be able to use the file again later, the reverse function must be applied. This is called *unzipping* or *extracting*.

Windows 7 offers a very easy way to zip files. *Windows 7*, *Windows Vista* and *Windows XP* users will be able to unzip a file that has been zipped that way.

You can try this with the website you saved earlier to the folder *My Documents*. If you did not save the website, you can choose any other file:

⊕ **Click** [ ], **Documents**

⊕ **Right-click**

Information on Anne Frank

A menu appears:

⊕ **Click** Send to

⊕ **Click** Compressed (zipped) folder

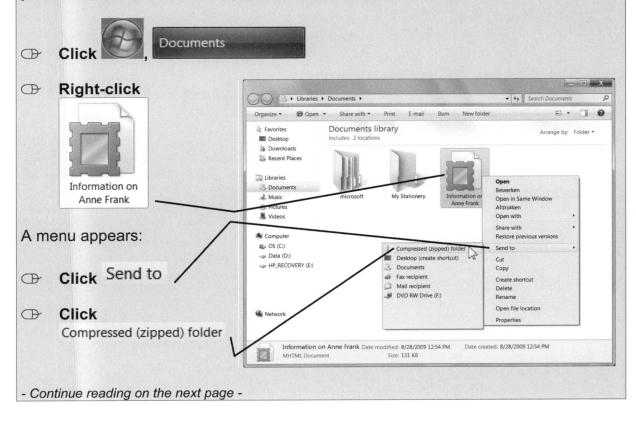

- *Continue reading on the next page -*

The zipped folder appears in the list. You can recognise the zipped folder by the zipper 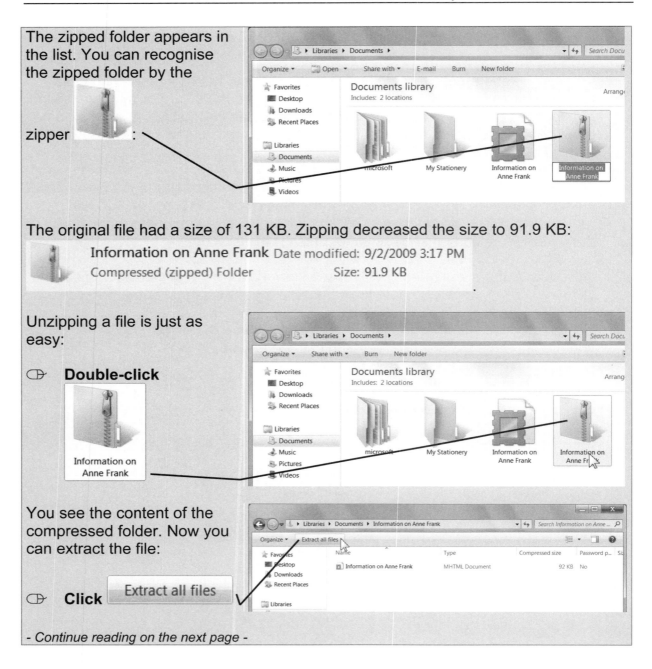 :

The original file had a size of 131 KB. Zipping decreased the size to 91.9 KB:

Information on Anne Frank Date modified: 9/2/2009 3:17 PM
Compressed (zipped) Folder   Size: 91.9 KB

Unzipping a file is just as easy:

☞ **Double-click**

Information on Anne Frank

You see the content of the compressed folder. Now you can extract the file:

☞ **Click** [Extract all files]

- Continue reading on the next page -

The *Extract Compressed (Zipped) Folders* window appears.

Here you can choose a new folder for the extracted files:

You do not need to do that now:

☞ **Click** [Extract]

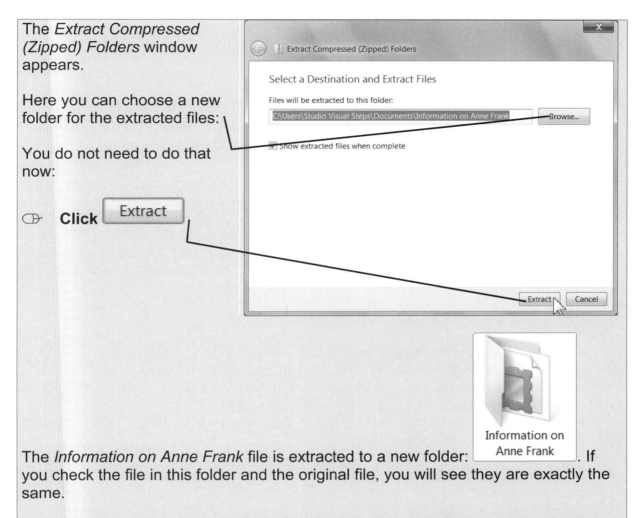

The *Information on Anne Frank* file is extracted to a new folder: [Information on Anne Frank]. If you check the file in this folder and the original file, you will see they are exactly the same.

If you plan to send photos or drawings by e-mail, it is advisable to zip them first before sending them. This saves you and the recipient a lot of time. Make sure to check if the recipient knows how to unzip a compressed folder.

Tip

Opening an attachment
When you double-click the attachment, the program to open the attachment in question is automatically opened.

Which program is opened depends on your computer's settings. Your computer may have a different program assigned to open a particular type of file.

If the attachment is a text document, *Microsoft Word* will automatically be opened. If you do not have *Microsoft Word* on your computer, then *WordPad* will be opened. If the attachment is a photo, *Windows Viewer* will be opened. If another photo editing program has been installed on your computer, that program will be opened instead. If the attachment is a computer program (a *.exe-file for example), then that program itself will be opened.

 Tip

How do I find an e-mail address?
The Internet is such a dynamic medium that there is no telephone book containing everyone who has an e-mail address. People also frequently change Internet Service Providers. When you switch to a new ISP, you usually get a new e-mail address. In addition, not everyone wants his or her private e-mail address to be published, to avoid unwanted e-mails, for example.

There are websites such as *Bigfoot Directories* and *Yahoo Search* that offer the possibility to search for e-mail addresses. Unfortunately, most *Bigfoot* and *Yahoo* search results come up empty. They only contain links to pages of commercial companies. These companies claim to have the information you want, but it is not free.

💡 **Tip**

CC and BCC
You can send an e-mail to multiple addresses in different ways. You see two more buttons beneath the [To ->] button.

[Cc ->]

Use the *CC* (*Carbon Copy*) button if you want to send a copy of the e-mail to others. The names of both the main addressee and the people in the CC field are visible to others who receive the e-mail.

[Bcc ->]

Addressees in the BCC (*Blind Carbon Copy*) field are invisible to the others who receive a copy of the e-mail.

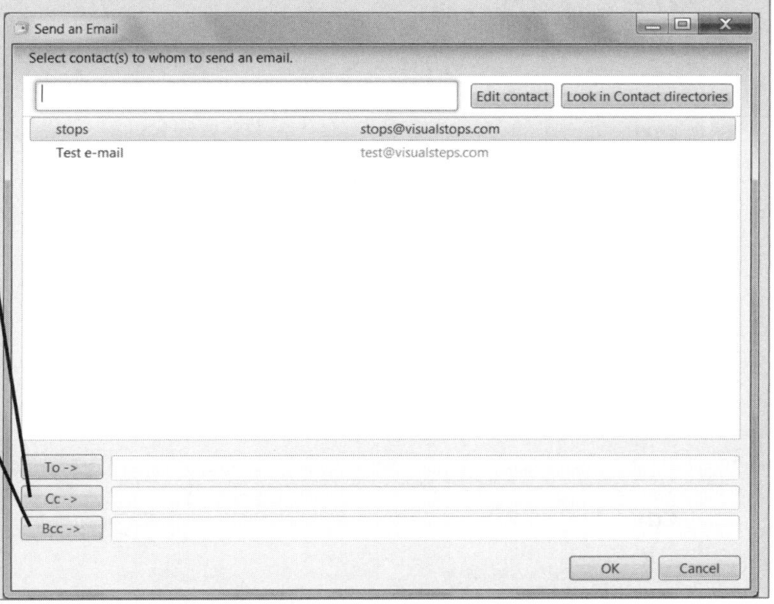

Send an Email

Select contact(s) to whom to send an email.

[   ] [Edit contact] [Look in Contact directories]

| stops | stops@visualstops.com |
| Test e-mail | test@visualsteps.com |

To ->
Cc ->
Bcc ->

[OK] [Cancel]

Tip

Keyboard control

If you prefer, you can use the keyboard to operate *Windows Live Mail* rather than the mouse. The most important keys and their functions are listed below.

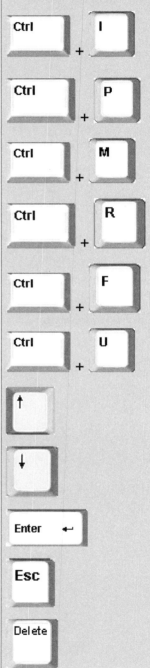

Ctrl + I
Open the *Inbox*.

Ctrl + P
Print the selected e-mail message.

Ctrl + M
Send and receive e-mail messages.

Ctrl + R
Reply to the selected message.

Ctrl + F
Forward the selected message.

Ctrl + U
Go to the next unread message.

Go to the previous message in the list.

Go to the next message in the list.

Enter
Open the selected message.

Esc
Close the message window.

Delete
Delete the selected message.

7. Special Functions in Windows Live Mail

Up to this point, you have created e-mails that consist only of text without any formatting. It is customary in the business world to send e-mails containing short texts without frills. For personal use however, it can be a lot of fun to send more interesting e-mails to your friends, children or grandchildren.

In fact, almost all the formatting you can use in a text-editing program can also be applied to an e-mail. You can choose different fonts and larger or smaller letters. This is called *Rich Text*.

It is also possible to quickly create an e-mail message using *Internet Explorer* to let someone know about an interesting website.

With *Windows Calendar*, the calendar application that comes with *Windows Live Mail*, you can easily keep track of your appointments. You can add an appointment. You can also share your calendar with anyone in your *Windows Live Contacts* folder by using e-mail to send and receive appointments.

In this chapter, you will learn how to:

- format an e-mail
- choose a different font, size and color
- use emoticons
- send e-mail using *Internet Explorer*
- use *Windows Live Mail* to keep track of your appointments
- invite someone else for an appointment by e-mail
- receive the details regarding an appointment

7.1 Formatting E-mail

There are two kinds of e-mail:

- e-mail with unformatted text and no images, also called *plain text*
- e-mail with formatted text and images, also called *Rich Text* or *HTML*

You can format your e-mails. *Windows Live Mail* offers all the same options as a text editing program like *WordPad* or *Microsoft Word*. In fact, it has more options, for example: the use of stationery. First, create a plain new e-mail message:

☞ **Start** *Windows Live Mail* 🦶³⁵

☞ **Create a new message** 🦶³⁶

In this chapter, *Windows Live Mail* does not need to connect to the Internet. Of course, you can check your e-mail if you would like.

You see the options for formatting:

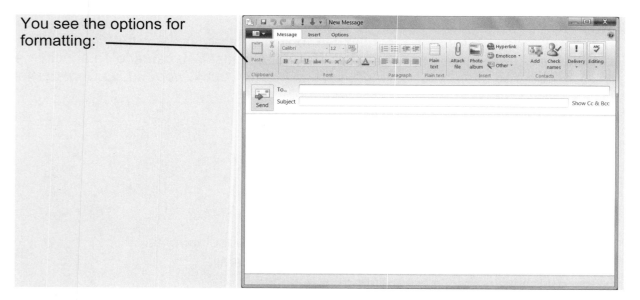

Most of the formatting you can do in *WordPad*, for example, is also available in *Windows Live Mail*. You can see your options on the tab | Message |:

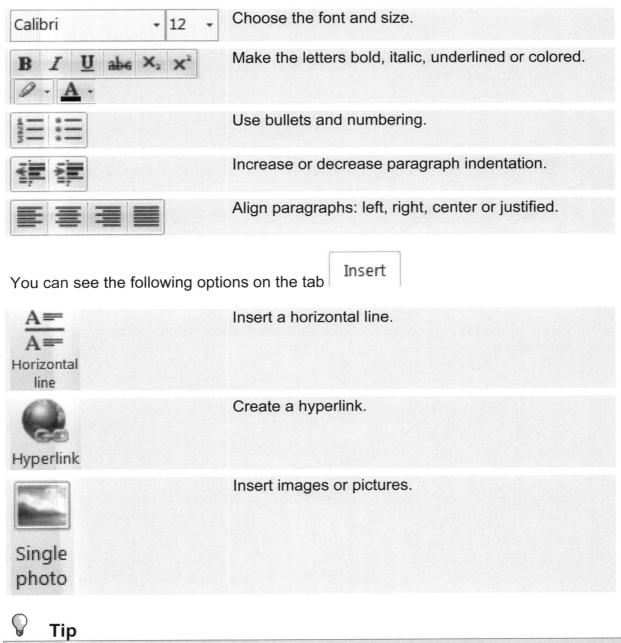

Calibri ▼ 12 ▼	Choose the font and size.
B *I* U abc X₂ X² ⌀ ▼ **A** ▼	Make the letters bold, italic, underlined or colored.
	Use bullets and numbering.
	Increase or decrease paragraph indentation.
	Align paragraphs: left, right, center or justified.

You can see the following options on the tab | Insert |

A≡ A≡ Horizontal line	Insert a horizontal line.
Hyperlink	Create a hyperlink.
Single photo	Insert images or pictures.

💡 **Tip**

Would you like to know more about text formatting and fonts?
Read the Visual Steps book **Windows 7 for Seniors**.
See **www.visualsteps.com/windows7** for more information.

7.2 The Font Size and Font Color

You can write your e-mails using a larger font size to increase readability. The default setting is a smaller font. You can choose a larger font size like this:

On the Message tab you see a button with a number 12 ▾ on the toolbar.

This means the current font is 12 (*points*) large:

☞ **Click** 12 ▾

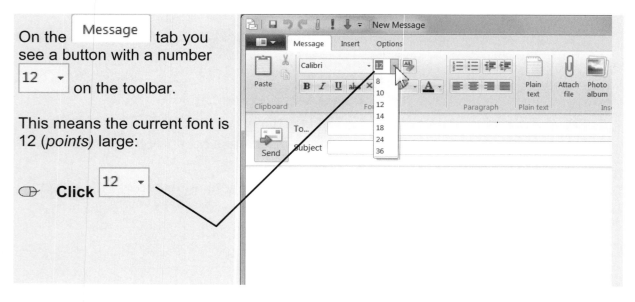

Now you see a list of numbers. A low number means smaller letters; a large number larger letters:

☞ **Click** 14

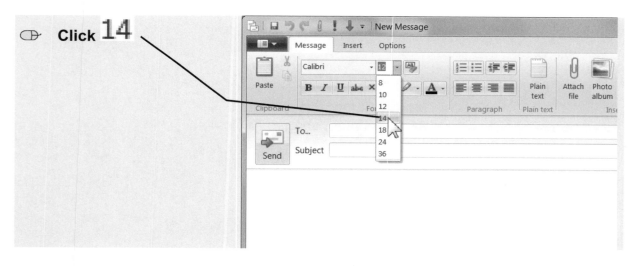

From now on, the text you type will be in a larger font.

Click the main message area

Type: This is a larger font size, 14 points.

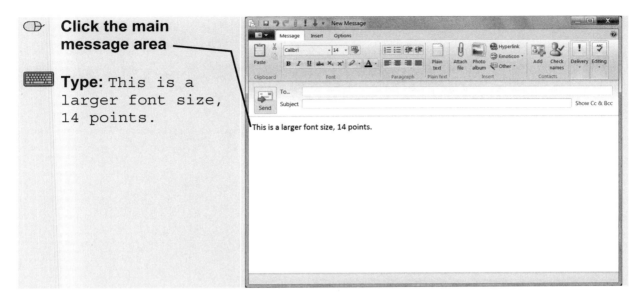

You see that the letters are larger. You can also change the font color. For example, you can make it red:

Type: The font color of these letters is red.

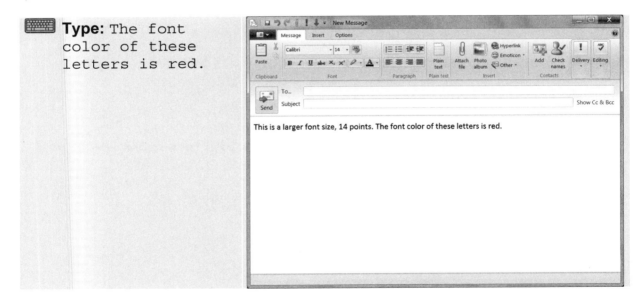

Place the mouse pointer before the word 'red'

Click and keep the mouse button pressed

Drag the mouse over the word 'red'

Release the mouse button

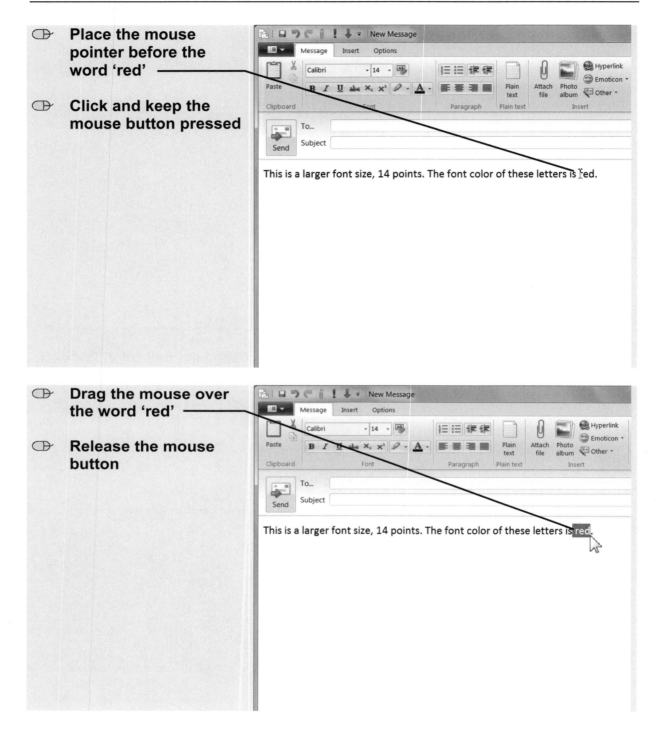

At 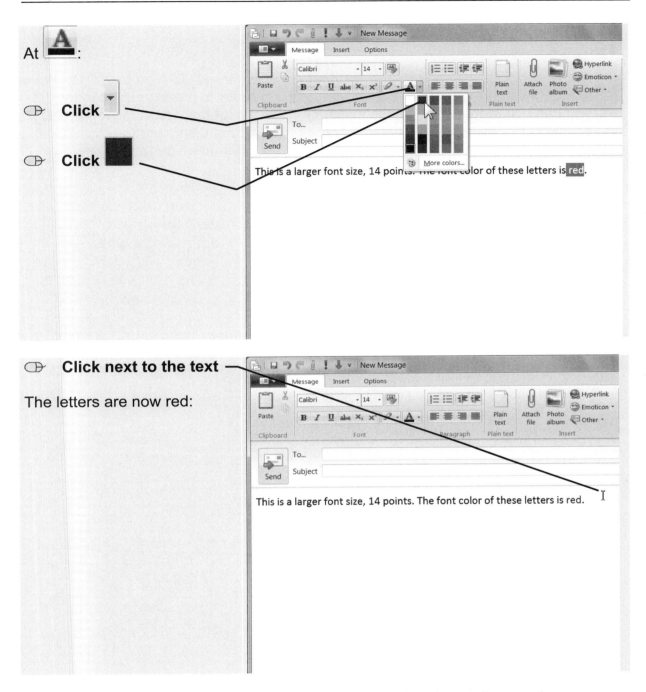:

☞ **Click**

☞ **Click**

☞ **Click next to the text**

The letters are now red:

You can do all kinds of formatting this way. You can also draw a line or place an image into the e-mail text. Go ahead and experiment.

7.3 Emoticons

E-mail is primarily used to send short letters and messages. You usually type shorter sentences than you would in a regular letter. In order to make your intentions clear, you can use *emoticons*. Emoticon is a combination of the word emotion and icon. Emoticons show what you think of something, without using words. They are also known as *smileys*. The following emoticons are often used on the Internet:

:-) or :)	happy, smiling, joking	;-)	winking
:-(or :(	frowning, unhappy	:-p	sticking out your tongue
:-D	laughing	:-c or :-<	very unhappy
>:-<	angry	:-x	not saying anything
|-O	yawn	{:-@	angry
:-*	kiss	:,-(	crying
:-|	indifferent or ambivalent	:-o	surprised or concerned

If you lean your head to the left, you can see that these icons could be little faces. You can type these smileys using the letters and symbols on the keyboard.

Type: *; -)*

A smiley has been attached to the e-mail message:

You can use these techniques to send an eye-catching e-mail to someone for special occasions like birthdays and holidays.

 Close the message window $\mathcal{QQ}^{32}$

 Do not save the changes to the message $\mathcal{QQ}^{55}$

 Tip

Will they be able to see it?
You can easily send a formatted e-mail to anyone that has *Windows* and uses *Windows Live Mail* for their e-mail program.
If you are not sure whether the recipient uses this program, it is possible he or she will not be able to view your handsome e-mail.
You can send them a test e-mail first. They will let you know if they were able to read the message.

 Close *Windows Live Mail* $\mathcal{QQ}^{43}$

7.4 E-mail Using Internet Explorer

The *Internet Explorer* program contains several functions that make it easy to send an e-mail when you are out on the World Wide Web. This can be useful if you have found an interesting website and want to send the web address to a friend. You can make use of this function as follows:

☞ **Start *Internet Explorer*** 🐾¹

☞ **Open the *Internet for Seniors* practice website for this book** 🐾⁵²

Now you see this page:

In *Internet Explorer 9*:

⌨ **Press** **Alt**

In *Internet Explorer 8 and 9*:

👆 **Click** **File**

👆 **Click** **Send**

You see two options for e-mail:

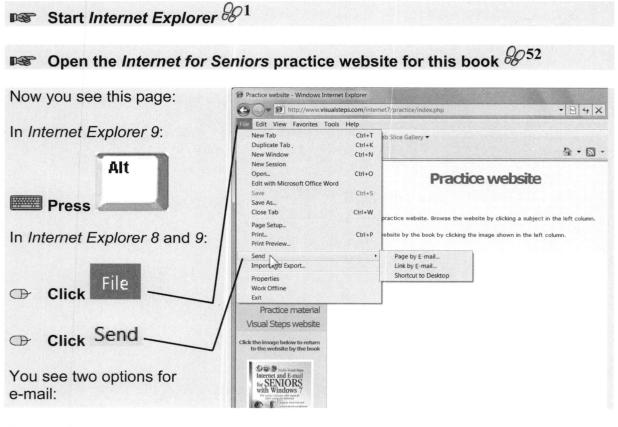

These two options are:

- send the page by e-mail
- send the web address (the link) by e-mail

You can send an *entire web page* to someone by e-mail. It is more convenient, however, to send only the web address (the *link*). By clicking on the web address, the recipient of your e-mail can connect to the Internet and view the page in question. The great advantage of sending the link by e-mail is that the chance for error from typing the address (URL) is minimized. Try this:

Click Link by E-mail...

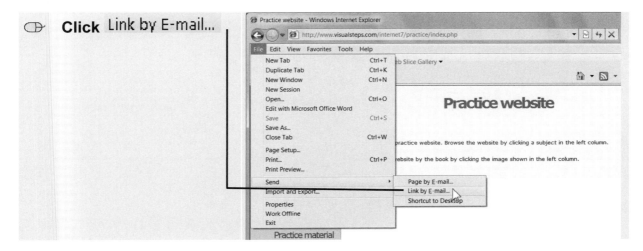

Windows Live Mail starts in the background and a new e-mail message is immediately created for you.

The subject has already been added in this new e-mail message:

The web address (the link) is already listed in the body of the message:

The recipient of this message just needs to click the link to view the web page.

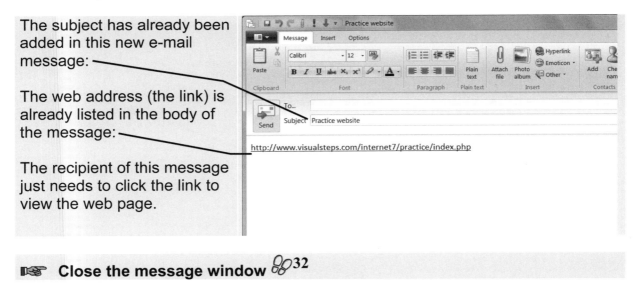

Close the message window ✏️**32**

7.5 An E-mail Address on a Website

Many websites list e-mail addresses you can use to contact a person, company or institution. Sometimes this is set up so that *Windows Live Mail* is started on your own computer with a new message. Give it a try:

There is a special link for creating an e-mail message:

☞ **Click** Test e-mail

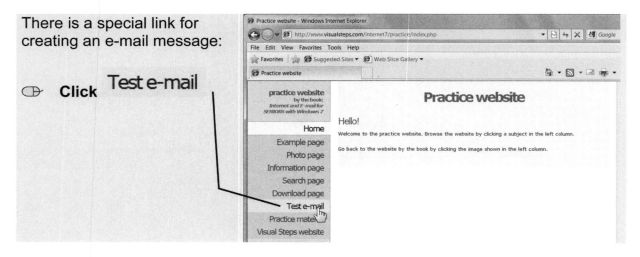

The standard program for e-mailing will be opened. In this case it is *Windows Live Mail*.

A new message is created.

The correct e-mail address has already been filled in:

You do not need to send this message, so:

☞ **Click** X

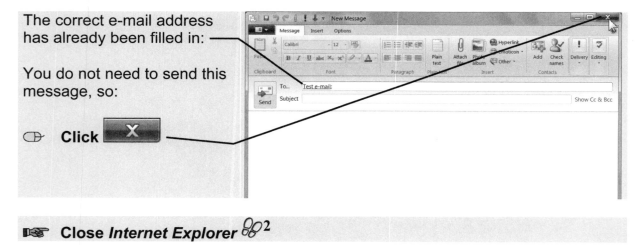

☞ **Close *Internet Explorer* ꙮ²**

7.6 Calendar - Windows Live Mail

Calendar is a calendar application included in *Windows Live Mail*. You can open the calendar like this:

☞ **If necessary, start *Windows Live Mail*** 🦶 **35**

At the bottom left-hand side of the window:

☞ **Click** 🗓 Calendar

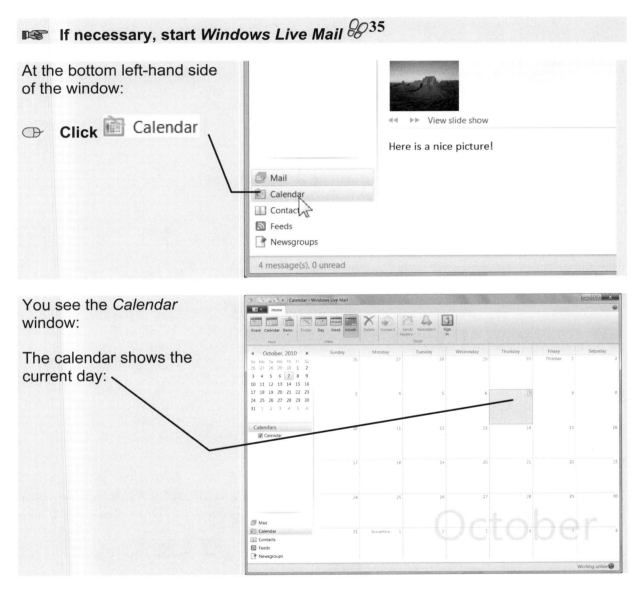

You see the *Calendar* window:

The calendar shows the current day:

7.7 Adding a New Appointment

Just like your paper calendar, you can use the calendar to keep track of your appointments. Give it a try:

☞ **Click** Event

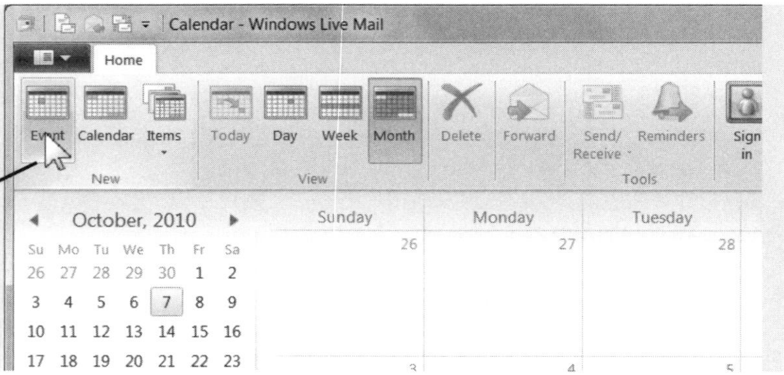

Now you will see the *New Event* window:

You will be adding a new appointment for the next week.

You can type the title of this appointment right away:

Next to Subject:.

⌨ **Type:** Meeting

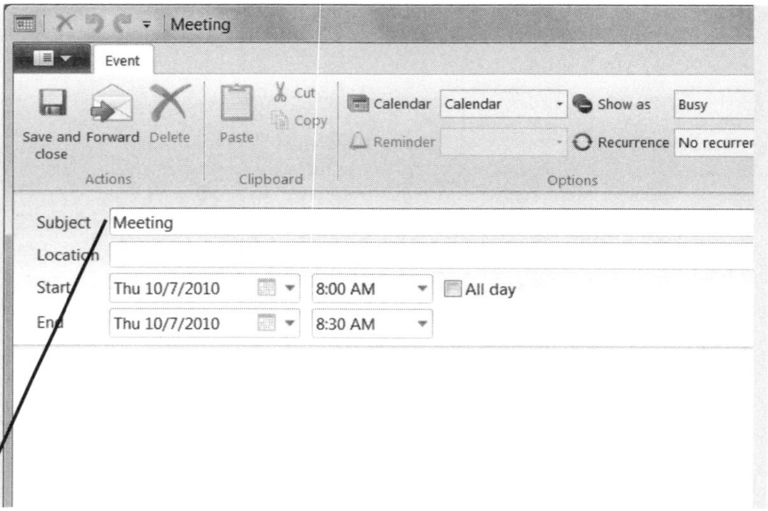

In the same window, you can add details to the appointment. First enter the location of the meeting:

Next to Location:.

☞ **Click the box**

⌨ **Type:** Office

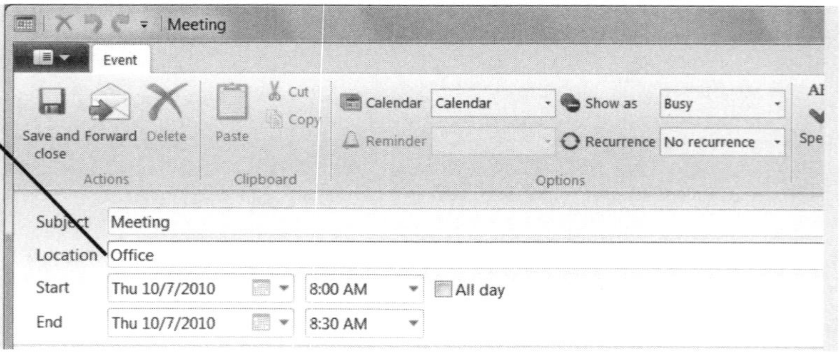

You can quickly set a date and a time for a new appointment like this:

Next to the date:

☞ **Click** ▾

☞ **Click on a date, for example** 11

The date changes into the 11th.

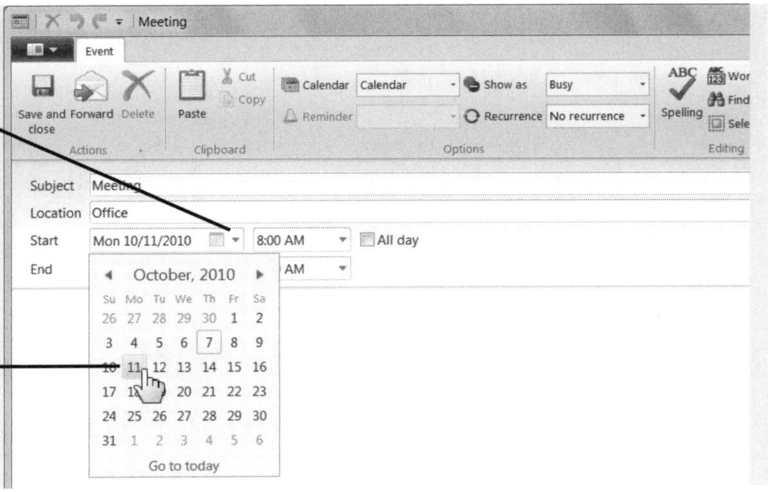

Next to the time:

☞ **Click** ▾

☞ **If necessary, drag the scroll bar down**

☞ **Click on a time, for example** 11:00 AM

A new appointment is created that will last from 11:00 AM until 11:30 AM:

You can save the appointment:

☞ **Click** Save and close

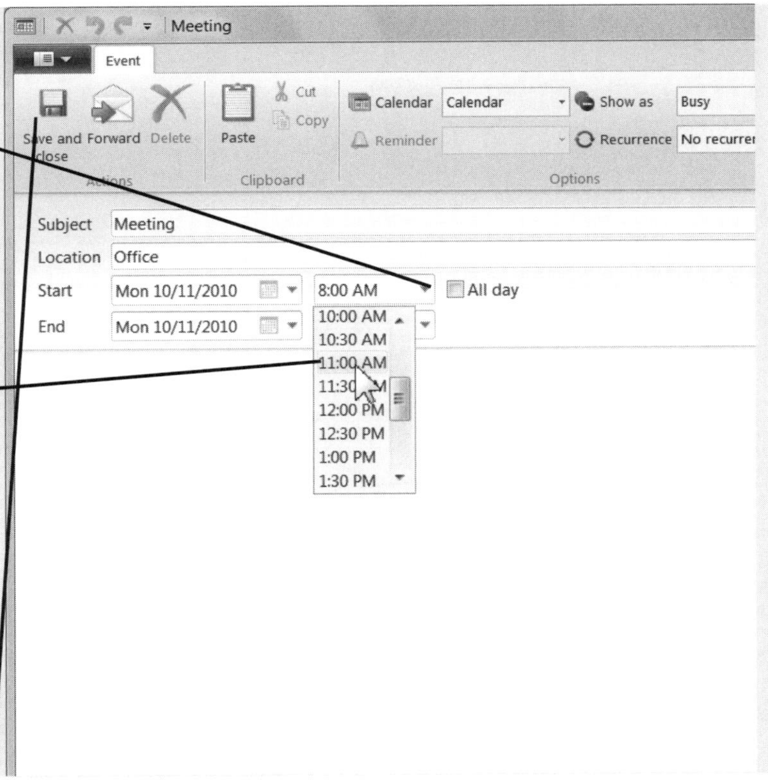

💡 **Tip**

All day appointment

For an appointment that will last all day, check the box ☐ All day.

For repeating appointment, set 🔄 Recurrence to weekly, monthly, etcetera.

Now you will see that the appointment has been added the the calendar:

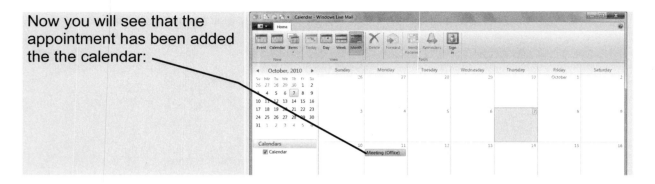

7.8 Inviting Someone for an Appointment

If you want other people to take part in a meeting, you can invite them by e-mail.

☞ **Double-click the appointment**

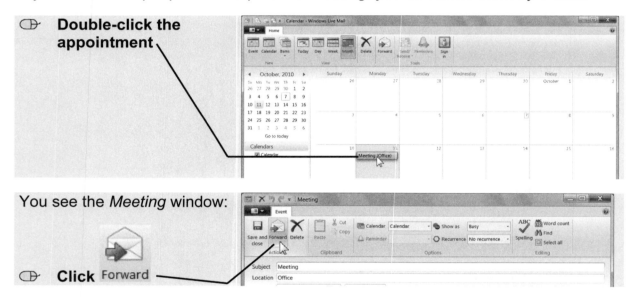

You see the *Meeting* window:

☞ **Click** Forward

A new e-mail message is created. To be able to see what happens when you receive an invitation, first add your own e-mail address:

Next to To...:

⌨ **Type your own e-mail address**

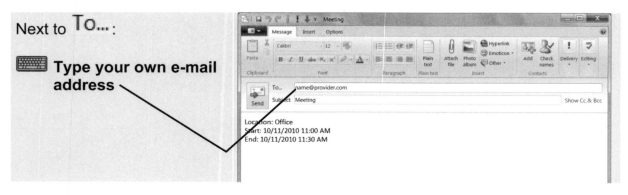

If necessary, you can always invite more people for he meeting. You do this by clicking the To... button, and then selecting the contacts you want to invite.

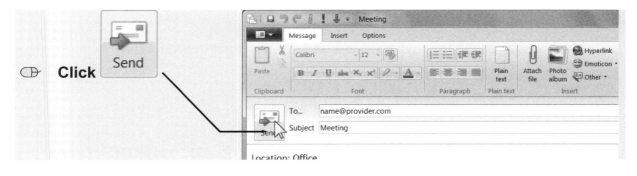

Click Send

☞ **Tip**

More information
Before sending the message, you can add a text to the e-mail message concerning the appointment.

Your message is placed in the *Outbox*.

You can save the appointment and close the window:

☞ **Click** Save and close

To view the e-mail message with the appointment:

At the bottom left-hand side of the window:

☞ **Click** Mail

☞ **If necessary, send and receive your e-mail** ⬤⬤^39

☞ **If necessary, connect to the Internet** ⬤⬤^3

The message with the invitation will be sent to you immediately.

☞ **Check your mail in the *Inbox*** ⬤⬤^39

7.9 Receiving the Details Regarding an Appointment

The details regarding the appointment have been received in your *Inbox*:

👉 **Double-click the**
   message Meeting

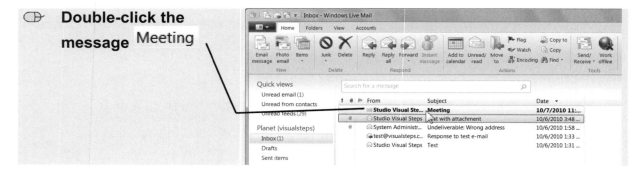

An appointment you receive can be merged with your own calendar, or created in a new calendar.

👉 **Click** Add to calendar

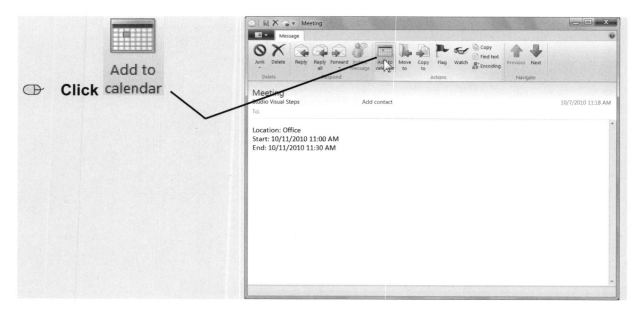

In this window you can add the appointment to your own calendar:

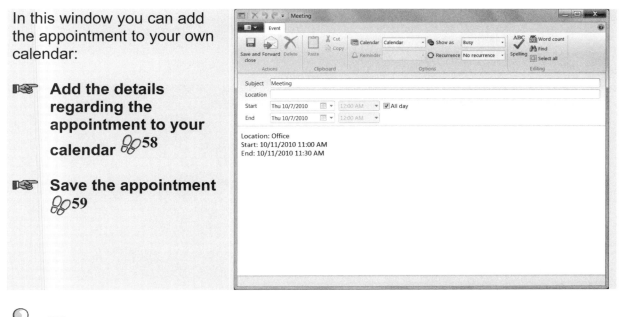

☞ **Add the details regarding the appointment to your calendar** 🐾58

☞ **Save the appointment** 🐾59

💡 **Tip**

Deleting
It is very easy to delete an appointment:

◑ **Click on the appointment**

◑ **Click** Delete

☞ **Close the message window** 🐾32

☞ **Close** *Windows Live Mail* 🐾43

Now you have learned how to make up your e-mail messages. Furthermore, you have learned how to use the *Windows Live Calendar*.

You can practice what you have learned in this chapter by doing the following exercises.

7.10 Exercises

Have you forgotten how to do something? Use the number beside the footsteps to look it up in the appendix *How Do I Do That Again?*

Exercise: Creating a Formatted E-mail

In this exercise, you will practice creating a formatted e-mail.

☞ Start *Windows Live Mail*. $\mathscr{C}\!\mathscr{C}^{35}$

☞ Create a new e-mail message addressed to yourself. $\mathscr{C}\!\mathscr{C}^{36}$

☞ Choose a larger font size of 16 points. $\mathscr{C}\!\mathscr{C}^{47}$

☞ Type in the following message:
Larger letters are easier to read.

☞ Send this e-mail to the *Outbox*. $\mathscr{C}\!\mathscr{C}^{37}$

Exercise: Planning a Day Off

In this exercise, you will practice using *Windows Live Calendar*.

☞ Open *Windows Live Calendar*. $\mathscr{C}\!\mathscr{C}^{49}$

☞ Click on tomorrow.

☞ Create a new appointment. $\mathscr{C}\!\mathscr{C}^{50}$

☞ Type the following name for the appointment: Day off

☞ Set the appointment to last all day. $\mathscr{C}\!\mathscr{C}^{66}$

☞ Save the appointment. $\mathscr{C}\!\mathscr{C}^{59}$

☞ Close *Windows Live Mail*. $\mathscr{C}\!\mathscr{C}^{43}$

7.11 Background Information

Glossary

Emoticons	Sequences of keyboard characters that symbolize facial expressions. For example, :-) looks like a smiling face when you look at it sideways.
Font	A font is a collection of numbers, symbols, and characters. A font describes a certain typeface, along with other qualities, such as size and spacing.
Formatting bar	The toolbar that you can use to format the text of your e-mail message.
HTML	A language used to create documents for the web. The term HTML is also used for an e-mail with formatted text and images, also called *Rich Text*.
Rich Text	E-mail with formatted text and images, also called *HTML*.
Webmail	E-mail service that is offered through a website. If you have a webmail address, you can read your e-mail anywhere in the world, as long as Internet access is available.
Windows Live Calendar	Calendar application that comes with *Windows Live Mail*. It can be accessed via *Windows Live Mail*.

Source: Windows Help and Support

E-mail abroad

Almost everywhere in the world, you can find public places with access to the Internet. There are Internet cafés where you can access the World Wide Web for a fee. Many libraries have Internet enabled computers, and more and more hotels are offering similar services.

For sending and receiving e-mails while you are away from home, it is useful to have an e-mail address you can access via the World Wide Web. This is called *webmail*. The most well known webmail services are *Hotmail*, *G-Mail* (from *Google*) and *Yahoo! Mail*.

If you have a webmail address, you can read your e-mail anywhere in the world.

Internet abroad

If you will be traveling abroad for a long time and want to have Internet access while you are away, you will need to arrange for local access. It would be very costly to have your computer connect through your dial-up number in the United States. There are several options.

- Ask your ISP if it has dial-up numbers in the countries where you will be traveling. This is called *roaming*. Many American ISPs have foreign dial-up numbers. If your Internet Service Provider does not have options for a local dial-up connection where you will be traveling, you can explore other options.

- You can consider using an ISP with a worldwide presence. For example, *Compuserve* is a worldwide organization with local dial-up numbers around the world. If you have a subscription in the US, you will also have access abroad.

- Another possibility is a temporary subscription with a free ISP abroad, such as *FreeSurf* in France, *Wanadoo* in the Netherlands, or *LiveDoor* in Japan. You can keep your regular Internet subscription and have your mail forwarded to your new free e-mail address in the other country. One disadvantage is that the instructions and installation software will probably be in a foreign language.

E-mail services from ISPs
Many ISPs offer various kinds of services for processing your e-mail.

- **Webmail**
  Many Internet Service Providers offer the option of using *webmail*. You can view and send your e-mail from your regular account on your ISP's website by navigating to their *Webmail* option. You do this using *Internet Explorer*. You will need your account information: user name and password on hand. In this way, you have access to your e-mail on any computer with internet access.
- **Forwarding your e-mails**
  Every incoming e-mail is sent through (forwarded) to an e-mail address you specify. For example, you can have your e-mails forwarded to your *Hotmail* address if you have one.
- **Automatic reply**
  Every incoming e-mail is automatically answered with a message you have written beforehand. This is useful if you are on vacation, to let people know that you are away and will not be able to reply immediately to an e-mail. This service is also called *Vacation Service*. But be careful, by using this option you will also reply to every spam e-mail you receive. This confirms to the company sending the spam that your e-mail address is in use, which will lead to even more spam.
- **A second e-mail address**
  Many ISPs give you the opportunity to request multiple e-mail addresses, for example, for additional family members. It can also be useful to have multiple e-mail addresses if you want to keep your e-mails separated; for example, your private correspondence and the e-mail you receive as secretary for a club. You can read how to set up multiple e-mail addresses (accounts) in *Windows Live Mail* in *Bonus Online Chapter Setting up a Webmail Account in Windows Live Mail* on the website that goes with this book.
- **Changing your e-mail address**
  You can usually change your e-mail address if it works better for you. You may need to do that if you use multiple e-mail addresses to help prevent confusion.
- **Changing your password**
  Your ISP probably gave you your own password for your e-mail account. In most cases you did not choose this password yourself. It can be useful, however, to choose a password you can easily remember.
- **Links to other communication media**
  Some ISPs provide a service for sending e-mail to cellular phones, for example.
- **Spam filter**
  Some ISPs can filter out unwelcome commercial e-mails for you.

You can read which services are available on your ISP's subscriber service website.

Newsgroups

There is a special kind of e-mail called *newsgroups*, or *discussion groups*. These are comparable to bulletin boards where people place messages and others react to them. There are thousands of newsgroups covering nearly every subject imaginable. If you have subscribed to one of these newsgroups, you can read the messages and response to them in *Windows Live Mail*. You can participate in the discussion by posting a message of your own if you so desire.

In order to set up *Windows Live Mail* to read newsgroups, you must first have the name of a *news server*. You can get this from your Internet Service Provider. Then you can download all available newsgroups from that server.

That is an enormous list containing thousands of groups:

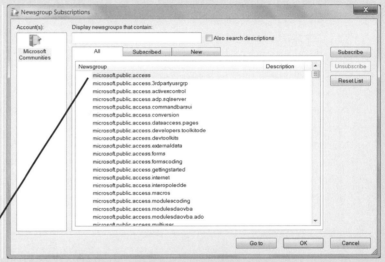

You can then subscribe to one or more of these newsgroups. "Subscribe" is actually a confusing word, because your name and so forth are not recorded. The only thing that happens is that all the messages in the newsgroup you have chosen are downloaded.

When you open the newsgroups in *Windows Live Mail,* you can *synchronize* the messages. That means that your list is updated with the current list of messages on the news server.

The content and quality of each newsgroup differs tremendously from one subject to the next, and a word of warning is in order. In some newsgroups, the "dark side" of the Internet emerges: the most extreme subjects are "discussed" by strangers, and it often becomes clear that someone is hiding behind anonymity. On the Internet, you can never be certain of someone's identity.

7.12 Tips

💡 **Tip**

Unusual fonts
Try to use only well-known fonts such as *Times New Roman* and *Arial* in your e-mails. Not everyone has the same fonts installed on his or her computer. Some drawing programs, for example, will install the most beautiful fonts, but that does not mean the recipient of your e-mail has the same font on his computer. In that case, your handsome e-mail will be shown in a default font.

💡 **Tip**

Sending a photo message
With *Windows Live Mail* you can easily send a photo:

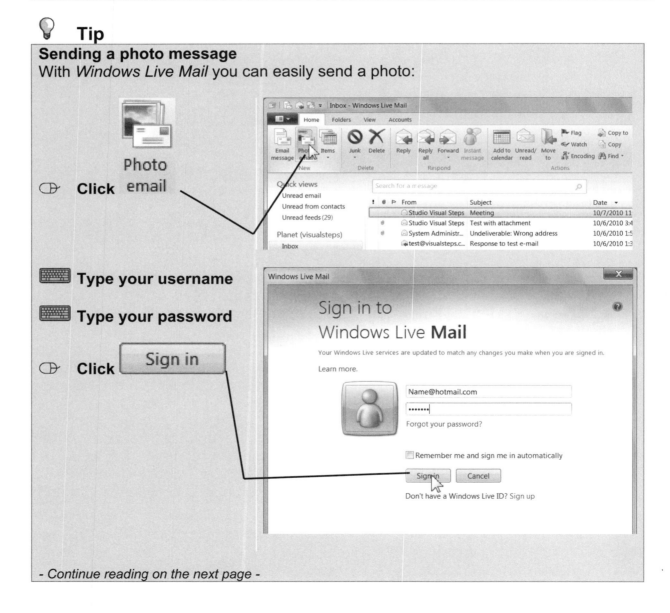

Click **Photo email**

Type your username

Type your password

Click **Sign in**

- Continue reading on the next page -

The *New Message* and *Add Photos* windows will be opened simultaneously. You can now select the photo you want to send:

☞ **Select the folder you want to use**

☞ **Select the desired photo**

☞ **Click** | Open ▼ |

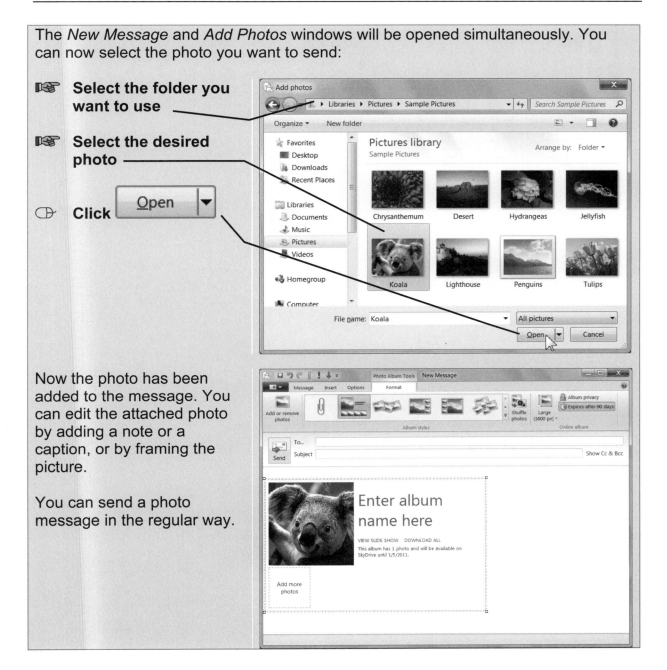

Now the photo has been added to the message. You can edit the attached photo by adding a note or a caption, or by framing the picture.

You can send a photo message in the regular way.

Notes

8. Downloading Files

There is a vast amount of information on the Internet that you can copy onto your own computer. This copying is called *downloading*. The opposite of *downloading* is *uploading* (sending files from your computer to the Internet).

You can download just about anything: computer programs, music, video films and more. After you have downloaded something, you usually save it to your computer's hard drive so that you can use it again later.

For computer programs, the second step after downloading is usually installing the program onto your computer. Installation makes the program ready for use so that you can work with it. For example, the program gets added to the Start menu so you can start it easily.

There is a separate web page for this chapter on the *Internet for Seniors* website. Here you will find different kinds of files to practice downloading. In addition, we have included a small computer program, the *Alarm clock*, to demonstrate how you install a program that you have downloaded. Once you know how to do this, a wealth of (free) computer programs lies waiting for you on the Internet. Not only programs that are enjoyable or useful for you, but also for your grandchildren, for example.

The Internet is also becoming an increasingly important medium for computer and software manufacturers. You can often download the latest versions of software from the Internet, and it is frequently the best way to replace faulty software with the most recent improved version. In short, downloading is becoming more and more important in the maintenance of your computer.

In this chapter, you will learn how to:

- download the *Alarm clock*
- install the program
- remove the installation program from the *Downloads* folder

8.1 The Practice Website

There is a practice page for this chapter on the *Internet for Seniors* website. To work through this chapter, you will first connect to the Internet and then open this web page.

☞ **Start** *Internet Explorer* 👣¹

☞ **If necessary, connect to the Internet** 👣³

☞ **Open the** *Internet for Seniors* **website** 👣⁵²

There is a page for practicing downloading on the website. Take a look at this page:

☞ **Click**

Download page

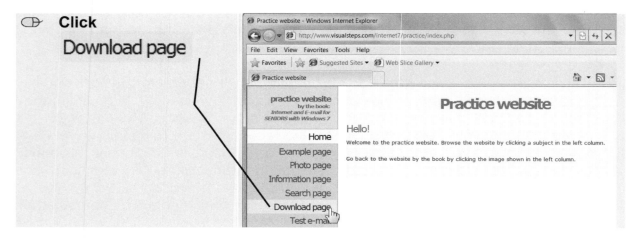

8.2 Downloading the Alarm Clock

In order to practice downloading software, there is a small program on the website called the *Alarm clock*. You will see how to download this program and then install it.

You see a page with different kinds of files:

Among them is the *Alarm clock* program. You can start downloading it by clicking on the name:

☞ **Click** `Alarm clock`

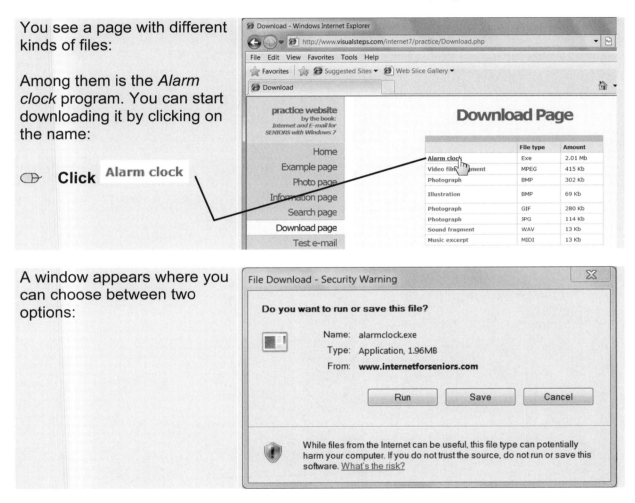

A window appears where you can choose between two options:

You can choose to:

- *run* the file.
  In this case, the installation program is immediately started.
- *save* the file.
  Then the file will be saved to your computer first. Afterwards, you have to start the installation program yourself.

In this case, it is a good idea to save the file first:

Click [Save]

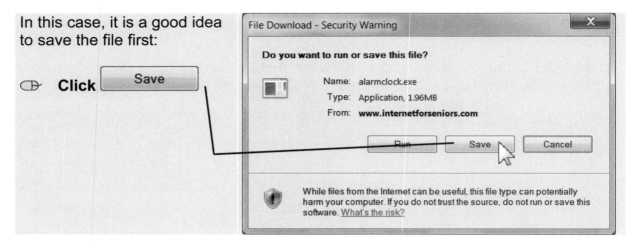

A window appears in which you can specify where you want to save the file:

By default, a downloaded file will be saved in the ▶ Downloads folder in your *Personal folder*.

The file already has a name, alarmclock:

Click [Save]

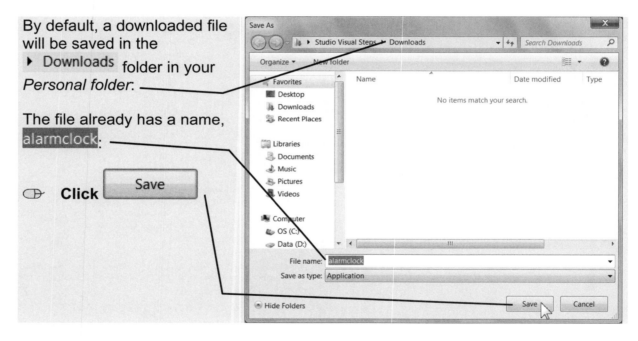

The file download begins automatically. You can follow the progress of the download by watching the green bar:

In the window, you can see roughly how long the download will take and how large the file is (1.96 MB).

99% of alarmclock.exe from www.internetforseniors.com Comp...

alarmclock.exe from www.internetforseniors.com

Estimated time left: 1 sec (1.80MB of 1.96MB copied)
Download to: C:\Users\Studio Visual Ste...\alarmclock.exe
Transfer rate: 841KB/Sec

☐ Close this dialog box when download completes

Open   Open Folder   Cancel

SmartScreen Filter checked this download and did not report any threats.
Report an unsafe download.

Has the entire file been downloaded?

☞ **Click** ⟦ Close ⟧

Now you can close *Internet Explorer* and disconnect from the Internet.

☞ **Close *Internet Explorer*** 👣²

☞ **If necessary, disconnect from the Internet** 👣⁵

The *Alarm clock* program has been downloaded and is stored on your computer's hard drive. Now you can install the program on your computer.

💡 **Tip**

Downloading? Always save to the same folder.
It is a good idea to save the files you have downloaded in the same folder, for example in ▶ Downloads . It makes it easier to find your files later on.

8.3 Installing the Program

Most computer programs contain several parts. In order for the program to work properly, all these parts have to be correctly installed on your computer. The different parts are then copied to the right place on your hard drive and the program name is added to the Start menu in *Windows*. All this work is done by the installation program. This is also how the *Alarm clock* installation works.

➡ Please note:

If you are working on a 64 bits computer, the installation process might not complete well. If so, only read through this section.

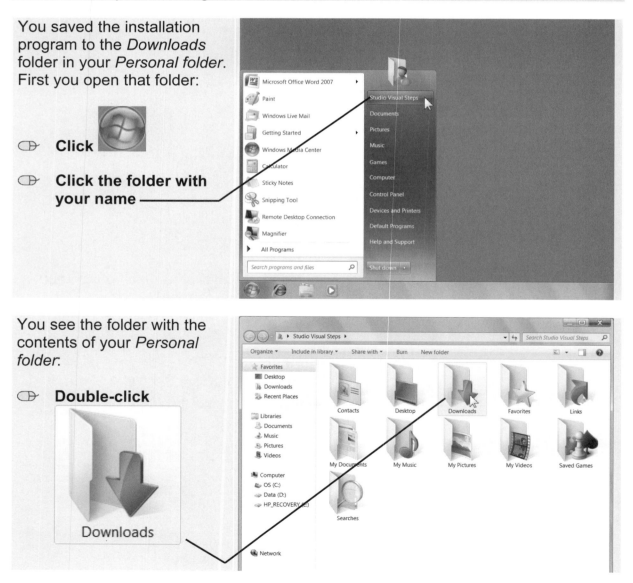

You saved the installation program to the *Downloads* folder in your *Personal folder*. First you open that folder:

☞ **Click**

☞ **Click the folder with your name**

You see the folder with the contents of your *Personal folder*:

☞ **Double-click**

The file 📦 alarmclock has been stored in this folder.

☞ **Double-click**
  📦 alarmclock

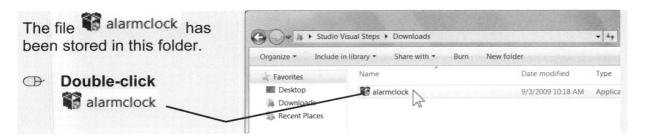

First you see a security warning. *Windows 7* wants to verify that you really want to run the installation program:

Possibly you will see this window:

☞ **If necessary, click**
  ┌─────────┐
  │   Run   │
  └─────────┘

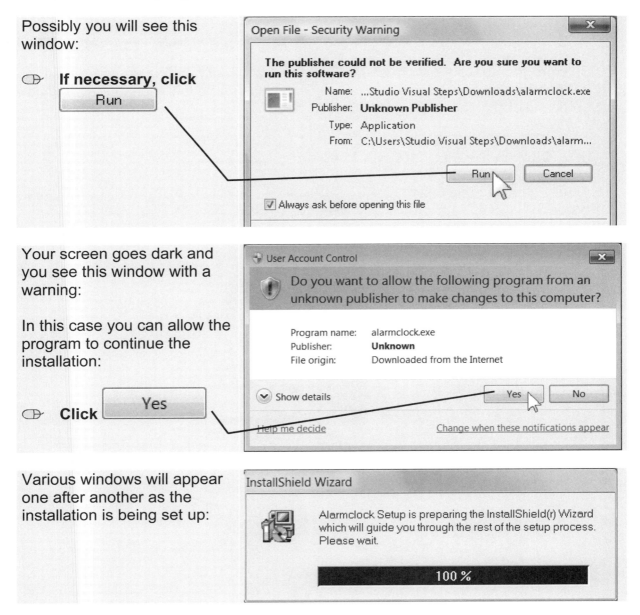

Your screen goes dark and you see this window with a warning:

In this case you can allow the program to continue the installation:

☞ **Click** ┌─────────┐
            │   Yes   │
            └─────────┘

Various windows will appear one after another as the installation is being set up:

Then you see this window:

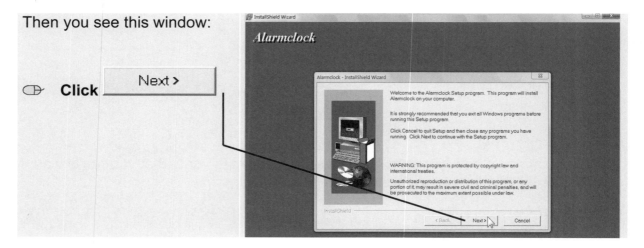

👆 **Click** [Next >]

This program uses the word *setup*. This means the same thing as *installation*. You will see four more windows in a row, all of which can be left unchanged. This means you can keep going to the next window:

👆 **Click in the next four windows on** [Next >]

Finally, you see this last window:

👆 **Click** [Finish]

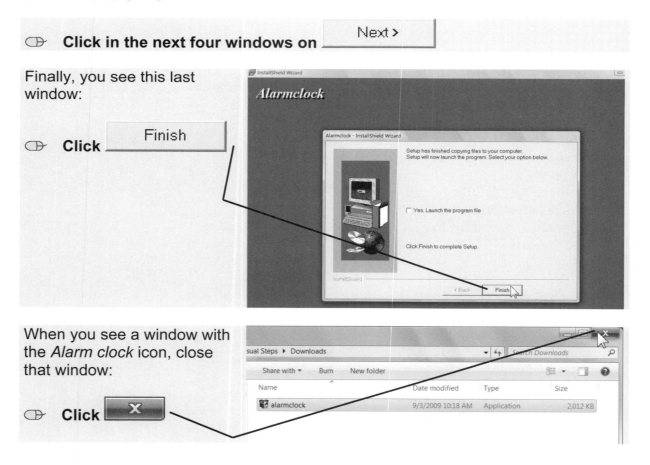

When you see a window with the *Alarm clock* icon, close that window:

👆 **Click** [X]

You see the *Downloads* folder window again:

You can close this window as well:

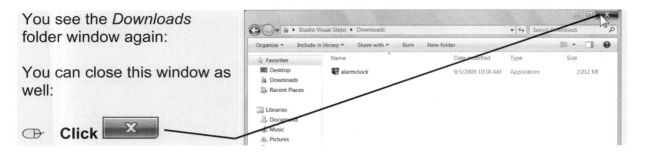

 **Click**

Most installation programs work more or less the same way as the *Alarm clock*. You have seen how this kind of installation works. Now you can start the *Alarm clock* program.

➥ **Please note:**

You do not need the installation program anymore. A little further in the book, you will read how you can remove the installation program.

8.4 Starting the Alarm Clock

You use the Start button to start a new program:

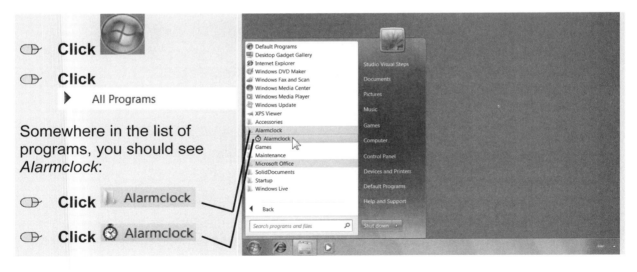

Click

Click

▶ All Programs

Somewhere in the list of programs, you should see *Alarmclock*:

Click Alarmclock

Click 🕐 Alarmclock

The program starts.

You see this little window:

🔆 Tip

How does the alarm clock work?

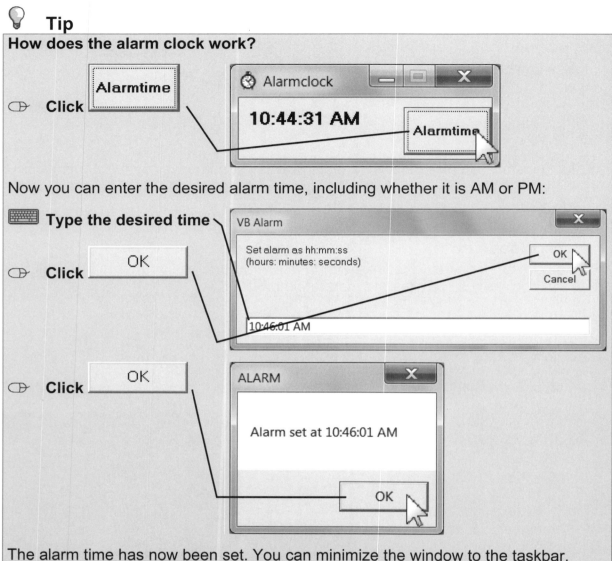

☞ **Click** Alarmtime

Now you can enter the desired alarm time, including whether it is AM or PM:

⌨ **Type the desired time**

☞ **Click** OK

☞ **Click** OK

The alarm time has now been set. You can minimize the window to the taskbar. As soon as the time you set is reached, a small pop-up window appears and you hear a sound.

The *Alarm clock* comes in handy when you need to be reminded of an appointment, or for example, when you want to keep track of how long you are working at the computer. This way you can prevent RSI from developing in your hands and wrists.

You can close the program:

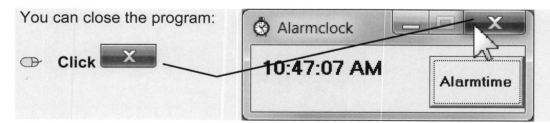

☞ **Click** X

8.5 Deleting the Installation Program

Now that the *Alarm clock* works, you can remove the installation program.
You can delete it as follows:

☞ **Open the *Downloads* folder** ⏱60

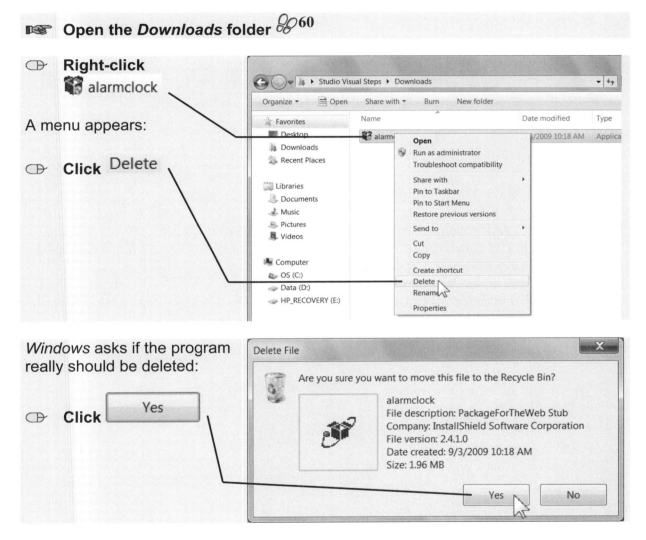

☞ **Right-click**
🟦 alarmclock

A menu appears:

☞ **Click** Delete

Windows asks if the program really should be deleted:

☞ **Click** Yes

The installation program is removed.

☞ **Close the *Downloads* folder** ⏱32

8.6 Open or Save?

When you download a file, you will usually be asked if you want to *run* it or *save* it on the hard drive. Then you see this window:

> **File Download - Security Warning**
>
> **Do you want to run or save this file?**
>
> Name: alarmclock.exe
> Type: Application, 1.96MB
> From: www.internetforseniors.com
>
> [Run]   [Save]   [Cancel]
>
> While files from the Internet can be useful, this file type can potentially harm your computer. If you do not trust the source, do not run or save this software. What's the risk?

You have seen how you can save a program file and then start the installation process. If you download a different type of file, however, what happens depends upon the kind of file and your computer's settings.

- If your computer recognizes the file type, the file will sometimes be opened right away, and you will not be able to choose between *run* and *save*.
- Depending on the programs available on your computer, the appropriate program may be started and the file opened.

There are various other types of files to practice with on the *Internet for Seniors Download page*:

> **Download - Windows Internet Explorer**
> http://www.visualsteps.com/internet7/practice/Download.php
> File   Edit   View   Favorites   Tools   Help
> Favorites | Suggested Sites ▾ | Web Slice Gallery ▾
> Download
>
> practice website
> by the book:
> *Internet and E-mail for*
> *SENIORS with Windows 7*
>
> Home
> Example page
> Photo page
> Information page
> Search page
> Download page
> Test e-mail
>
> **Download Page**
>
> | | File type | Amount |
> |---|---|---|
> | Alarm clock | Exe | 2.01 Mb |
> | Video film fragment | MPEG | 415 Kb |
> | Photograph | BMP | 302 Kb |
> | Illustration | BMP | 69 Kb |
> | Photograph | GIF | 280 Kb |
> | Photograph | JPG | 114 Kb |
> | Sound fragment | WAV | 13 Kb |
> | Music excerpt | MIDI | 13 Kb |

These are photos and music in different file formats. Some of these files will open on the web page itself, others require another program to be opened.
In the following exercises, you can download these files and see what happens with them on your computer.

8.7 Exercises

Have you forgotten how to do something? Use the number beside the footsteps to look it up in the appendix *How Do I Do That Again?*

Exercise: Downloading

In this exercise, you will practice downloading files.

☞ Start *Internet Explorer*. ₰**1**

☞ If necessary, connect to the Internet. ₰**3**

☞ Open the *Internet for Seniors* practice website. ₰**52**

☞ Click Download page.

☞ Open a video clip (MPEG). ₰**51**

☞ Open a photo (JPG). ₰**51**

☞ Open a photo (GIF). ₰**51**

☞ Open a music file (MIDI). ₰**51**

☞ Close *Windows Media Player*. ₰**13**

☞ Close *Internet Explorer*. ₰**2**

☞ If necessary, disconnect from the Internet. ₰**5**

8.8 Background Information

Glossary

AVI	Filename extension for compressed video files. The acronym stands for *Audio Video Interleave*.
BMP	*BMP* was developed by *Microsoft* and is the native graphics format for *Windows* users. The files are usually not compressed and can be quite large. Also known as *bitmap*.
Cable Internet	Cable Internet access is a broadband connection that uses the same wiring as cable TV. To use cable, you need an account with a cable Internet Service Provider in your area. The ISP usually provides any necessary equipment, and often sends a technician to set it up for you.
CDA	Filename extension for a small (44 bytes) file generated by *Microsoft Windows* for each track on an audio CD. Tells where on the disc the track starts and stops.
Download	Copying a file from one computer to another using a modem or network. For example, copying software from a website.
Installation	In order for a program to work properly, all parts have to be correctly installed on your computer. This means that the different parts are copied to the right place on your hard drive and the program name is added to the Start menu in *Windows*. All this work is done by the installation program. How you add a program depends on where the installation files for the program are located. Typically, programs are installed from a CD or DVD, from the Internet, or from a network.
JPG, JPEG	Filename extension for compressed image files such as photographs, in the format developed by the *Joint Photographers Experts Group*.
EXE	Filename extension for an executable file, a program that can be installed or run on your computer.
MPG, MPEG	Filename extension for compressed video files, in the format developed by the *Moving Pictures Experts Group*.

- Continue reading on the next page -

MP3	Filename extension for compressed audio files, in the *MPEG Audio Layer 3* format. MP3 is the most popular way for compressing audio files and exchanging them on the Internet.
Setup	Installation.
WAV	Filename extension for uncompressed audio files, the acronym stands for *Waveform Audio Format*. The system sounds on your computers are also stored in this format.
WMA	Filename extension for compressed audio files in the *Windows Media Audio* format.

Source: Windows Help and Support

Types of software
Various types of software are available on the Internet:

Freeware
This software may be freely used and copied. It is sometimes also called *Public Domain* software.

Shareware
The program may be used free of charge for a period of time so you can try it out. If you would like to keep using it after the trial period, you must pay.

Cardware
Similar to shareware, but the maker wants you to recognize that this is his or her intellectual property. The user is expected to send a postcard indicating that he or she is using the program. Also called postcardware.

Demos
Demos are free software in which some functions have been disabled. The functions that still work give a good idea of the software's capabilities.
Sometimes the demo works fully, but only for a limited time.

Updates
These are additions, patches or improvements to existing software. They are often provided free of charge to people who have a license for the original program.

Cookies
Cookies are small text files that websites put on your computer to store information about you. This information can be requested by websites in order to determine various things, such as your settings or user name for that website. Using cookies, you only have to enter that information once. Cookies can be misused, however. Information about your browsing behavior may be made available to marketing companies.

Plug-ins
A *plug-in* is an accessory program which can be installed as an extra in *Internet Explorer*. Plug-ins are often required for viewing video clips and animations or listening to music. You usually download them free of charge from the Internet. The following programs are required in order to open specific file types:

- *Adobe Flash Player*: for viewing and interactive use of animations on websites.
- *RealPlayer:* for playing sound and music; among other things, this program makes it possible to follow radio broadcasts over the Internet.
- *Adobe Reader*: reads PDF documents; many manuals and brochures on the Internet are distributed in this file format.

Windows Media Player
You can play music and video without plug-ins, too: *Media Player* is installed when you install *Windows*.

This program can play various file types:
- WMA, MP3, WAV, ACC: music and sound
- CDA: CD Audio Track
- WMV, MPEG, AVI, WTV: video files

Windows Live Messenger
You can use *Windows Live Messenger* to stay in touch with friends, colleagues and family.

The principle is simple. When you are connected to the Internet, the *Live Messenger* window shows which one of your contacts is online. Your contacts can also see if you are online or not.

You can start up an online conversation with a contact by typing and sending instant messages (IM). This is also called *chatting*.
It is also possible to start a conversation using a microphone and by using a webcam you can have a *face-to-face* experience.

You can download the *Messenger* program free of charge at download.live.com

Do you want to know more about the *Messenger* program? In *Chapter 9* of the book **Interesting Online Applications for Seniors** (ISBN 978 90 5905 285 7) this subject will be discussed.

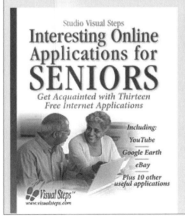

Interesting Online Applications for SENIORS
Get acquainted with thirteen free internet applications
Author: Studio Visual Steps
ISBN 978 90 5905 285 7
Book type: Paperback
Nr of pages: 392 pages
Price: US $22.95, Canada $24.95
Website for this book: www.visualsteps.com/online

The cable modem

A cable company offers Internet access by using the same cables which are used for TV broadcasts to transmit both upstream and downstream data from the Internet.

The cable TV outlet   *An external cable modem*

The way in which your computer connects differs greatly from one cable provider to the next. Sometimes a mechanic will install an *internal cable modem* into your computer. Alternatively, an *external modem* might be placed between your computer and the cable outlet. The modem is then connected to your computer with another cable.

The ISDN Modem

ISDN has a number of advantages over the regular telephone line. First, its speed is greater than that of the regular telephone network. This is particularly evident when you are surfing the Internet. Another advantage is that you have two telephone lines. This means that you can use the telephone and the Internet at the same time.

If you choose ISDN, you will need to buy an ISDN modem in order to benefit from the increased speed. There are external and internal ISDN modems. They look just like regular modems, with a slightly different telephone jack. An internal modem is sometimes called an *ISDN card*.

An ISDN card in the computer   *An external ISDN modem*

DSL

With DSL, the telephone line coming into your home is split. Your telephone connects to one jack, and your computer connects to the other through a modem. The big advantage of DSL is that, just as with a cable connection, you are connected to the Internet twenty-four hours a day. The DSL connection is very fast and you can call on the telephone and use the Internet all at the same time.

8.9 Tips

Tip

Updating Windows 7
Updating means replacing your system files with the very latest versions. The *Windows Update* program scans your computer, creates a list of files that can be updated, and then installs the files. These files are automatically downloaded from the *Microsoft* website. Here is how you start *Windows Update*:

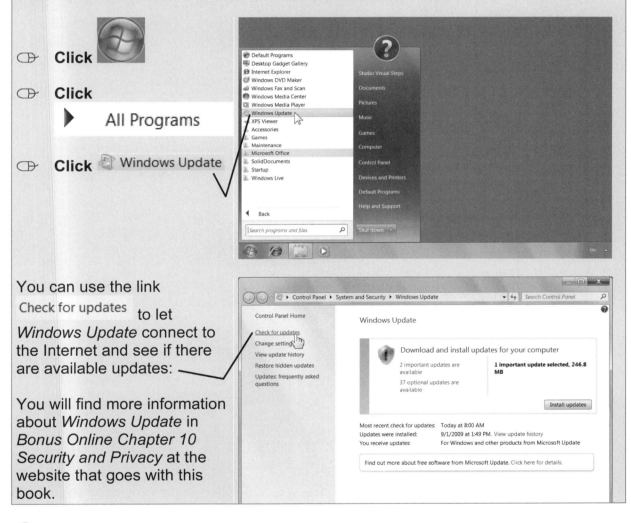

Click

Click

▶ All Programs

Click Windows Update

You can use the link Check for updates to let *Windows Update* connect to the Internet and see if there are available updates:

You will find more information about *Windows Update* in *Bonus Online Chapter 10 Security and Privacy* at the website that goes with this book.

Tip

Where can I find programs?
There are websites with huge software libraries.
On the *Internet for Seniors* website, you will find a special software page with information on locations where you can find interesting programs.

💡 Tip

Uninstalling a program

You can uninstall a program from your computer if you no longer use it or if you want to free up space on your hard drive. This is the safest way to uninstall a program:

☞ **Click** [Control Panel],

In the group Programs :

☞ **Click** Uninstall a program

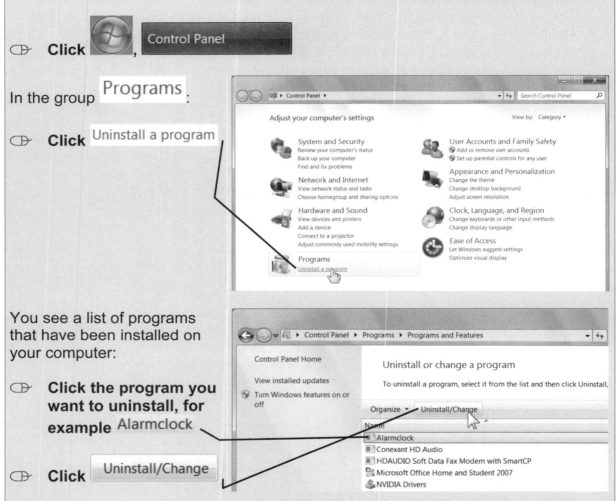

You see a list of programs that have been installed on your computer:

☞ **Click the program you want to uninstall, for example** Alarmclock

☞ **Click** Uninstall/Change

First, *Windows 7* wants your permission to continue the operation. To grant permission you click the *Yes* button.

As a safety measure, you must confirm again that you want to remove the program. You do that by clicking the *Yes* button.

Finally, the *Uninstall Shield* window appears. You see the various components of the program being removed. When you see the message 'Uninstall successfully completed', the program has been removed from your computer.

9. Bonus Online Chapters and Extra Information

Now you have come to the last chapter of this book. However, on the website that goes with this book you can find a bonus online chapter and appendix. In this chapter you will learn how to open these additional chapter and appendices.

Furthermore, you will take a look at the Visual Steps website. You will see that this website contains lots of useful, extra information.

In this chapter, you will learn how to:

- open the Bonus Online Chapter
- visit the Visual Steps website

9.1 Opening the Bonus Online Chapter

The website that accompanies this book contains a bonus online chapter, namely:

- *Chapter 10 Security and Privacy*

You will also find an extra appendix:

- *Extra Appendix Setting Up a Webmail Account in Windows Live Mail*

This chapter and appendix are provided as PDF files. These files can be opened with the free *Adobe Reader* software program. This is how you open these files on this book's website:

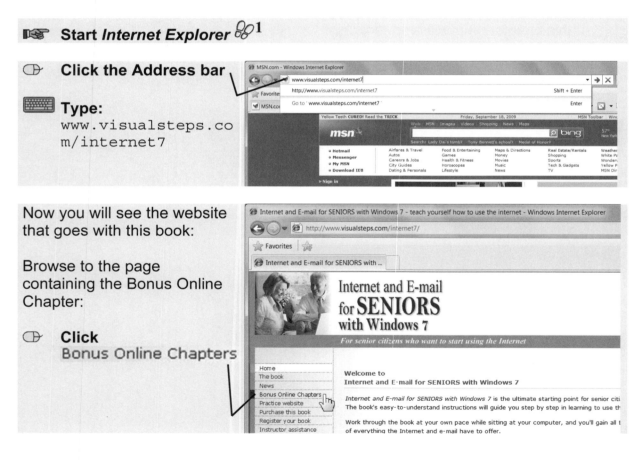

☞ **Start** *Internet Explorer* 𝄞¹

☞ **Click the Address bar**

⌨ **Type:**
www.visualsteps.co
m/internet7

Now you will see the website that goes with this book:

Browse to the page containing the Bonus Online Chapter:

☞ **Click**
Bonus Online Chapters

Now you will see this web page:

To open a chapter:

⊕ **Click**
   Start downloading »»

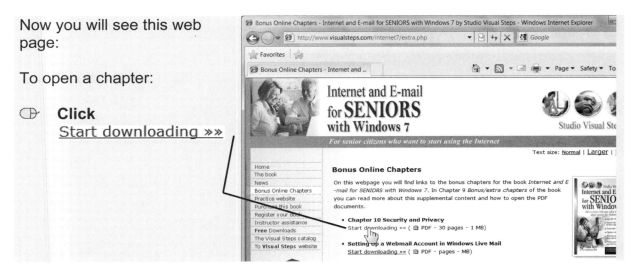

You can use the free *Adobe Reader* program to open these PDF files. This program allows you to view the files and even print them, if you wish.
The PDF files are secured by a password. To open the PDF files, you need to enter the password:

⌨ **Type:** 69462

⊕ **Click** OK

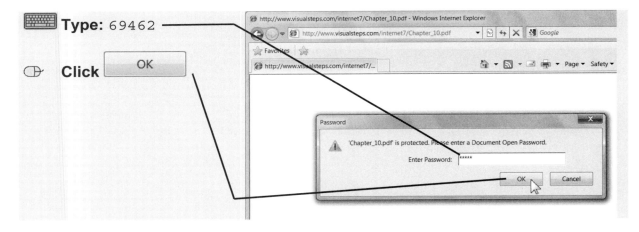

HELP! I see a different window.

If the window below is displayed on your screen, the *Adobe Reader* program has not yet been installed to your computer. In that case you need to follow a number of steps to install the program:

Click [Cancel]

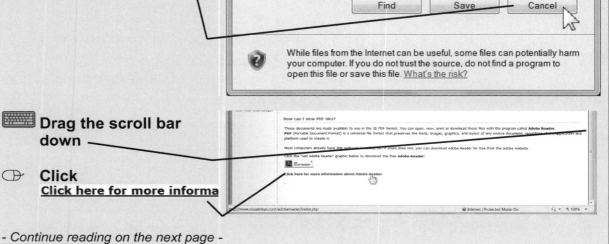

Drag the scroll bar down

Click

Click here for more informa

- Continue reading on the next page -

Now you will see a web page with information on downloading *Adobe* Reader in an easy way:

☞ **Follow the steps in this window**

Now you will be guided through the installation procedure, step-by-step. After the installation has been completed:

☞ **Close the *Internet Explorer* window about installing *Adobe Reader* ✂️³²**
☞ **Open the Bonus Online Chapter as described in this section**

🩹 HELP! I see a different window.

When you open the program *Adobe Reader* for the first time, you see a window like the following:

⊙ **Click** [Allow]

Internet Explorer Security   ❌

⚠️ A website wants to open web content using this program on your computer

This program will open outside of Protected mode. Internet Explorer's Protected mode helps protect your computer. If you do not trust this website, do not open this program.

Name: **Adobe End User License Agreement**
Publisher: **Adobe Systems, Incorporated**

☐ Do not show me the warning for this program again

⊙ Details   [Allow] [Don't allow]

- Continue reading on the next page -

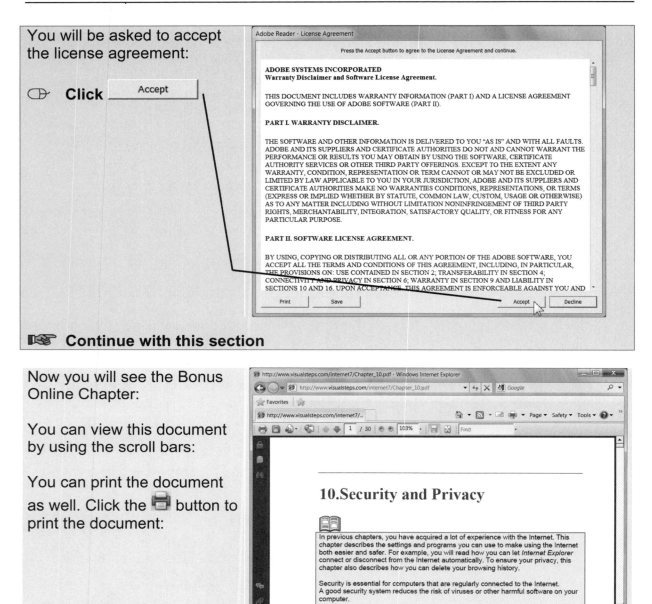

You will be asked to accept the license agreement:

☞ **Click** | Accept |

☞ **Continue with this section**

Now you will see the Bonus Online Chapter:

You can view this document by using the scroll bars:

You can print the document as well. Click the 🖶 button to print the document:

You can work through this online chapter in the same way you have worked with the chapters in the book. After you have read or printed the chapter, you can close the window.

☞ **Close all windows** ✂³²

The extra appendix can be opened in a similar way, by using the same password: 69462.

💡 Tip

More about Adobe Reader

On the **www.visualsteps.com/info_downloads** web page you will find a free PDF file with information on the use of *Adobe Reader*. This is how you open this file:

☞ **Start *Internet Explorer* ⚘1**

☞ **Open the www.visualsteps.com/info_downloads web page ⚘4**

If you already have a subscription to the Visual Steps Newsletter:

⌨ **Type your e-mail address here** ———

⌨ **Press** `Enter  ⏎`

If you have not yet subscribed to the Visual Steps Newsletter:

⌨ **Type your e-mail address here** ———

⌨ **Press** `Enter  ⏎`

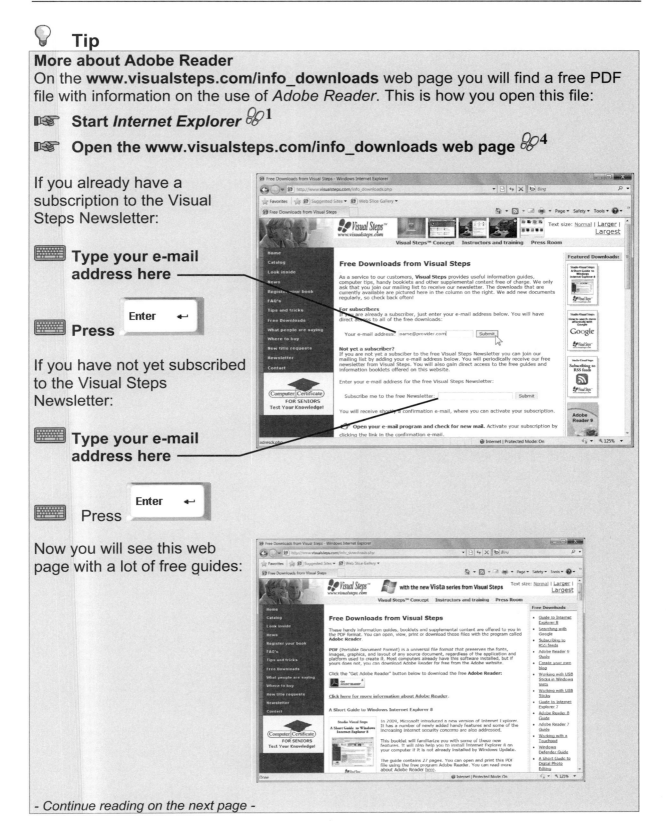

Now you will see this web page with a lot of free guides:

- Continue reading on the next page -

Click

Start downloading »»

The window with the PDF file will be opened:

You can view this document by using the scroll bars:

You can print the document as well. Click the 🖶 button to print the document:

Please note: all these free guides are free downloads, you do not need a password.

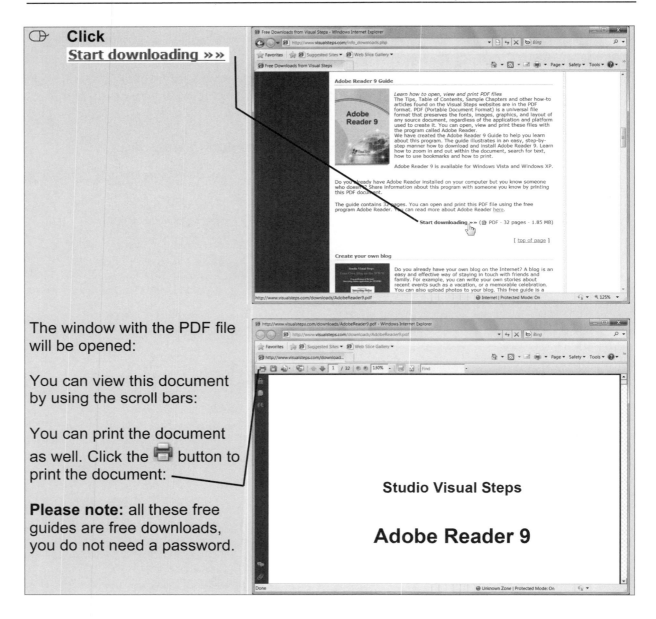

9.2 Visual Steps Website and Newsletter

So you have noticed that the Visual Steps-method is a great method to gather knowledge quickly and efficiently. All the books published by Visual Steps have been written according to this method. There are quite a lot of books available, on different subjects. For instance about *Windows*, photo editing, and about free programs, such as *Google Earth* and *Skype*.

Book + software

One of the Visual Steps books includes a CD with the program that is discussed. The full version of this high quality, easy-to-use software is included. You can recognize this Visual Steps book with enclosed CD by this logo on the book cover:

Website

Use the blue *Catalog* button on the **www.visualsteps.com** website to read an extensive description of all available Visual Steps titles, including the full table of contents and part of a chapter (as a PDF file). In this way you can find out if the book is what you expected.

This instructive website also contains:
- free computer booklets and informative guides (PDF files) on a range of subjects;
- free computer tips, described according to the Visual Steps method;
- a large number of frequently asked questions and their answers;
- information on the free Computer certificate you can obtain on the online test website **www.ccforseniors.com**;
- free 'Notify me' e-mail service: receive an e-mail when book of interest are published.

Visual Steps Newsletter

Do you want to keep yourself informed of all Visual Steps publications? Then subscribe (no strings attached) to the free Visual Steps Newsletter, which is sent by e-mail.

This Newsletter is issued once a month and provides you with information on:
- the latest titles, as well as older books;
- special offers and discounts;
- new, free computer booklets and guides.

As a subscriber to the Visual Steps Newsletter you have direct access to the free booklets and guides, at **www.visualsteps.com/info_downloads**

9.3 More Visual Steps Books

The **Internet and E-mail for Seniors with Windows 7** book has taken you through all the Internet features. Now you can download software, personalize your e-mail, send, receive, open and save attachments and save e-mail addresses in the *Windows Live Contacts* folder. Interested in gaining more skills? Try the following Visual Steps books in the *Windows 7 for SENIORS series*:

Windows 7 for SENIORS

For senior citizens who want to start using the computer

ISBN 978 90 5905 116 4

More Windows 7 for SENIORS

Get more out of your computer

ISBN 978 90 5905 346 5

Google for SENIORS

Get Acquainted with free Google Applications

ISBN 978 90 5905 236 9

Picasa for SENIORS

Get Acquainted with Picasa: Free, Easy-to-Use Photo Editing Software

ISBN 978 90 5905 246 8

Interesting Online Applications for SENIORS

Get acquainted with thirteen free Internet Applications

ISBN 978 90 5905 285 7

Windows Live for SENIORS

Get Acquainted with free Windows Live Applications

ISBN 978 90 5905 356 4

If you would like to know more about these books, please visit our website, **www.visualsteps.com**

Appendix A
Setting up a Dial-up Connection

If your dial-up connection has not yet been set up, you can use this appendix to configure the necessary settings. First, check if your modem is ready.

🖙 **Make sure your modem is connected to the telephone line**

Do you have an external modem?
🖙 **Turn the modem on**

Do you have an internal modem?
🖙 **You do not have to do anything**

➡ **Please note:**

If you have an Internet access subscription, your Internet Service Provider (ISP) has given you a **user name** and a **password**. Also, you should have received a **phone number** that can be used to contact your ISP's computer.
Make sure to have these details ready.

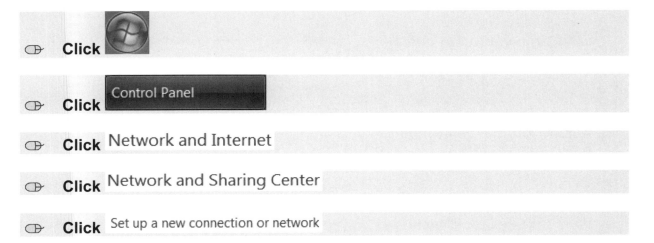

👆 **Click**

👆 **Click** Control Panel

👆 **Click** Network and Internet

👆 **Click** Network and Sharing Center

👆 **Click** Set up a new connection or network

You choose *Set up a dial-up connection*:

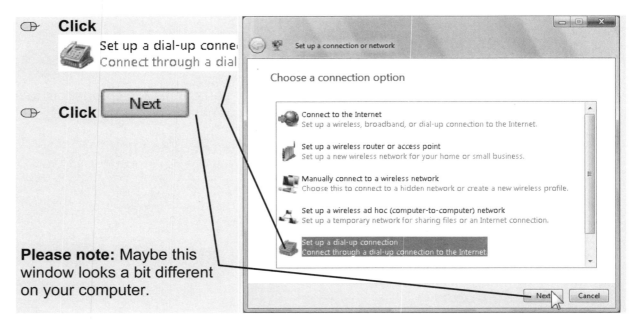

☞ **Click**

    Set up a dial-up conne
    Connect through a dial

☞ **Click**   Next

Please note: Maybe this window looks a bit different on your computer.

Now you can enter the details for your dial-up connection:

⌨ **Type the ISP's dial-up phone number**

⌨ **Type your user name**

⌨ **Type your password**

Please note: Maybe this window looks a bit different on your computer.

➥ Please note:

Whether you want *Windows* to remember your password or not depends a great deal on how accessible your computer is to others. If you are the only user and no one else has access to your computer, the situation is very different than when the same computer can be used by others.

Do not remember
If you choose not to let *Windows* remember your password, you will have to type it in yourself every time. This is recommended when you want to be certain that no one else can use your Internet connection.

Do remember
If you are the only person who uses your computer and you are reasonably certain no one else can use it, you can choose the convenience of letting the computer remember your password.

Do you want your password to be remembered?

☞ **Check the box**
☑ Remember this password

If you do not want your password to be remembered:

☞ **Make sure this box is not checked**

Please note: Maybe this window looks a bit different on your computer.

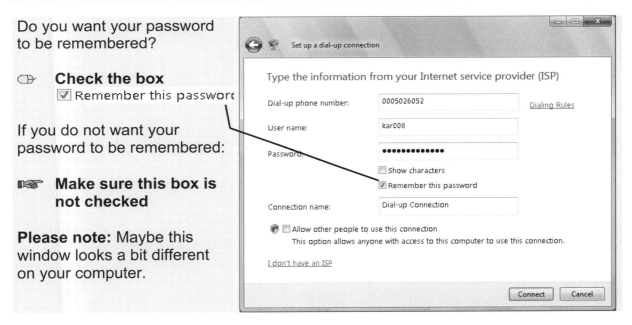

Windows 7 also offers the possibility to let other users with access to your computer use this same dial-up connection. This means that other people with a different account can see and use the connection you are setting up.

Do you want other users to be able use this dial-up connection?

☞ **Check the box**
    ☑ Allow other people to use

If you do not want your password to be saved:

☞ **Make sure this box is not checked**

Please note: Maybe this window looks a bit different on your computer.

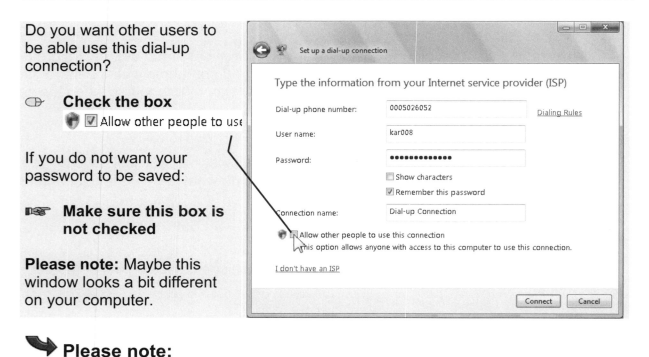

➡ Please note:

As soon as you check the box 🛡 ☑ Allow other people to use this connection, your screen goes dark and *Windows* asks your permission to continue. Click the *Yes* button if you want to apply this setting.

Now you can try the connection:

☞ **Click** Connect

Please note: Maybe this window looks a bit different on your computer.

The connection is being made:

After that your password is verified and the connection is tested.

Please note: Maybe this window looks a bit different on your computer.

When the connection is made, you see this window:

☞ **Click** [Close]

Please note: Maybe this window looks a bit different on your computer.

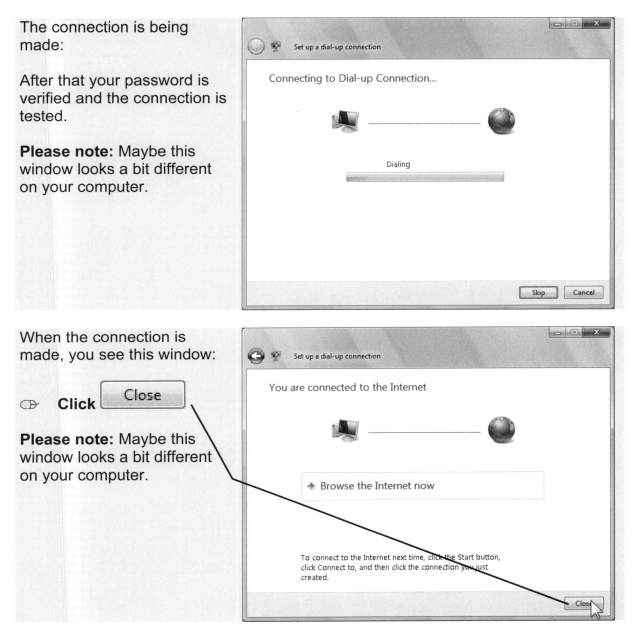

Now you see the *Set Network Location* window. The first time that you connect to a network, you must choose a network location. This automatically sets the appropriate firewall settings for the type of network that you connect to.

If you connect to networks in different locations (for example, a network at your home, at a local coffee shop, or at work), choosing a network location can help ensure that your computer is always set to an appropriate security level.

There are three network locations: *Home*, *Work*, and *Public location*.

Depending on where you are, click the location that describes your situation best.

For example:

☞ **Click**

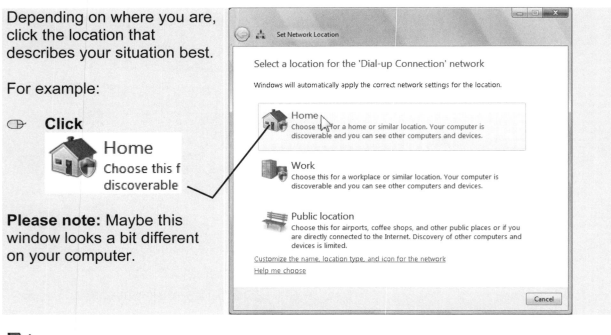

Please note: Maybe this window looks a bit different on your computer.

➥ Please note:

As soon as you choose one of the locations, your screen goes dark and *Windows* asks your permission to continue. Click the *Yes* button if you want to grant your permission and apply this setting.

The settings have been configured.

At the bottom of the window:

☞ **Click** Close

Please note: Maybe this window looks a bit different on your computer.

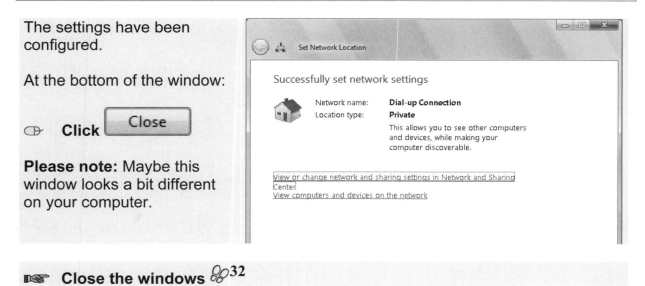

☞ **Close the windows** ⅋⅋³²

Now that your dial-up connection has been set up, you can begin surfing the web. If you want to save that for another time, simply click disconnect:

☞ **Disconnect from the Internet** ⅋⅋⁵

Appendix B
How Do I Do That Again?

As you work through this book you may have noticed these footsteps: 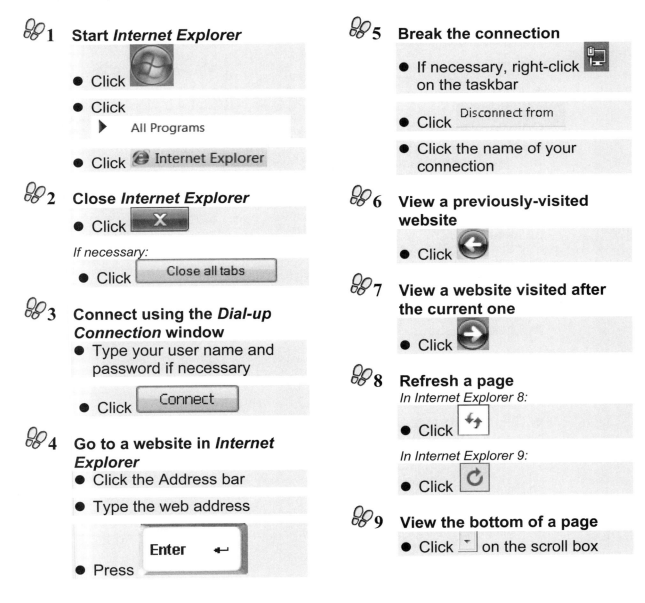x
with a number beside them. This number indicates that there is a listing in the
Appendix B. How Do I Do That Again?. Here you will find many short descriptions of
how to perform specific tasks. Use the number to find the listing here in this
appendix. This may come in handy when you have forgotten what is meant by a
certain computer term.

1 Start *Internet Explorer*

- Click

- Click
  - ▶ All Programs

- Click Internet Explorer

2 Close *Internet Explorer*

- Click X

If necessary:

- Click Close all tabs

3 Connect using the *Dial-up Connection* window

- Type your user name and password if necessary

- Click Connect

4 Go to a website in *Internet Explorer*

- Click the Address bar

- Type the web address

- Press Enter ↵

5 Break the connection

- If necessary, right-click on the taskbar

- Click Disconnect from

- Click the name of your connection

6 View a previously-visited website

- Click ←

7 View a website visited after the current one

- Click →

8 Refresh a page
In Internet Explorer 8:

- Click ↔

In Internet Explorer 9:

- Click ↻

9 View the bottom of a page

- Click ▾ on the scroll box

Or:
- Drag the scroll bar down

Or:
- Use the scroll wheel on the mouse

10 View the top of a page
- Click ⌃ on the scroll box

Or:
- Drag the scroll bar up

Or:
- Use the scroll wheel on the mouse

11 Minimize a window
- Click ▭

12 Open a window from the taskbar
- Click the button on the taskbar

13 Close a window and stop the program
- Click ✕

14 Open a website from *History*
- Click ⭐ Favorites or ⭐
- Click History
- Click the folder of the website
- Click the desired webpage

15 Make a website a favorite
- Click ⭐ Favorites or ⭐
- Click ⭐ Add to Favorites...
- Click Add

16 Temporarily break the connection
- Right-click 🖳 on the taskbar
- Click Disconnect from
- Click the name of your connection

17 Open a favorite website
- Click ⭐ Favorites or ⭐
- If necessary, click Favorites
- Click the website

18 Make a web address a favorite and save it in a folder
- Click ⭐ Favorites or ⭐
- Click ⭐ Add to Favorites...
- Click ▾ in
  ⭐ Favorites   ▾
- Click the folder 📁

19 Open a favorite in a folder
- Click ⭐ Favorites or ⭐
- Click the folder
- Click the website

20 Click the instant Search box or Address bar
In Internet Explorer 8:
- Click this box
  🔍 ▾

In Internet Explorer 9:
- Click the Address bar
  ℮

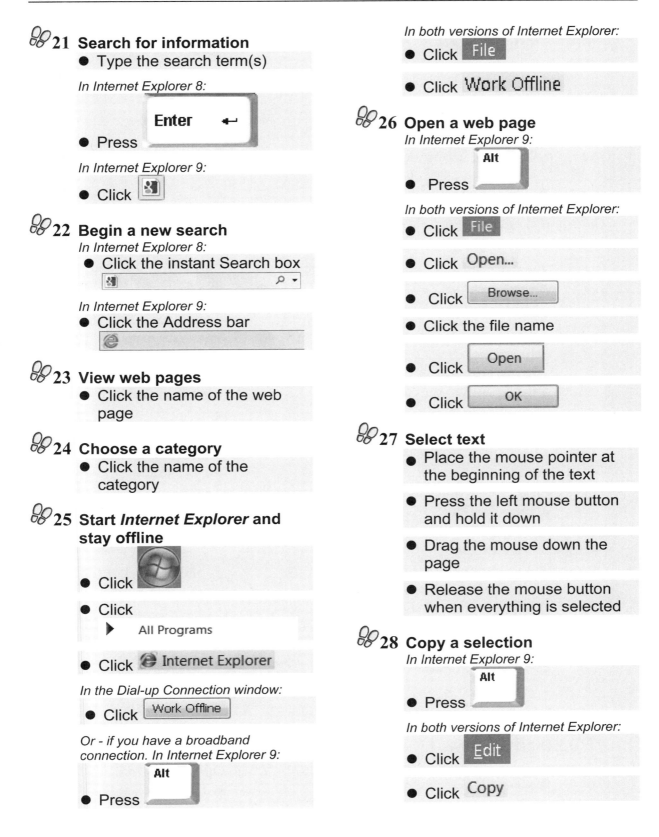

21 Search for information
- Type the search term(s)

In Internet Explorer 8:

- Press **Enter ←**

In Internet Explorer 9:
- Click

22 Begin a new search
In Internet Explorer 8:
- Click the instant Search box

In Internet Explorer 9:
- Click the Address bar

23 View web pages
- Click the name of the web page

24 Choose a category
- Click the name of the category

25 Start *Internet Explorer* and stay offline
- Click
- Click
  ► All Programs
- Click 🔵 Internet Explorer

In the Dial-up Connection window:
- Click Work Offline

Or - if you have a broadband connection. In Internet Explorer 9:
- Press **Alt**

In both versions of Internet Explorer:
- Click File
- Click Work Offline

26 Open a web page
In Internet Explorer 9:
- Press **Alt**

In both versions of Internet Explorer:
- Click File
- Click Open...
- Click Browse...
- Click the file name
- Click Open
- Click OK

27 Select text
- Place the mouse pointer at the beginning of the text
- Press the left mouse button and hold it down
- Drag the mouse down the page
- Release the mouse button when everything is selected

28 Copy a selection
In Internet Explorer 9:
- Press **Alt**

In both versions of Internet Explorer:
- Click Edit
- Click Copy

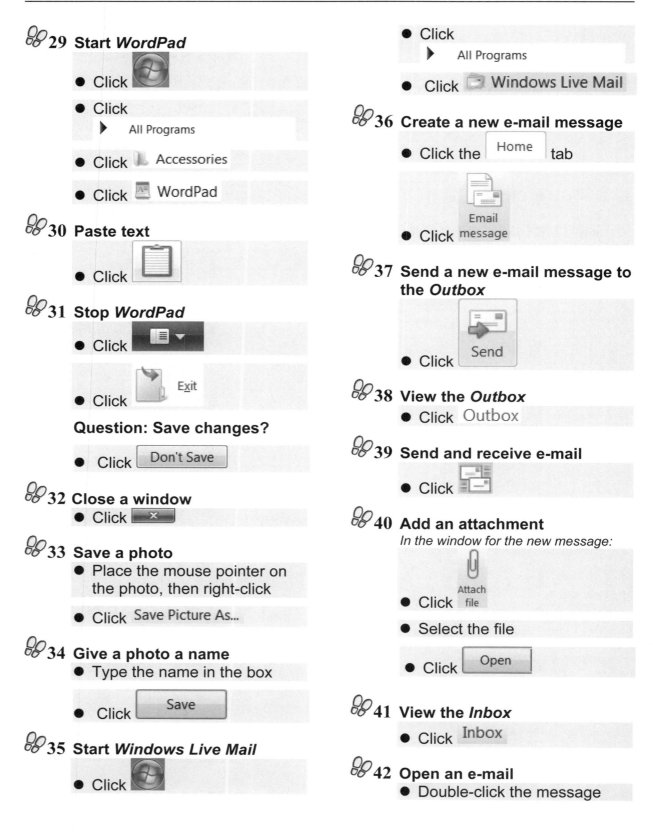

⚇29 Start *WordPad*

● Click

● Click

  ▶ All Programs

● Click Accessories

● Click WordPad

⚇30 Paste text

● Click

⚇31 Stop *WordPad*

● Click

● Click Exit

Question: Save changes?

● Click Don't Save

⚇32 Close a window

● Click x

⚇33 Save a photo

● Place the mouse pointer on the photo, then right-click

● Click Save Picture As...

⚇34 Give a photo a name

● Type the name in the box

● Click Save

⚇35 Start *Windows Live Mail*

● Click

● Click

  ▶ All Programs

● Click Windows Live Mail

⚇36 Create a new e-mail message

● Click the Home tab

● Click Email message

⚇37 Send a new e-mail message to the *Outbox*

● Click Send

⚇38 View the *Outbox*

● Click Outbox

⚇39 Send and receive e-mail

● Click

⚇40 Add an attachment

In the window for the new message:

● Click Attach file

● Select the file

● Click Open

⚇41 View the *Inbox*

● Click Inbox

⚇42 Open an e-mail

● Double-click the message

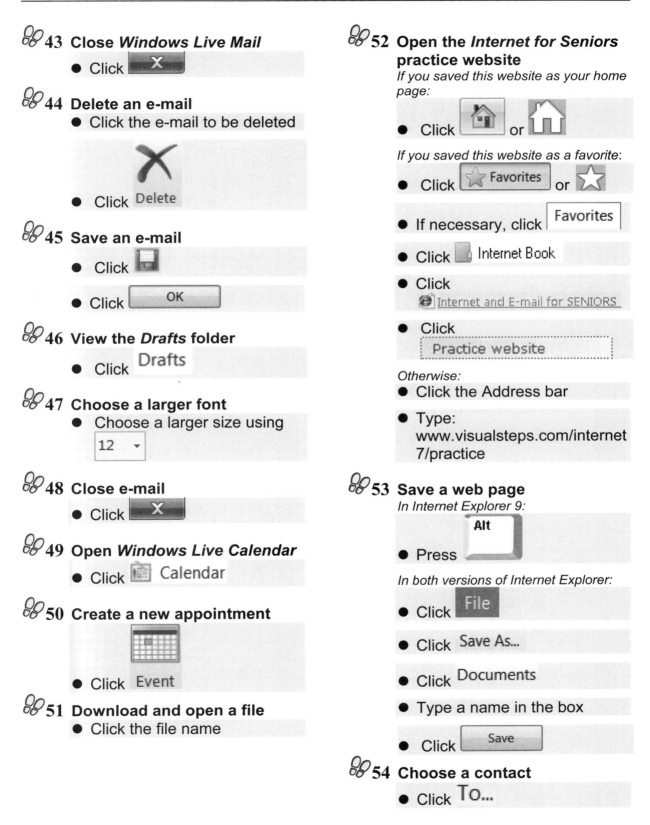

43 Close *Windows Live Mail*
- Click [X]

44 Delete an e-mail
- Click the e-mail to be deleted
- Click Delete

45 Save an e-mail
- Click 💾
- Click OK

46 View the *Drafts* folder
- Click Drafts

47 Choose a larger font
- Choose a larger size using [12 ▾]

48 Close e-mail
- Click [X]

49 Open *Windows Live Calendar*
- Click 📅 Calendar

50 Create a new appointment
- Click Event

51 Download and open a file
- Click the file name

52 Open the *Internet for Seniors* practice website
If you saved this website as your home page:
- Click 🏠 or 🏠

If you saved this website as a favorite:
- Click ☆ Favorites or ☆
- If necessary, click Favorites
- Click Internet Book
- Click 🌐 Internet and E-mail for SENIORS
- Click Practice website

Otherwise:
- Click the Address bar
- Type: www.visualsteps.com/internet7/practice

53 Save a web page
In Internet Explorer 9:
- Press Alt

In both versions of Internet Explorer:
- Click File
- Click Save As...
- Click Documents
- Type a name in the box
- Click Save

54 Choose a contact
- Click To...

- Click the name

- Click | To -> |

- Click | OK |

55 Save changes to this message?
- Click | No |

56 Maximize a window
- Click 🔲

57 View an attachment
- Double-click the attachment

58 Add details
- Type the location next to Location:

- Add the date

- Add the time

59 Save the appointment
- Click 💾 Save and close

60 Open the *Downloads* folder
- Click ⊕

- Click your *Personal folder*

- Double-click *Downloads*

61 Open a new tab
- Click ▢

62 Open a link in a new tab
- Press and hold | Ctrl |

- Click the link

- Release | Ctrl |

63 Switch to another tab
- Click the tab

64 Close a tab
- Click ✕ on the tab

65 Open a website from the Address bar *History*
- Click the small arrow ▾ at the end of the Address bar

- Scroll down the list and click the desired address (URL)

66 Make an appointment last all day
- Check the box ☐ All day

67 Reconnect to the Internet
- Double-click 🖥 on the taskbar

- Click | Connect |

68 Display the menu bar
In Internet Explorer 8 you can display the menu bar permanently:
- Click | Tools ▾ |

- Click Toolbars

- Click Menu Bar

In Internet Explorer 9:
- Press | Alt | every time you want to display the menu bar

Appendix C Downloading and Installing Windows Live Mail

If you want to be able to execute all the operations in *Chapter 5 E-mail, Your Electronic Mail*, you will need to use the free *Windows Live Mail* program. If you are not yet using this program, you need to download and install the program first. Downloading means copying the files from the Internet to your own computer. Installing means putting the program on your computer's hard disk drive. All the files will be copied to the correct folder, and the program will be included in the list of installed programs.

This is how you do it:

☞ **Start *Internet Explorer*** ✂¹

👆 **Click the Address bar**

⌨ **Type:**
download.live.com

Enter ⏎

⌨ **Press**

👆 **At** Mail **click**
Learn more

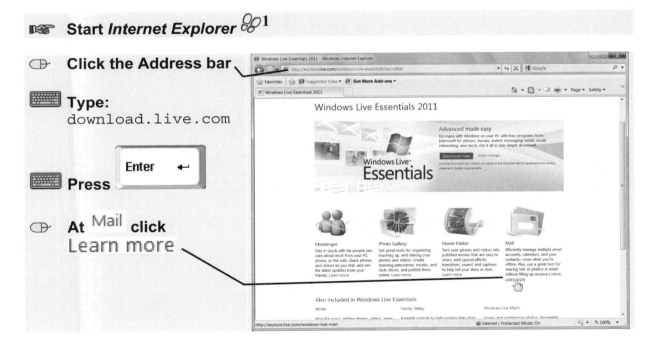

On the right-hand side of the window you will see the Download now button. By clicking this button you will start downloading the files:

☞ **Click** Download now

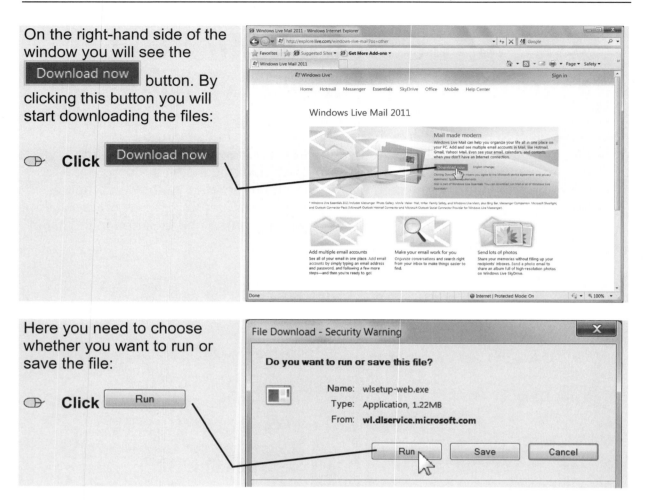

Here you need to choose whether you want to run or save the file:

☞ **Click** Run

Now your screen will turn dark and you will be asked for permission to continue:

☞ **Click** Yes

You can choose the programs you want to install:

☞ **Click**
→ **Choose the program**

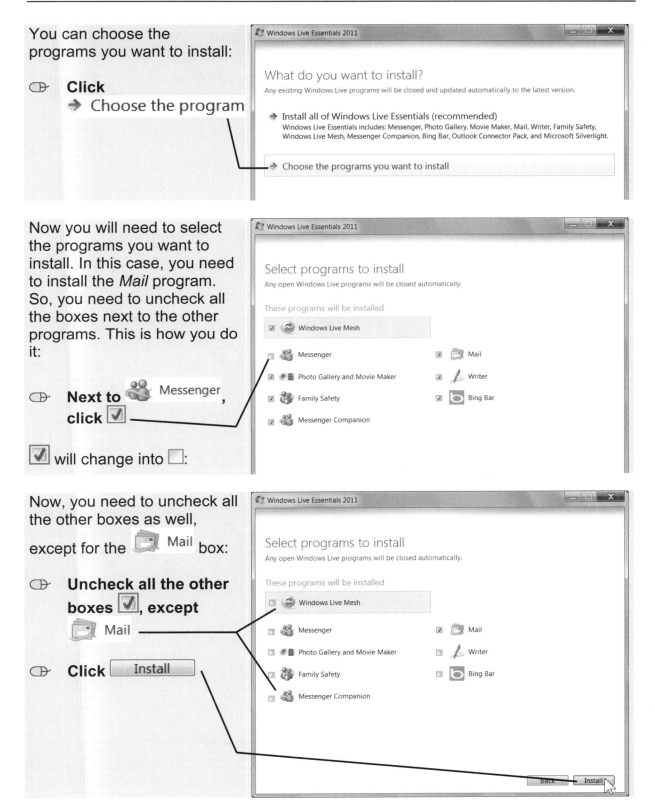

Now you will need to select the programs you want to install. In this case, you need to install the *Mail* program. So, you need to uncheck all the boxes next to the other programs. This is how you do it:

☞ **Next to** 👥 Messenger,
click ☑

☑ will change into ☐:

Now, you need to uncheck all the other boxes as well, except for the 🗔 Mail box:

☞ **Uncheck all the other boxes** ☑, **except**
🗔 Mail

☞ **Click** Install

It is possible that you will see this window:

☞ **Click** [Continue]

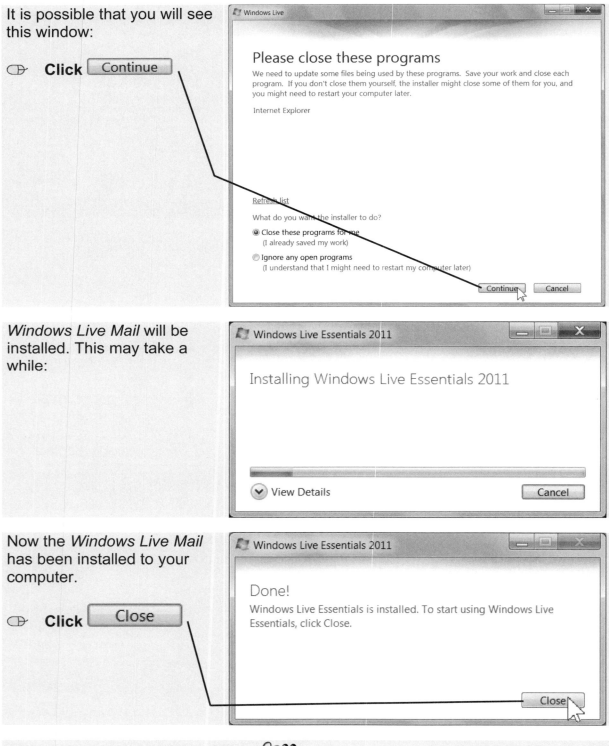

Windows Live Mail will be installed. This may take a while:

Now the *Windows Live Mail* has been installed to your computer.

☞ **Click** [Close]

☞ **Close all the other windows** 🦶³²

Appendix D Index